SUNY Series in Hindu Studies
Wendy Doniger, Editor

LITERARY INDIA

Comparative Studies in Aesthetics, Colonialism, and Culture

Edited by
Patrick Colm Hogan
and
Lalita Pandit

STATE UNIVERSITY OF NEW YORK PRESS

Production by Ruth Fisher
Marketing by Nancy Farrell

Published by
State University of New York Press, Albany

Printed in the United States of America

For information, address the State University of New York Press, State University Plaza, Albany, NY 12246

Library of Congress Cataloging-in-Publication Data

Hogan, Patrick Colm.
Literary India : comparative studies in aesthetics, colonialism, and culture / edited by Patrick Colm Hogan and Lalita Pandit.n
p. cm. — (SUNY series in Hindu studies)
Includes bibliographical references and index.
ISBN 0-7914-2395-6 (alk. paper). — ISBN 0-7914-2396-4 (alk. paper : pbk.)
1. Literature, Comparative—Indic and English. 2. Literature, Comparative—English and Indic. 3. Indic literature (English)—20th century—History and criticism. 4. Criticism—India—History—20th century. I. Pandit, Lalita. II. Title. III. Series.
PK5408.H64 1995
891′.1—dc20 94-16097
CIP

10 9 8 7 6 5 4 3 2 1

The editors wish to dedicate this volume to their parents:

Patrick Hogan	B. N. Pandit
Madonna Hogan	Kamalavati Pandit

CONTENTS

ACKNOWLEDGMENTS

"The Postcolonial Critic: Homi Bhabha Interviewed by David Bennett and Terry Collits" was previously published in *arena: a marxist journal of criticism and discussion* 96 (Spring 1991): 47–63. We are grateful to professors Bhabha, Bennett, and Collits and to the editors of the journal for permission to reprint.

Ashis Nandy's "Culture, State, and the Rediscovery of Indian Politics" was previously published in *Interculture* (April 1988) and, in an earlier version, in the *Economic and Political Weekly* (December 8, 1984). We are grateful to Professor Nandy for permission to reprint.

The essays in this volume, and the overall shape of the volume itself, benefited greatly from the comments of four anonymous readers for the State University of New York Press. We are grateful for their care in reading the manuscript and for their suggestions. We are also grateful to William Eastman for choosing such scrupulous readers and for his more general support of the manuscript. In addition, thanks are due to Michael A. Baker for his great care in copy-editing the manuscript, and Ruth Fisher for her work on the production of the manuscript.

This project would never have come to fruition had it not been for the patience and encouragement of Wendy Doniger. Working with her on this project has proven almost as rewarding as reading her invaluable analyses of myth or her lucid and beautiful translations of literary and religious texts.

INTRODUCTION: MULTICULTURAL COMPARATISM

In the last decade, Indian and other non-Western literatures have begun to work their way into the mainstream of English and American literary study. Not unrelated to this, there has been a more generalized interest in placing works of literature—both Western and non-Western—within broader cultural contexts. However, comparative studies involving non-Western works have remained relatively narrow, focusing almost entirely on contemporary literature in European languages. Moreover, much of the critical work in this field has concentrated exclusively on colonialism and the attempts of Anglophone and Francophone writers to respond to European cultural hegemony through anticolonial or postcolonial writings. Thus, with a few exceptions, mainstream comparatists have paid little attention either to indigenous literary traditions in non-Western countries or to the range of noncolonial issues important to contemporary non-Western literatures.

Our broad goal in assembling this collection is, then, to think more encompassingly about comparative literature, to consider a wider range of similarities and differences, interactions and reactions, in order to understand better both the artistic form and the social import of any literature. To this end, we have designed the volume to present an overview of the major issues—aesthetic, political, and more inclusively cultural—that define or should define a comparative field of study. Our more narrow goal in this collection is to advance comparative work in the specific area of South Asian literature. Literature of the Indian subcontinent is particularly appropriate for broadly comparative study because it includes one of the oldest literary traditions in the world and, even more importantly, because it includes the most fully developed and the most sophisticated tradition of poetic theory prior to the modern age.

Work in comparative literature may proceed in one of two ways. First, it may examine literary works, tradtitions, etc., in parallel. Partially modeled on the important linguistic work of Noam Chomsky, Joseph Greenberg, and others, this approach considers similarities (and, to a lesser extent, differences) in the properties and structures of diverse traditions, focusing in particular on those properties and structures that arose independently. This approach is most obviously relevant to pre-colonial works. However, colonial and postcolonial literatures that retain indigenous elements may be fruitfully studied in parallel with Western or other literatures as well.

The second approach examines works, traditions, etc., in sequence. This approach, already common in the comparative study of European literatures, focuses on historical relations—not only what one tradition has taken from another, but also what it has rejected or transformed. In the case of former European colonies, this form of study most often seeks to locate such interactions within the cultural matrix of colonial dominantion, though it may also invoke aesthetic or other contexts. Moreover, its focus has typically been on non-Western responses to Western literature (whether as colonial imitation or anticolonial "writing back"—on the latter, see, for example, Ashcroft, Griffiths, and Tiffin). However, it may just as readily examine the effects of non-Western literatures in the West (on the model of, for example, Martin Bernal's important cultural/intellectual history, *Black Athena*).

The value of the parallel approach is in isolating both cross-cultural constants and cultural variance, allowing us to see what is common across unrelated literatures and what is idiosyncratic to given literatures; at its best, this sort of study allows us insight into both our shared humanity and our cultural diversity. The value of the sequential approach is that it allows us insight into the historical interaction of cultures; at its best, it helps us to understand the historically defined particularities of different cultures as well as their often surprisingly intercultural origins and development.

The following essays may be divided roughly along these lines. The first essay, by Hogan, touches on both approaches to comparative study in an overview of political and aesthetic issues. The next six essays take up the parallel approach more narrowly. Ebbesen, Chari, and Lehmann draw on precolonial Indian literature and poetics in order to address some broad, theoretical issues.

Pandit, Holland, and Chaudhuri turn to specific works—precolonial, colonial, and postcolonial, in that order—to examine common structures that are not the product of historical interaction. The interview with Anita Desai provides a sort of transition between the parallel and the sequential, for Desai discusses both "universal" literary concerns—of the sort isolable in parallel studies—and her own historical situation as an Indian novelist drawing upon European literary models to write about India. The next three essays take up the sequential approach. Saha examines the nexus of translation, the central point of literary contact for different cultures. Swann considers two approaches to theater, one Indian and one European, in connection with the impact of Eastern drama in the West. Pandit looks at contact in the opposite direction, examining one Indian response to European colonial literature and culture. The interview with Bhabha provides another transition, this time between the narrowly literary concerns of the earlier chapters and the broader sociopolitical issues that are important to any sequential study and that are particularly crucial in the context of colonial and neocolonial hegemony. In a final essay, Ashis Nandy goes further in this direction and examines the possibility of a truly postcolonial culture, taking us from the relatively narrow topic of literary relations to the larger and more pressing issue of understanding and restructuring the culture in which literature can arise and function.

More exactly, Patrick Hogan begins the volume with an analysis and criticism of the dichotomizing view of East and West. Maintaining that an emphasis on difference has distorted our understanding of both Indian and European literatures, Hogan argues that a more circumspect study of cultural difference should be complemented by two sorts of study: reconstructive work on common ancestors of Indian and European literary forms (on the model of historical linguistics), and, even more importantly, the isolation of literary universals (on the model of universal grammar).

Jeffrey Ebbesen takes up a similar theme, though with a very different method, in his discussion of Indian and European conceptions of authorship. Employing deconstructive principles, he, too, argues against a dichotomizing view and concludes that Eastern and Western notions are both more similar to one another and more internally different than has previously been recognized.

Turning from the author, first to poetic form, then to the audience, V. K. Chari considers the theory of genre in Indian poetics, emphasizing the ways in which aesthetic response was more important to Indian writers than merely formal properties. Chari notes both differences and similarities between Indian and European theories, going on to employ Sanskrit theory in rethinking not only Indian, but European problems in this area.

Moving from author and audience to the artistic and communicative medium that links them, W. P. Lehmann examines the dominant views of language, particularly literary language, in India and the West. Specifically, Lehmann argues that these traditions are diametrically opposed on the nature of linguistic representation—an opposition with significant consequences for literary study. On the other hand, Lehmann notes that the dominant Western conception is present in India and has been for many centuries, while the dominant Indian conception has held a strong minority position in the West.

As already noted, the following three essays turn from theory to practical criticism, while retaining the focus on parallelism. In the first of these essays, Lalita Pandit examines two similar, but historically unrelated dramas: Bhavabhūti's *Uttararāmacarita* and Skakespeare's *The Winter's Tale.* As Pandit points out, these two plays, and other Sanskrit and Shakespearean romantic tragicomedies, share a range of generic properties. Rather than outlining these in general terms, Pandit concentrates on a common theme of considerable political and psychological importance in both India and Europe: man's paranoia about woman's infidelity, his consequent brutality toward her, his subsequent remorse, and his final fantasy of her as a purified and romanticized savior.

Holland, too, takes up common psychological and political motifs, in this case looking at Oedipal structures and the theme of religious belief in Satyajit Ray's *Devi* (a film based on P. K. Mukherjee's novella of colonial Bengal).

In a final study of parallelism, Una Chaudhuri considers the issue of postcolonial exile from the perspective of deconstruction. Concentrating, like Holland, on Oedipus and a recent South Asian film and returning us to the issues of linguistic representation raised by Lehmann, Chaudhuri argues that both *Oedipus the King* and *Sammy and Rosie Get Laid* effectively deconstruct the identitarian metaphysics of presence so frequently associated with a romanticized view of home, expecially as presented in realistic drama.

Again, the interview with Anita Desai functions as a sort of bridge between those essays adopting a parallel approach and those engaging in a sequential investigation. Half German and half Indian, writing about India but in English, Desai embodies what postcolonial critics and theorists have referred to as the "hybridity" of the colonial/postcolonial writer. Yet Desai is perhaps less concerned with her European and Indian influences than with a sort of common fund of themes (e.g., the struggle of the individual against large impersonal forces) and techniques (e.g., cyclical structure) on which she draws in crafting her novels.

Turning to the sequential approach, P. K. Saha examines what is perhaps the most fundamental issue in cross-cultural literary influence: translation. He carefully distinguishes cultural, aesthetic, and linguistic impediments to adequate translation, illustrating each variety with examples from Bengali and Sanskrit. He then goes on to suggest a number of practical, though necessarily partial solutions to the problem of translating Indian literature into English.

Darius Swann takes up Eastern influence on the West, considering the more particular issue of similarities between *Nauṭankī* theater and the drama of Bertolt Brecht. While Brecht was not directly influenced by *Nauṭankī*, he was influenced by another Asian form of theater: the Chinese opera. Swann examines not only the similar antirealist techniques that derive from Brecht's interest in Eastern drama, but also the very different aims toward which these techniques are used in Brecht and *Nauṭankī*. As Swann emphasizes, *Nauṭankī* retains a classical Indian concern with the emotional effect of the drama, a concern at odds with Brecht's pursuit of the "alienation effect."

In the following essay, Pandit takes up an Indian response to colonial European literature. Specifically, she considers Tagore's *Gora* and its precursor *Kim* in order to explore the problem of Indian cultural identity after British colonization. Identity is perhaps the most widely thematized topic in postcolonial criticism, and *Gora* is a particularly crucial text on this topic, for, in this novel, Tagore sought to portray the impossiblity of complete indigeneity and, simultaneously, the indecency and injustice of full Westernization.

The last two essays return to broad theoretical concerns. The critical currency of the term "hybridity" is to a great extent the result of the writings of Homi Bhabha. In his interview with David Bennett and Terry Collits, Bhabha reconsiders this influential notion in relation to a variety of more contemporary issues, from multiculturalism in the academy to the Rushdie affair. In each case, critically stressing a politics of signification, he seeks to isolate an internal disruption that indicates that widely presupposed cultural unities are deeply disunified.

Probably most comparatists and writers on postcolonial literature would agree that literature only arises, is sustained and disseminated, within the structures of a more encompassing culture. For example, Pandit's and Bhabha's discussions of identity and hybridity clearly presuppose this point. In the case of a former colony such as India, the question of the form of that culture is particularly pressing. In the final essay, Ashis Nandy turns to this larger issue. Arguing for the primacy of culture over statist politics, he sets forth a specifically Indian alternative to the current hegemonic and Western structures, which operate to stifle the human and cultural aspirations of most people throughout the world today.

Nandy's essay should remind all of us that, though many of the most crucial political issues may be broadly cultural, they are not necessarily narrowly literary. Nonetheless, what we read and teach, and how we read and teach it, have political repercussions. It is our hope that the following essays will help to encourage a broadened study of comparative literature, more rigorous attention to both the similarities and differences between Indian and European traditions, and a fuller understanding of the historical relations between these traditions. On the other hand, our aims are as much aesthetic as they are political. Thus we hope equally that the following essays will foster in readers a fuller appreciation of the beauty of Indian literature—an appreciation that is itself, perhaps, not without political consequences.

Bibliography

Ashcroft, Bill, Gareth Griffiths, and Helen Tiffin. *The Empire Writes Back.* London: Routledge, 1989.

Bernal, Martin. *Black Athena: The Afroasiatic Roots of Classical Civilization.* 2 vols. New Brunswick: Rutgers University Press, 1987.

Part I

India and the Study of Comparative Literature

1

Beauty, Politics, and Cultural Otherness: The Bias of Literary Difference

Patrick Colm Hogan

When one imagines the possibilities of comparative literature in the context of recent developments in psychology, linguistics, and cognitive science, one of the first tasks that should come to mind is the isolation of universal principles of literary composition, structure, reception, etc. However, leaving aside a handful of valuable, but narrowly focused, linguistic/formal analyses, serious work in this potentially important field of study is almost nonexistent. There are a number of obvious reasons for this. First of all, students of literature are usually interested and educated in ways of examining single works or, at most, periods or movements. In general, they have neither the training nor the inclination to pursue large-scale abstractions on the model of the natural sciences. (A similar point is made by Kiparsky; see "Roman Jakobson" 36–37.) Second, comparative literature is in practice the study of European literature; as Earl Miner puts it, the world of comparative literature most often lacks "an eastern and a southern hemisphere" (20). Thus current work in the field does not provide an adequate basis for the study of literary universals, just as work on solely European languages would be inadequate for the study of linguistic universals. Finally, there is a deep-seated belief among humanists that European and non-European literatures are vastly different and that the study of universals is hopeless at best and somehow harmful at worst.

There are certainly other reasons for the neglect of universals in the study of comparative literature. However, these are perhaps the most significant. And of these, while the first and second are of great practical importance, the third is no doubt the most ideologically crucial factor inhibiting expanded comparatist work on Indic and other non-Western literatures. In the following pages, then, I should like to address this particular issue—along with some related political concerns—by focusing on both the nature and representation of Indian literature in a comparatist context. By way of a discussion and criticism of the notion of India's "Otherness," I hope to indicate some areas of research that contain rich potential for increasing our understanding of the human mind, human society, human communication, etc.

The Ideology of East and West

There has been a consistent strain in Western ideology, which has defined the East as absolutely Other. Whether it is judged to be execrable or laudable, India, China, Japan, and other countries in the area, have been seen as mystical, inscrutable lands "where even the most ordinary actions were imbued with symbolism," as Romila Thapar puts it (16). Rudyard Kipling formulated this dichotomous view most famously with his line "East is East, and West is West, and never the twain shall meet." But such a global East/West opposition is not confined to the Kiplings and has been accepted by those who celebrate Eastern difference as well as by those who deplore it; it has been affirmed by Orientalists, by imperialists, by ordinary men and women alike. Jean-Paul Hulin, in his essay *"L'Inde dans les premiers écrits de Kipling: Orthodoxie et Deviance,"* describes the social circumstances in which Kipling came to formulate his views. During the 1880s, the Anglo-Indian community in India was feeling an increasing estrangement and isolation. Within this group, "One came to posit, as an axiomatic truth, the existence of an unbridgeable gulf, an irreducible discontinuity, between the two cultures." This confirmed "the Anglo-Indians in their conviction of their superiority, and in the essential strangeness or foreignness of the indigenous culture" (161–62; my translation). Thus Hulin sees the dichotomization of East and West as in part a response by insecure Anglo-Indians to changing circumstances, a response designed to affirm their superiority and thereby bolster their superior social, political, and economic position.

No doubt, Hulin is to a degree correct. But the conceptual opposition of East and West did not begin in the late nineteenth century. We already find Montesquieu writing in the early eighteenth century that "Everything with the natives of India . . . is marked by the seal of paradox"—a flaw that ultimately results in passivity, cowardice, and feminization on the one hand, and wild fantasy, luxuriousness, and cruelty on the other (quoted in Weinberger-Thomas, 20; my translation here and below). In the early nineteenth century, G. W. F. Hegel found the Indian spirit dreamy due to the "fluidity" and arbitrariness of "an imagination with neither check nor law" (Weinberger-Thomas 21), and, as Roger-Pol Droit points out, Hegel stressed "the specificity of . . . Indian texts in order to deny them any claim to universality" (195). Somewhat later in the century, Ernst Renan wrote that Indians were a "race of the infinite, dreamy, lost, led astray by its imagination" (Weinberger-Thomas 22). In a similar vein, near the turn of the century, S. H. Butcher claimed that the "Oriental" imagination—presumably including the Indian—was not under the "control of reason" and thus had a strong inclination to "run riot" (393). Nor did Kipling's oppositional view come to an end with the decline of the Anglo-Indian ascendancy. To take only a small and in many ways peripheral example, in his introduction to *New Writing in India,* Adil Jussawalla, citing reviews of John Alphonso-Karkala's 1971 *Anthology of Indian Literature,* argues that even today "the view of the liberal section of the British public"—the section of the British mainstream most favorably inclined to things Indian—is that Indian literature is "tedious" and "other-worldly" (17).

As Catherine Weinberger-Thomas indicates in her study "*Exotisme indien et representations occidentales,*" however, disparaging opinions such as those we have just cited are frequently paired with laudatory counterparts. Thus, she points out, the criticism of India as immutable and stagnant is paired with praise of India for its eternalness (24). In this way, Indologists and others who laud India are almost as likely to urge the extremity of East/West differences as imperialists who denigrate India. For example, in what is no doubt the best introduction to Indian literatures for nonspecialists, Edward Dimock insists that Western drama is "irrelevant" when reading Indian drama, and that Western epic "should be far from one's mind" when reading Indian epic (Dimock et al. 43).[1] In fact, sticking only to Hegel and the authors of this introduction—the former colonial and critical, the latter postcolonial and laudatory, both focusing on Indian literature or art—we may uncover many striking similarities. While Hegel deplores the presumed fact that Indian poetry is "always one and the same thing over again" due to the "similarity of content," which makes it "extremely monotonous and, on the whole, empty and wearisome" (368; compare the contemporary "liberal" view just cited), a writer such as A. K. Ramanujan emphasizes the putatively non-Western repetition of imagery in Tamil lyrics while insisting that it "adds nuances" (Dimock et al. 171). In contrast with Greek drama, Hegel argues, "there is no question of the accomplishment of a free individual action" in Indian theater (1206). In a similar vein, J. A. B. van Buitenen maintains that "the Indian has never been pleasurably attracted, as Western man has been, by psychological variety, individualistic introspection, and moral ambiguity" (Dimock et al. 45). (Regarding the last, it is interesting to note that a writer such as P. Lal, equally enthusiastic about East/West differences, maintains the position opposite to that of van Buitenen; specifically, for Lal, one major difference between Indian drama and Greek drama is that Greek drama has moral absolutes, presumably leaving moral ambiguity for the Indian writers; see Lal xvii.) Hegel decries the "confusion" of Indian writing, its failure to "assert the laws of nature" and follow the "natural course of events" (375). Edwin Gerow insists that, in Indian drama, the "action does not have to be subjected to canons of probability" and it is "not real" (Dimock et al. 134). Hegel objects to the predominance of coincidence in Sanskrit drama and the incoherence of its plot developments, for example, the mixing of the natural and the supernatural in *Śakuntalā* (339 1176). Van Buitenen maintains that "chance becomes an important factor in the Indian play," again unlike Western drama, and goes on to discuss the function of coincidence in *Śakuntalā* (86–7), while Edwin Gerow emphasizes the plethora of dei ex machina in Indian drama (219).

We shall turn to a discussion of some of these theses below. In each case, my view is that the stated or implied claim of profound East/West difference involves beliefs that are either mistaken with regard to the East or mistaken with regard to the West. For the moment, however, I should like to emphasize that, historically, as Thapar points out, the celebration of Indian Otherness—by, for example, the German romantics—"was to do as much damage to India as [the] rejection of Indian culture" (16). This is because the affirming and the rejecting views are not unrelated, but share the most important descriptive presuppositions, differing primarily in terms of evaluation. As Ashis Nandy points out in a different but closely related context, "There is a perfect fit . . . between many versions of Indian nationalism and the worldview of the Kiplings. Both share what the Mādhyamika [school of Buddhist philosophy] might call the tendency to absolutize the relative differences between cultures. Both seek to set up the East and the West as permanent and natural antipodes. Both trace their roots to the cultural arrogance of post-Enlightenment Europe which sought to define not only the 'true' West but also the 'true' East" (73–4). Edward Said is similarly critical of the global distinction between East and West and condemns "the altogether regrettable tendency of any knowledge based on such hard-and-fast distinctions as 'East' and 'West': to channel thought into a West or an East compartment" (46). "[S]uch divisions," he argues, "are generalities whose use historically and actually has been to press the importance of the distinction between some men and some other men, usually towards not especially admirable ends" (45). They should be superceded by scholarship in which "racial, ethnic, and national distinctions [are] less important than the common enterprise of promoting human community" (328).

Moreover, due to the identity or near identity of descriptive presuppositions across the imperialist and Indophilic claims, even the seemingly opposed evaluations are not unrelated. It is a commonplace of feminist criticism that the elevation of woman and the degradation of woman are two sides of one coin—both imprison, but, in one case, the cage is gilded. When Homi Bhabha argues that the colonized subject is split into fetish and phobic object, he is, in part, redeveloping this idea. Bhabha's formulation of this ideological structure brings to the fore the perverse sexualization of the Other, a real and destructive phenomenon, discussed most famously by Franz Fanon (see especially Fanon, chapters 2 and 3) and more recently examined by a number of other writers (see, for example, Gilman). But in some ways, the analogy linking the colonized subject with woman is more revealing (in part because it subsumes Bhabha's division, insofar as that division is valid). Of course, there are important differences between patriarchal and colonial ideology, but, in their conceptual structure, these two ideological complexes are closely parallel and genetically related. To say that someone is in thought illogical or antilogical and intuitive; in literature, unbound by rules or incapable of rigor; in desire, bestial or transcendental—to say this is in effect to say that such a person conforms to the ideological stereotype of woman. If such a claim is made about an entire race or culture, one may infer that that race or culture has been assimilated to an imaginary structure of femininity. As Ashis Nandy argues, "Western colonialism invariably used" a "homology between sexual and political dominance," which made the latter "congruent with existing Western sexual stereotypes" (4).

Clearly, in both cases—that of colonialism and that of patriarchy—this ideological complex may be accepted and reviled or accepted and celebrated. Those who seek to affirm and valorize the putative irrationality of the East, its sexual luxury—or asceticism—and so on, like those who seek to celebrate the putative irrationality of woman, her "thousand and one thresholds of ardor" (Hélène Cixous's phrase; see Cixous 256), or, conversely, her chastity, and so on—in other words, a great number of those who see themselves as struggling against imperialism, racism, and sexism—share with their professed antagonists the bulk of relevant ideological belief. Specifically, they presuppose, and thus reenforce, a certain "problematic," a set of fundamental, ideologically functional principles that serve to define the dominant and subject groups (male and female, white and black, Western and Eastern, etc.) and to represent these groups as internally homogenous and mutually contradictory.[2] Certainly it makes some difference whether one supports a given hierarchization, whether one approves of racial or sexual subjugation. But it also makes a difference whether one accepts the descriptive component of a dichotomizing ideology, whether one affirms beliefs that have served historically to justify subjugation. In other words, it makes a difference whether one says that women or Indians are irrational (i.e., more irrational than men or Europeans) and therefore should not be allowed to vote, or one says that women or Indians are irrational and should still be allowed to vote. But, in both cases, one is accepting as true a factual claim that, first of all, is false, and that, second, has in fact served to justify the denial of suffrage to women, Indians, and so on.

Having said this, it is important to emphasize that any judgments about India and Europe, men and women, etc. are matters for historical, scholarly, and empirical investigation, not political legislation or a priori speculation (including that based on "personal experience" or introspection, both of which are entirely unreliable; see Hogan "Some Prolegomena" and *Politics* 136–37, 192, and citations).[3] That a certain idea has been used for purposes of oppression (e.g., the idea that Western medicine is broadly superior to non-Western alternatives) does not show that this idea is false or even that oppression is its necessary consequence. However, the dichotomous view of East and West, with the descriptive content it entails, is in fact false, just as is the correlate dichotomization of male/female, with its descriptive content (on the latter, see Fausto-Sterling, Epstein, or Faludi). And like the male/female dichotomy, that of East and West is indeed disabling, both politically and intellectually—and to all parties. While it is clearly beyond the scope of the present essay to consider all claims of East/West opposition, I should like to examine and criticize two examples of common stereotypical beliefs about Indian literature before going on to look at some of the political and intellectual possibilities that open up when the oppositional view of East and West is discarded.

Pseudodifferences between East and West: Indian Literary Otherness

From the views quoted at the outset, we can isolate two broad tendencies in the standard descriptions of Indian literary art. The first is that Indian literature is incoherent/free in structure, lacking the Western attention to/obsession with necessity. The second is that it is monotonous/traditional, free from the Western concern for/obsession with novelty. (In each case, which evaluative alternative one chooses depends upon one's aesthetic and ideological preferences—within, again, a single problematic.) S. H . Butcher succinctly expressed the derogatory version of these views when he wrote that "India has produced vast poems which pass under the name of dramas, wanting, however, both the unity of action and the spiritual freedom which the drama proper implies" (366). The first conception (of Indian literary incoherence) takes part in the view of India as hypermystical and irrational; the second conception (of Indian literary monotony) is an aspect of the view that India is stagnant or ossified. Both, as I shall argue, are mistaken.

Literary Innovation

Let us begin with the question of novelty. In general, the belief in the peculiar Westernness of innovation is misguided. W. J. Bate, at the beginning of his *The Burden of the Past,* quotes a lament made 4,000 years ago by an Egyptian scribe: "Would I had phrases that are not known, utterances that are strange, in a new language that has not been used, free from repetition, not an utterance which has grown stale, which men of old have spoken" (3–4). Similar sentiments have been expressed by poets in many traditions, and similar sentiments have no doubt been felt by poets in all traditions. As the prominent Dutch anthropologist, A. A. Gerbrands, argues, "an artist . . . in any society," due to the nature of his/her occupation, "must be to some degree the non-conformist" (151). Indeed, any time a society endorses aesthetic evaluation, it thereby virtually guarantees that poets will seek to differentiate themselves from one another. And this necessarily involves innovation—if frequently innovation justified by an appeal to the past, as Bate has indicated (see 21–22). Gerbrands points out that "even in the most conservative societies the margin of freedom which is allowed the individual in practice is much greater than ethnological theory was formerly willing to accept" (151). It has to be. It is clear that, for example, classical Sanskrit comic poets are not only very different from one another, but that their dramas often drastically differ from their sources—something that is probably untrue of our two great Roman comic writers, Plautus and Terence, who seem to have functioned more as adaptors of Menander than as poets or makers in their own right. Interestingly, Sir William Jones, one of a handful of scholars who seem not to have held to the dichotomous view of East and West, recognized that "The Hindus and Arabs are perfectly original" in contrast to the Romans (quoted in Mukherjee, 119).

Thus, for example, Bhavabhūti totally changes the ending of the *Rāmāyaṇa* in his *Uttararāmacarita*. In the original, when Rama asks Sītā to undergo a second fire ordeal in order to prove her chastity, she refuses and, abandoning Rāma, miraculously returns to her mother, the earth. They are finally reunited when Rāma commits suicide by jumping in the river. In Bhavabhūti's version, however, there is no question of a second fire ordeal or multiple suicides. While Western playwrights such as Shakespeare, writing many centuries later, may sometimes have considerably altered their sources—and, we might add, sometimes remained very close to those sources—it seems unlikely that they would have completely altered the ending of a sacred narrative.[4] In India, in contrast, the restructuring of this sacred text is almost commonplace, as can be seen not only in Bhavabhūti's play, but in the multiplicity of regional *Rāmāyaṇas*, the extremely popular fifteenth-century revision by Tulsīdās, etc. (on the variety of Rāmāyaṇas, see Richman).

A perhaps more striking example may be found in the most celebrated of Indian dramas, *Śakuntalā*. In this play, Kālidāsa does not simply retell the story of Śakuntalā and Duṣyanta as recounted in the *Mahābhārata*. Rather, he takes a minimal story, with two flat characters and a slim, rather cynical plot line, and develops it extensively. For the benefit of readers unfamiliar with either version and because we shall have occasion to return to the plot of *Śakuntalā* below, I shall summarize both.

In the original, Duṣyanta meets Śakuntalā in the woods. His desire is aroused and, in order to sleep with her, he agrees to award the kingship to their son, should their union result in conception. His lust sated, he leaves. When Śakuntalā shows up at his court, he pretends not to recognize her. As she is being escorted out, a voice booms forth from the heavens announcing that Śakuntalā's claims are true. Duṣyanta recants, explaining his deception by reference to fear of scandal. Though the original tale is doubtless realistic—except for the divine intervention, of course—and engaging in a cynical sort of way, it is also very distanced and uninvolving. In comparison, Kālidāsa's version is more romantic, more psychologically developed, and more moving. Beyond the elaboration of courting, etc., Kālidāsa develops characters who are more sympathetic and more "rounded" than the lust-driven Duṣyanta and ambition-driven Śakuntalā of Vyāsa.[5]

Specifically, in Kālidāsa's version, Duṣyanta is gentle and Śakuntalā demure, and their relationship is one of mutual affection, not mutual exploitation (at least in the commonly translated Devanāgarī recension; the Bengali recension is somewhat closer to the *Mahābhārata* version in this respect; see Rajan 13–20 and Miller 333–35 for discussion and Rajan 208–13 for an example). But, from the outset, a vague curse casts a shadow of foreboding over their love. Śakuntalā's adoptive father has gone to Somatīrtha in order to pray that Śakuntalā's undesirable fate be averted, or at least qualified. Meanwhile, Duṣyanta and Śakuntalā unite in something that is much more like a marriage than the business contract of the *Mahābhārata* original. Duṣyanta leaves, saying that he will call for Śakuntalā in a few days' time, after he has made appropriate preparations for her arrival in the palace. Absent-minded due to love, Śakuntalā fails to welcome a visiting guest, the sage Durvāsas, known throughout Indian myth and legend for his scrupulousness about duty even in the smallest details (for example, those pertaining to greetings) and for his phenomenal ill humor. Angered, Durvāsas curses Śakuntalā, saying, "That one you are thinking of with thoughts for no one else,/Because of whom you do not notice that I, a holy sage, am here—/He shall not remember you however much reminded/Any more than a drunken man remembers what was said" (Coulson 89). Priaṁvadā and Anasūyā manage to convince Durvāsas to modify the curse, so that Duṣyanta will recognize Śakuntalā upon seeing the ring he has given her. Due to the curse, Duṣyanta fails to send for Śakuntalā. Eventually, Śakuntalā sets out for the court despite hearing no word from her beloved. On the way to the capital, she bathes in a stream and loses Duṣyanta's ring.

At the court, Duṣyanta predictably rejects Śakuntalā. After she has been spurned by her scandalized escorts and forbidden from returning home, he reconsiders, deciding to house her and have her taken care of until the child is born. However, when Śakuntalā is led away, she is assumed into the heavens by her mother, an *apsaras*, or celestial nymph. In the next scene, two police officers bring to Duṣyanta a fisherman who has been caught with a royal ring. The police assume that the man stole the ring. He insists that he found it in the belly of a fish. Duṣyanta sees the ring and recalls everything. He is plunged into despair due to his grief over losing Śakuntalā and his guilt over rejecting her. After an interestingly self-referential sequence when Duṣyanta relates his love to an artistic representation of Śakuntalā, and after some amusing antics with the buffoon and Duṣyanta's jealous wives, he and Śakuntalā are reunited by the gods in the heavenly hermitage of Mārīca. Here Duṣyanta meets his child, who has the royal birth mark and whose magical amulet—designed to kill anyone who touches it, excepting the child's parents—does not harm Duṣyanta, who thus receives incontrovertible proof of his paternity.

There should be little doubt that Kālidāsa's treatment of this story radically alters the source. There should also be little doubt in the minds of readers of such authors as Kālidāsa, Bhavabhūti, or Bhāsa that each author revises sources differently, individually. Moreover, it should be clear that the romantic tragicomedies of these writers differ greatly from such works as *The Little Clay Cart* or *The Minister's Seal*, which are distinct both in genre and in origin.

Not surprisingly, Indian aestheticians have not been silent on the issue of innovation—or on the related issue of the individuality of the poet, the importance of which is also widely viewed as Western. Thus, for example, the tenth-century theorist, Kuntaka, in his *Vakrokti-Jīvita*, makes the innovative "turn" (*vakrokti*) of speech or idea, as generated by a poet of genius (*pratibhā*), the centerpiece of his aesthetic. He writes of "words and meaning or sense, which together contain a certain striking turn of idea given to it by the poet's imagination or fancy and which gives pleasure to the Sahṛdaya [or connoisseur]" (quoted in Rajamannar 27) and continually stresses *navatya*, or newness. Indeed, as P. V. Rajamannar points out, "It is this quality of eternal newness which [according to Kuntaka] accounts for the continuous production of works of art" (29). Kuntaka tells us that originality "should be understood in a two-fold manner:—Firstly, something which never existed before might be invented. Secondly, that which lacks propriety as it exists in the source, should be modified suitably. The object in both cases remaining the same, namely, aesthetic effect on readers" (544). Moreover, he argues that a literary work "reveals the essence of creative originality which is most aesthetic only in the case of a very rare poetic genius who is endowed by nature with the gift of an extraordinary inventive imagination" (Kuntaka 545). And in this, as R. S. Pathak points out in his *Vakrokti and Stylistic Concepts*, Kuntaka is by no means alone; many Indian aestheticians—including Bhaṭṭatauta, Mahimabhaṭṭa, Ānandavardhana, Bhoja, and Abhinavagupta—affirm the individuality of the poet (68–9).

In a related manner, the great ninth-century theorist Ānandavardhana distinguishes three ways in which a literary work may resemble that of a precursor. As Amaladass explains, the resemblance may be "like a reflection" or "like a painted picture of a person" or "like two living persons resembling each other" (74). Of these, Ānandavardhana claims that only the third is acceptable. Amaladass summarizes: "An intelligent man should avoid the first two varieties but not the third. The reason is, as long as there is a separate life of its own, even a poetic theme bearing close resemblance to an earlier one will acquire exceeding beauty. . . . [S]imilarities . . . don't become flaws . . . as long as the poetic theme as a whole shines with novelty" (74–5). Chapter IV of Ānandavardhana's *Dhvanyālokā* deals extensively with novelty. And in his classic commentary, Abhinavagupta maintained that "Since we call a poem that is built on a meaning that has been used by another poet a poem of that other poet, one should strive for originality of meaning" ("Locana" 703); poetry, in consequence, should be "ever new" (706; see also 410–11). Great art is the product of "Genius," which is to say, "an intelligence capable of creating new things" (120).

It would appear, then, that individual invention is not foreign to Indian literature, either in practice or in theory. On the other hand, it is no doubt the case that the degree of innovation in Indian literature varies from writer to writer, from period to period, from genre to genre, as does the degree of innovation in Western literature. Sometimes works are like reflections, sometimes like portraits, sometimes like resemblances of living people. For example, the standardized imagery of the Tamil anthology poems—outlined and discussed by A. K. Ramanujan—shows the extent to which some Indian literature can be highly constrained. Thus Ramanujan is right to emphasize the conventionality of this verse (as noted above). But that does not mean that this conventionality is peculiarly Indian or Eastern or that it supports a dichotomistic view of Western and Indian literature. (Of course, Ramanujan does not claim this, though much of his discussion does seem to point in that direction.)

First of all, sticking to the anthologies, Ramanujan's own discussion of the rigid structuration of *akam* and *puram* poems ("interior" poems dealing with feelings, etc. and "exterior" poems dealing with actions, events, etc., both involving fixed patterns of imagery) indicates that quite a few anthology poems, perhaps the majority, were exceptions to this classification and the strict standarization it implies (see Ramanujan 262–69). Moreover, Ramanujan himself points out that anthology poets strove to create new effects within the conventionalized frameworks in which they were working (see Dimock et al., 174). Indeed, it is hard to see how this might *not* have been the case. Again, it would seem that some minimal degree of innovation would be necessary, if only to assure that individual poems were distinguishable from one another. Of course, this does not mean that the preferred poems of the period were the most radically innovative. But then, the preferred works of the Western tradition have not necessarily been the most wildly innovative either, at least until the twentieth century, and then only in very small, "elite" circles (and then sometimes for only the crudest economic reasons relating to the publishing needs of academics). It certainly appears plausible that, say, first-century Tamil tastes favored a lesser degree of innovation than ours do today. On the other hand, given the amazing monotony of popular culture (e.g., popular song), most famously analyzed by Horkheimer and Adorno, and given the extremely formulaic nature of "pulp" fiction, it seems unlikely that this is true in general. Indeed, it may not even be true for our literary "elite," for it is very easy to see even postmodern fiction, putatively the paradigm case of radical innovation, as absurdly formula-ridden. Perhaps we just like to think of ourselves as valuing innovation.

In any case, even if first-century Tamil readers desired a lower proportion of innovation to tradition than we do, this says nothing about putative East/West differences. First of all, Tamil anthology poetry is highly oral in provenance, as K. Kailasapathy has argued at length. George Hart has convincingly maintained that

Kailasapathy is mistaken in concluding that the anthology poems were originally oral compositions (see Hart 152–154). However, it is clear that they were composed in a society that was predominantly oral. They enormously evidence what Walter Ong calls "residual orality"—formulaic phrasing, dense use of epithets, etc. (for a list of oral characteristics, see Ong 33–57)—which is certainly no more Eastern than it is Western. All oral societies, East and West, prize innovation, but, at least in certain respects, they do so in a more limited degree than chirographic and print cultures. This tendency toward literary conservatism has to do with the risk of losing the wealth of knowledge that oral lore preserves and that can vanish entirely in a single generation if it remains untold. No doubt, habits of mind formed in this context continue long after the invention of writing. Moreover, due to the fleeting nature of sound, we all have a much higher tolerance for repetition and a much lower tolerance for innovation in oral speech, even in highly literate societies. At the time of their composition, Tamil anthology poems may well have been heard as frequently or more frequently than they were read. If so, that alone would predict a relatively high degree of repetition or conventionality.

But in fact we need not invoke orality to see that an East/West aesthetic dichotomy is unnecessary to account for the standardized imagery of the Tamil anthologies. There are many instances of remarkably convention-bound poetry in the Western tradition. An obvious case is medieval troubadour poetry, of which Arnold Hauser writes that "all the poems employ the same rhetorical formulae to such an extent that one could take them to be the work of one and the same poet" (215). Less extreme comments could be made about other periods and movements, even such recent work as late Romantic and Celtic Twilight poetry. Indeed, writers such as Eliot see the crystallization of poetic idiom as an inevitably recurrent property of poetry, including, of course, European poetry (see Eliot 23). A particularly relevant case of Western conventional/formulaic poetry may be found in the Petrarchan love sonnet, which flourished a millennium or more after the Tamil anthology poems. The conventional, formulaic nature of these sonnets is obvious—and was indeed so obvious at the time that Shakespeare, who used the standard imagery frequently and effectively, was able to parody its conventions in one of his most beautiful poems, Sonnet 130, "My Mistress' Eyes are Nothing Like the Sun." Indeed, Shakespeare's attitude in the poem directly parallels that of some classical Indian poets. For example, in the fifth century, Bhartrihari parodied conventionalized imagery in love poems, or "poets' hyperbole," with such lines as "her face, a vile receptacle of phlegm,\is likened to the moon" (69, 87). Such points are, of course, rarely made in discussions of Indian lyrics. Moreover, while we would not ordinarily introduce a selection of Shakespearean sonnets with an extended discussion focusing on stereotyped imagery, such imagery is precisely the aspect of Indian lyrics that is most emphasized in otherwise parallel introductory material, as we have already seen.

Finally, while Western critical theory is thought to advocate constant innovation—much like Kuntaka—in fact, many of the major treatises on poetics are conservative and rule-bound. Aristotle does not emphasize either individuality or innovation, but consistency, a quality also emphasized by many Sanskrit theorists (see Gerow 232). As Umberto Eco has pointed out, "the tragedies of which [Aristotle] had knowledge were many more than have come down to us, and they all followed (by varying it) one fixed scheme" (99). Aristotle's enormously influential interpreter, Horace, introduced the rigidity of the three unities. Terence, partially in justification of his and Menander's use of stock comic characters, insisted in the prologue to *Eunuchus* that "nothing is said that has not been said before" (238; 11.40–41), a claim supported in this context by Northrop Frye's observation that "The plot structure of Greek New Comedy, as transmitted by Plautus and Terence," a structure that "has become the basis for most [Western] comedy . . . down to our own day," is "in itself less a form than a formula" (171). Similarly, such famous poetic dicta as Pope's definition of successful poetry, "what oft was thought but ne'er so well expressed" ("An Essay on Criticism," 1.298), can hardly count as advocating innovation any more radical than the very minimum that must be granted to the Tamil lyricists. Finally, beyond these points, it should be clear that the degree of innovation in art varies anywhere with social, economic, and political circumstances. It has risen and fallen in the West and in the East. The history of these Western fluctuations has been discussed by a number of writers, for example Arnold Hauser in his *Social History of Art*. Indian literature has no doubt experienced similarly explicable alterations.

Thus it is apparent that innovation was valued in Indian literature, both theoretically and practically, just as it was in Europe, though the degree to which writers and theorists valued innovation varied in both regions. Those who admire the eternal changelessness of the Orient as well as those who disparage the Eastern arts for their ossification will no doubt be disappointed with this conclusion. However, the basic facts of Indian and Western literature do not appear to lend support to such traditional views.

Structural Unity

Turning to the question of the unity of Indian literature, we find precisely the same situation. As to theoretical statements, in the very passage where he is extolling the virtues of originality or uncommonness, Kuntaka affirms the importance of the "unity which strikingly underlies the various incidents described in different parts of the work leading to the ultimate end intended, each bound to the other by a relation of mutual assistance" (545). Indeed, he goes on to say that the presence of such unity in a work "reveals the essence of creative originality." Gerow notes a number of writers who explicitly isolate errors in logical and causal connection as poetic flaws (see 232). Although these may not make specific reference to structural unity per se, that is clearly one aspect of a literary work to which causal and logical connections are crucial. In a related vein, Gerow points out that the eighth-century theorist, Vāmana, viewed poetry as "an organic whole" (236), and that the authors of the *Nāṭyaśāstra* were "interested in the *rasa* [sentiment] . . . because it offers a rationale for stating the unity of this complex form which is the play" (248).[6] Abhinavagupta and Ānandavardhana stressed both causal unity and unity of sentiment as crucial to aesthetic success (see "Locana" 438 and *Dhvanyālokā* 478).

Clearly, then, unity has a significant place in the theoretical principles of classical Indian literature. There seems to be no reason to believe that it is less important in practice, or that structural unity in particular is less successfully pursued in the East than in the West (or, conversely, that Eastern literature has more successfully managed to evade draconian rigors of structure). Certainly there are structural flaws—improbabilities, contradictions, etc. (i.e., logical and causal errors, as mentioned above)—in any number of Indian literary works. However, there are such flaws in any number of Western literary works. And, once the general pattern of similarity is seen, the burden of proof is on those who would maintain that there is still a difference in frequency, that Indian works more frequently involve improbabilities when matched with Western works for genre, degree of textual corruption, etc.

The Problem of Genre. The mention of genre in this context—a relevant concern as our demands for structural unity vary with genre—brings us to an issue that it is important to address before going any further. The commonplace that tragedy is un-Indian is at best misleading, at worst false. This is shown not only by the speed with which Indian novelists and writers of short fiction have taken up the tragic format in the past century, but by a number of earlier developments as well. For example, both major epics of the Indian tradition, the *Rāmāyaṇa* and the *Mahābhārata,* involve very clear tragic elements (as do the Purāṇas; see Nandy 20–21). In the former, there is not only the story of Karṇa, but also the deaths of Kṛṣṇa and of all the Pāṇḍavas excepting Yudiṣṭhira. The *Rāmāyaṇa* focuses on a war fought by Rāma to regain his abducted wife Sītā. But Rāma's subsequent concern with reputation results in a second and now lifelong separation, a separation that Rāma then bitterly regrets. There are tragic incidents as well, such as the murder of Vali. Admittedly, each poem involves a final moment of (posthumous) joy. But then this sort of qualification is common in Western tragedies; witness, for example, the reconciliation of the Montagues and Capulets following the deaths of Romeo and Juliet, the hopeful accession of Edgar after the battle of France and England in *King Lear,* the assumption of Oedipus (in *Oedipus at Colonus*) with its implication of success and prosperity for Athens (a connection pointed out by Barbara Stoler Miller; see Miller 36), the vindication of Orestes and the concurrent founding of the Areopagus (in *The Eumenides*), and so on. (For a fuller discussion of tragic elements in a broader range of Sanskrit literature, see Bhat 36–67).

More importantly, there were at least two brief classical Sanskrit tragedies, both by Bhāsa (see Bhat), both drawn from tragic elements in the *Mahābhārata.* Prima facie, it seems unlikely that there were not many others, now lost; as J. A. B. van Buitenen has written, "It has been remarked that 90 percent of Indian literature has been eaten by white ants" (Dimock et al. 12). In any case, *Karṇabhāra* (*Karṇa's Burden*) and *Ūrubhaṅga* (*The Breaking of Thighs*) fit the Western tragic pattern well, the former presenting the events leading to Karṇa's death, the latter depicting the death of Duryodhana. (We shall have occasion to return to *Karṇabhāra* below.)

Edwin Gerow has maintained that these plays are not in fact tragedies in the Western sense. However, they are tales about the fall of a central character with whom we in some degree sympathize, and this is fundamentally what we mean by tragedy. Gerow adopts a much more limited definition than this, based upon a very narrow (and questionable) interpretation of Aristotle and involving such elements as a necessary "alienation" of the main character "vis-à-vis the community," a "flaw in terms of which he might be said to have brought about his own downfall" ("Bhāsa's Ūrubhaṅga" 411), etc. Perhaps—and this is debatable—*Karṇabhāra* and *Ūrubhaṅga* are not "true" tragedies according to Gerow's definition. But then one might equally argue that, according to this definition, most of the putatively paradigmatic tragedies of Greece, France, England, and other European countries are not "true" tragedies either. In this way, Gerow's argument is irrelevant, perhaps trivial, a mere terminological quibble with no bearing on issues of comparative literary study.

Beyond this definitional issue, Gerow bases his conclusions on two very questionable—indeed, in my view, clearly false—assumptions about Indian culture and Indian people. The first is that "Indian culture, which admits no ultimate divorcement of man's good from the good of all, and considers the separation—indeed, even the death—of man to be a temporary and resolvable condition. The status we call 'individual' is, insofar as can be determined, simply a defective condition, requiring remedy, and is not in itself significant, apart from its treatment" (411). As far as theology goes, this is true enough. Similar claims could be made concerning Christian views of death. But at the level of the human emotion of real Indian people—clearly what is relevant here—this is absurd, just as it would be for Christians.[7]

Gerow's second assumption is that, for Indians, or rather Hindus, "all consequences are deserved" and that pity, in Indian culture, is directed at suffering because it is "universal," not because it is "deserved or not deserved" (412). Again, a theologically plausible claim, but one that implies Indians will feel pity for a jailed murderer just as they will feel pity for the family of his or her victim, that they will not discriminate between a real criminal justly convicted and an innocent person framed for a crime and falsely convicted. This is just not true.

Despite Gerow's claims to the contrary, Bhāsa's two plays are as clearly tragedic as any Western play we might care to cite.[8] Moreover, they are as *rigorously* structured as Western tragedies, a point I shall try to demonstrate below in the case of *Karṇabhāra*. There is, in other words, no difference in kind between Indian and Western literature either in the existence of tragedy or, as we shall see, in its structural necessitation.

On the other hand, it does seem fair to say that Sanskrit drama was far more oriented toward romantic comedy. And this fact has at least one relevant implication. In interpreting and evaluating Western drama, we allow for greater leeway in comic emplotment than in tragic emplotment. It is commonplace to remark that comedy is less rigorous in its structural unity and that it has less of a need to be rigorous. As Helen Gardner puts it in an essay on *As You Like It*, "Tragic plots must have a logic which leads to an inescapable conclusion. Comic plots are made up of changes, chances and surprises. Coincidences can destroy tragic feeling: they heighten comic feeling. It is absurd to complain in poetic comedy of improbable encounters and characters arriving pat on their cue, of sudden changes of mind and mood" (208). As Susanne Langer notes in *Feeling and Form*, "The illusion of life which the comic poet creates is the oncoming future fraught with dangers and opportunities, that is, with physical or social events occurring by chance and building up the coincidences with which individuals cope according to their lights" (331). Or, as Northrop Frye argues, "Unlikely conversions, miraculous transformations, and providential assistance are inseparable from comedy" (170). Indeed, Frye goes so far as to say that "there can hardly be such a thing as inevitable comedy" (170).

Thus, by usual Western standards, a considerable degree of chance and improbability is not only permissible in comedy, but quite *characteristic* of comedy. It is important to keep in mind both the evaluative and descriptive points when examining the structure and unity of Sanskrit comedy. On the other hand, the best Sanskrit comedies, though comedies, are in my view as rigorously structured as most Western tragedies—indeed, more rigorously structured than many of the most famous Western tragedies, such as *Romeo and Juliet*, which, under the guise of astrology ("star-crossed lovers," I.6) is in fact a tragedy of bad luck, or Euripides' *Andromache*, a play well known for its episodic looseness.

Varieties of Unity. In order to discuss the relative structural unity of Sanskrit drama, I should like first to look at some relevant passages from Aristotle's *Poetics*, the work that, more than any other, has helped to define what Western writers and critics understand as structural unity. In book VII, Aristotle maintains that "tragedy is a representation of an action that is whole and complete" (31; VII.2). He continues

> A whole is what has a beginning and middle and end. A beginning is that which is not a necessary consequent of anything else but after which something else exists or happens as

> a natural result. An end on the contrary is that which is inevitably or, as a rule, the natural result of something else but from which nothing else follows; a middle follows something and something follows from it. (VII. 3–6)

In referring to "necessary" (*anankēs*) consequence (or "natural result"), Aristotle is asserting that there is some sort of necessity that links the three parts of a drama and communicates to the viewer/reader a sense of completeness or wholeness. The most obvious way in which such necessity can be achieved with a sense of wholeness is if a causal sequence unfolds that leads a main character from some normal or lasting state through a change of state to another normal or lasting state, a state that, the audience may assume, will continue along predictable, ordinary lines (cf. VII.11 and XIII). Moreover, this causal sequence should proceed out of the initial situation (including both circumstances and character) and not out of subsequently introduced elements that are themselves unexplained.

More exactly, for Aristotle, a causal sequence in a plot is first of all a sequence of events that imitates similar sequences in the world, following the same principles. It is "a *representation* [or imitation—mimēsis] of an action that is whole and complete" (31; VII.2). It is a common view that a concern with imitation is very Western. However, Indian theorists make significant reference to imitation as an important, even crucial element in literary composition. For example, in the *Nāṭyaśāstra*, we read that "[t]he drama . . . is a mimicry of actions and conducts of people" (15; I.111). In the *Abhinavabhāratī*, we find Abhinavagupta objecting strongly to drama that lacks verisimilitude (*Aesthetic* 63; I.9), and in his commentary on Ānandavardhana, Abhinavagupta writes that "Matters should be so described that there may be no breach in the credence of the audience" ("Locana" 430). (For a more detailed response to the idea that "imitation is alien to Indian aesthetics," see Sukla.)

Moreover, while imitation is more important to Indian theorists than is widely thought, it is less crucial to Aristotelian poetics than is commonly thought. Thus Aristotle emphasizes that successful drama need not be good science, for the causal and other principles that result in dramatic "wholeness" may accord with facts or with common beliefs or with ideals. As Aristotle puts it, "Since the poet represents life . . . he[/she] must always represent one of three things—either things as they were or are; or things as they are said and seem to be; or things as they should be" (101; XXV.2). Thus, in examining the structure of a drama, we may seek either realistic causal connections or unrealistic but widely accepted or widely desired causal connections.

In later centuries, the recognition that the experience of literature involves a "willing suspension of disbelief" added to these a form of causal necessity dictated by the internal principles of the fictional world itself. Aristotle perhaps hints at this possibility when he says that one may respond to a charge of falsehood not only by reference to ideals, but also by saying, "Such is the tale," instancing "tales about gods" as an example (103; XXV.12)—though he might have intended this as merely another reference to common beliefs. In any case, it is commonly acknowledged in the West that in, for example, various forms of fantasy literature, the causal principles may function well and give readers a sense of structural necessity without being true or believed true or seen as morally ideal.

It is important to emphasize that, for Aristotle and in respect to tragedy, any necessitation—actual, believed, or whatever—must derive from the initial situation, and the most effective form of necessitation from the initial situation is the inner flaw or motivated error of a fundamentally good or sympathetic hero, specifically an error that is the result of extremity, perhaps an extremity of a usually admirable quality. As Aristotle puts it, the best tragic hero is someone "who is no paragon of virtue and righteousness, and yet it is through no badness or villainy of his[/her] own that he[/she] falls into . . . misfortune, but rather through some flaw of character [or error, *hamartia*]" (47; XIII.5).

Beyond these forms of causal necessitation (actual, ideal, believed and internal), Aristotle points to a final, noncausal form: that of design. The most poetically effective occurrences that violate causal principles are, Aristotle tells us, "those which seem to have occurred by design [*epitēdes*], for instance when the statue of Mitys at Argos killed the man who caused Mitys's death by falling on him at a festival." "Such events do not seem to be mere accidents," Aristotle continues. "So such plots as these must necessarily be the best" (39 [altered]; IX.12–13).

Aristotle's example here clarifies the matter but, I think, is more narrow in its implication than the notion of design, which I would take to encompass cases of the sort Aristotle notes, but not to be confined to these. Specifically, I would distinguish four rough types of structuration or necessitation by design. I should emphasize that these are not absolutely distinct essences, but closely related literary practices, which are most often deployed in concert. The first of these four types is rhetorical and encompasses those techniques, such as foreshadowing or circularity (e.g., beginning and ending in the same place or same sort of place), which contribute to a feeling of the inevitability and finality of the ending. What range of techniques operate in this way and why they are effective is an important topic for investigation, but not crucial here.

The second category I should like to distinguish is that of metaphoric or symbolic connection. Frequently we are inclined to take a given event or act as necessary in part because we associate it ("symbolically") with other events—either within or outside of the story—and thereby link these events, consciously or unconsciously, as if they were causally connected. Cases of "poetic justice," such as Aristotle's example of King Mitys fall under this category.

A third type of design is the broader and more diffuse patterning of images and other associatively linked elements. These contribute to our sense that an event is "fitting," even if it is not well explained in causal terms. *Agamemnon* provides a good example of this: The recurrent imagery of nets and capture makes Agamemnon's entrapment in a robe seem appropriate and plausible as a means to his murder, though the scenario is somewhat questionable in terms of literal causality and mimetic realism. As with rhetoric, the diverse types that fall under this category are a potentially fruitful topic for future study. For the present, however, the patterning of imagery is well enough and widely enough understood to serve as a paradigm case.

Finally, I would add structural association or assimilation to this list of varieties of necessity by design. Here I have in mind the association of one story with another story that itself is conceived of as necessitated. I am not simply referring to allegory here. Rather, I am speaking of any sort of design by which a given narrative achieves a greater sense of structural necessitation by association with a second narrative—and for the most part this association is *not* allegorical. Perhaps the most obvious examples of this sort of nonallegorical design are those works that rely on classical parallels (e.g., Joyce's *Ulysses* in relation to the *Odyssey*) and those that involve the assimilation of a tragic hero to Christ (e.g., Makak in Derek Walcott's *Dream on Monkey Mountain*) or other Biblical figures, such as Job. It is important to note, however, that these parallels and assimilations may be quite effective, perhaps more effective, when not recognized self-consciously by the reader, or even produced self-consciously by the author.

Examples of each sort of design are obvious in Western literature. As I shall argue, the same techniques are employed in Indian literature—and just as obviously, once one sets out to look for them. Before turning to this "epitedic" necessitation, however, we should take a look at causal necessitation in its several varieties.

Causal and Mimetic Unity: The Example of *Karṇabhāra*. As I have already remarked, the two extant Sanskrit tragedies conform closely to Aristotelian principles of causal rigor. *Karṇabhāra* is a particularly striking example. The play concerns a simple event. Karṇa, who has been unjustly denied his birthright by his brothers, the Pāṇḍavas, and has joined their enemies, the Kauravas, is going forth to engage in the climactic battle between these two forces. As always, he wears a divine armor that protects him from death. Karṇa's character, we know beforehand, is extremely generous and strict in the fulfillment of obligations. At the outset of the play, he speaks briefly with his charioteer about a curse that will render his weapons useless just when he needs them. Indra—the father of Arjuna, whom Karṇa will face in battle—appears before Karṇa in the guise of a Brahmin requesting alms. Because of his sense of duty and because of his generosity, Karṇa agrees readily. After some discussion, Karṇa offers Indra the armor. Indra accepts and departs. When Karṇa's charioteer tells Karṇa that he has been duped, Karṇa replies that, in fact, it is Indra who has been duped. Karṇa indicates that, by unselfishly giving the armor, he has assured his own spiritual well-being, and thus he has ultimately been victorious. At the very moment he explains this, however, a messenger appears and offers Karṇa a powerful weapon that he can use only once. Karṇa initially refuses to accept the "counter-gift," which will render his earlier sacrifice meaningless. But the messenger insists that it is his duty to accept what the gods offer. Karṇa concedes. In the end, he calls to his charioteer to go forth, betraying no fear of the battle, though now he and the audience both know that he will be killed and that his weapon will be wasted.

In this play, the beginning and ending are only implied—subtly and powerfully. The causal middle that links these, centering on Karṇa's devastating loss of armor—and on the gods' worthless, self-exonerating, counter-gift—follows directly from Karṇa's flaw (excessive generosity linked with pride and blind commitment to duty), and the initial situation (including Indra's paternal commitments, etc.). Within the context of Hindu religious belief—or simply within the context of the fictional/mythological universe of the play—this brief and powerful tragedy follows Aristotelian principles of necessitation so closely that it would almost seem to have been based on them. (For an Aristotelian analysis of *The Breaking of Thighs*, see Bhat 78–79.)

As this reference to religious belief and fictional context indicates, Indian dramas do frequently involve what many of us would consider mimetic implausibilities. But what is important here is that precisely the same thing is true of European literature. Indeed, many of the things Western readers find most implausible in Sanskrit drama and other Indian fiction have close parallels in Greek drama, where they are, in contrast, readily accepted. Thus, for example, Hegel singles out the supernatural elements in *Śakuntalā*—when "we are suddenly snatched away from . . . concrete reality and carried up into the clouds of Indra's heaven" (339) or when Durvāsas curses Śakuntalā (1176)—as serious structural flaws. Presumably he would have said the same of *Karṇabhāra*. But it is inconsistent to find unconvincing the military and personal intervention of Indra in *Śakuntalā* or *Karṇabhāra* while accepting the in many ways more bizarre juridical intervention of Athena and the Furies in *The Eumenides*. Similarly, it is odd to question the miraculous assumption of Śakuntalā while not questioning the less clearly explained apotheosis of Oedipus at the end of *Oedipus at Colonus* (as, for example, Barbara Stoler Miller has noted; see Miller 36), or to be disturbed by the notion that sins are punished across the lives of one individual (karma) while viewing as quite natural the more evidently unjust Greek belief that sins are punished across generations (for example, recall that the tragedy of Oedipus goes back to a sin of Oedipus's father Laius, the abduction of Chrysippus—a sin that has tragic consequences for Oedipus's children as well). The same holds for the function of curses in Greek and Indian literature (recall, for instance, that the sufferings of Atreus's children and grandchildren, including Orestes, result in part from a curse pronounced by Thyestes).

Once again, there appears to be no substantive difference between Indian and European literature in the conception or value of causal necessitation.

Varieties of Design: The Example of *Śakuntalā*. But, again, not all necessitation or structural unity is causal in nature. Turning to rhetoric, the first of our four types of design, we find clear instances of such techniques as circularity and foreshadowing in a number of Sanskrit dramas. For example, *Śakuntalā* both begins and ends with Duṣyanta meeting Śakuntalā in a hermitage. Moreover, in both cases uncertainty and hope at the outset lead to union, the clear difference being that the second hermitage is more heavenly, in both literal and symbolic elevation, and the second union is public and spiritual rather than private and sexual (some ramifications of this point are examined in Gerow "Plot Structure"). Indeed, *Śakuntalā* is perhaps more tightly circular than any major Western drama in that not only do acts I and VII parallel one another (with the meeting in a hermitage), acts II and VI and acts III and V parallel one another as well, forming three concentric circles, with the center in the unpaired act IV (cf. Gerow "Sanskrit," 59).

Foreshadowing is evident in the same play at a number of points. For example, Duṣyanta's forgetting of Śakuntalā is prefigured at the very outset. The Director enters and announces that we are about to see a play called *Abhijñānaśākuntala, The Recognition of Śakuntalā*. But, after listening to an actress sing, he forgets the name of the play, just as Duṣyanta later forgets Śakuntalā herself (after he has heard one of his wives sing). Moreover, when reminded of the play, the director compares himself directly with Duṣyanta (Kale 6–13; references are to this edition unless otherwise noted). Similarly, we may glimpse the future separation of Duṣyanta and Śakuntalā in Gautamī's reference to the *cakravāka* birds, overheard by Śakuntalā just after Duṣyanta's proposal (115). Due to a curse, these birds are destined to be separated from one another every night (for a discussion of some elements of this myth, see Dave 450–53). Indeed, Śakuntalā explicitly identifies herself with the female *cakravāka* bird when leaving the hermitage to rejoin Duṣyanta (251). Moreover, the king is indirectly associated with the birds by the phonetic and semantic similarity between "*cakravāka*" (the ruddy goose, literally "*cakra*" or "wheel" bird) and the regal title "*cakravartin*" (the universal monarch characterized as turner of the *cakra*/wheel; Apte et al. note that this word may be used as a pun indicating resemblance with the *cakravāka*). This foreshadowing functions in further detail as well, for the birds are separated by a river and it is in entering a river that Śakuntalā loses Duṣyanta's ring and thus makes their separation inevitable. Finally, the fact that the birds are reunited in the day indicates that Duṣyanta and Śakuntalā, too, will ultimately be reunited.[9]

A final example of foreshadowing may be found when Kaṇva is said to have gone on a pilgrimage to Somatīrtha in order to avert some evil fate that threatens Śakuntalā. As Barbara Stoler Miller explains, it was at Somatīrtha that "Soma, the moon, was cured of consumption inflicted on him by the curse of his father-in-law,

Dakṣa" (338n.1.12+). Thus the mere mention of this place calls up a story of the moon being cursed by Dakṣa, suffering, and ultimately being cured at Somatīrtha. Duṣyanta is a king of the lunar race, and Durvāsas is a descendant of Dakṣa. Thus this play could be said to tell the story of how a lunar king suffered due to a curse by a descendant of Dakṣa but was ultimately cured due to a sacrifice at Somatīrtha—a series of events perfectly foreshadowed by the myth of Somatīrtha.

Turning to our second type of design, we may isolate an instance of metaphoric/symbolic connection in the peculiar manner of the ring's recovery. There are many reasons why a fish serves as the intermediary in causing Duṣyanta to recall Śakuntalā. Most importantly for our present concerns, a type of fish is one symbol or emblem of Kāma, the Hindu cupid. Indeed, at one point in the play, Kāma is referred to as "the fish-bannered god," thus making the connection explicit (see 90–91; actually the emblem of Kāma is a *makara,* "sea-creature," which is semantically but not etymologically connected with the word for the fish, "*matsya*"). In this way, the fish that functions to recall Duṣyanta's love for Śakuntalā is a sort of displacement of the god Kāma who (metaphorically or mythically) caused that love initially. This connection is not, of course, a powerful factor in the play. However, it is a significant detail that contributes, however slightly, to the overall sense of structural unity by giving the fish a sort of associative "rightness" and thus making its presence appear less arbitrary. Another example of this type may be found in the fact that Indra arranges the reunion of Śakuntalā and Duṣyanta, when it had been Indra's shrine at which Śakuntalā had lost her ring, thus giving rise to the initial separation. This is closer to the case of "poetic justice" cited by Aristotle.

Śakuntalā includes a range of more loosely associative image patterns as well. Many of these are fairly localized; for example, the early discussion of Śakuntalā as a divine work of art [72–73] connects and contrasts nicely with Duṣyanta's later attempt to reduce his feeling of loss by painting her (226–27). Other patterns, however, are more pervasive—for example, the elemental images of fire and water. Specifically, we may distinguish two sorts of fire in the play. The first is holy fire, the fire of ritual (personified in the god Agni), literal flames that allow and sanctify union. The second is sexual "fire," the fire of passion (personified in Kāma), a physiological heat that leads to physical union and procreation, or, if frustrated, leads to debilitating fever. For the most part, water, including the holy water of sacred pools, is linked with separation and death. In certain cases, water that is consumed—drinking water, rain water—is associated with the cooling of physiological heat and thus with union, life, and regeneration. In each case, though, water functions as the diametric opposite of fire.

As to the link between water and separation, we have already seen two examples in the *cakravāka* birds and the loss of the token ring. Other examples may be found in Śakuntalā's somewhat melodramatic insistence that her suffering (due to separation from her beloved) will result in her friends offering "sesamum-mixed-water" (101), which is to say performing her death ceremony, and in the fact that Śakuntalā's separation from her family takes place at "the margin of water" (251). As to fire, the ultimate reunion of Śakuntalā and Duṣyanta is guaranteed by the (literal and holy) fire offering of Kaśyapa (133). Śakuntalā's conception of Bharata, the concrete result of their initial union, is announced by a comparison of Śakuntalā with the *śamī* tree and the newly conceived Bharata with the (metaphorically sexual) "fire" in the "womb" (*garbha*) of that tree (132). Later, in a similar vein, when Duṣyanta first sees Bharata, he remarks, "The boy appears to me to contain within himself the germ of mighty energy, remaining like fire in the condition of a spark waiting for fuel [to display its blaze]" (267).

The *rohita* fish is particularly interesting in this context, for it is defined not by, but against the water that surrounds it, and this contrast operates both in plot function and in associative relations. In this way, the *rohita* fish neatly crystallizes the elemental pattern we are considering. First of all, "*rohita*" means "red," and the compound "*rohita-aśva*" ("red-horsed") refers to fire—specifically, Agni, the fire god. In this way, the *rohita* fish may be associatively linked with holy fire, appropriately in that it is what allows for Duṣyanta's recollection of Śakuntalā and thus ultimately his reunion with her. Moreover, as we have already noted, the *rohita* fish is also linked with Kāma and thus with sexual fire. Indeed, this association is strengthened—along with the fish/water contrast—by the fact that, just before referring to Kāma as the fish-bannered god, Duṣyanta speaks of the fire of Kāma as "like the submarine fire in the ocean" (88–89).

All of this is linked with other patterns of imagery and with religious motifs as well, further tightening the complex design of the play. Most strikingly, Duṣyanta concludes the play by asking Śiva to end his cycle of rebirth, a cycle that can be broken only when desire is overcome and one fully recognizes one's divine nature. Taking up the imagery of light and darkness—associated throughout the play with recognition and forgetting—Duṣyanta refers to Śiva as *"nīla-lohitaḥ"* (296), which is to say, combining darkness and light or, literally, blue and red. The "blue" here refers to a deadly poison held in Śiva's throat and thus fits well with the water imagery elsewhere in the play. The fiery *lohita*, the opposite of watery, thanatic *nīla*, also fits well with the patterns we have been examining, especially when one recalls that *"lohita"* is merely a variant of *"rohita."* But like other elements of the drama, these patterns are reoriented in this final scene. Specifically, the fire hinted at here is not divine Agni, the fire of ritual (including the ritual of marriage), nor is it Kāma, the fire of sexual longing. Rather, this is the fire that burned Kāma to ashes when he distracted Śiva from ascetic practices; it is the fire of yogic *tapas*, the fire of accumulated spiritual energy. In keeping with this spiritual reorientation of the play's conclusion, the union associated with this (suggested) fire, the union called for by Duṣyanta in these lines addressed to Śiva, is no longer the union of lover and beloved in procreative marriage or in carnal desire. Rather, it is the union of ātman and Brahman, the individual soul and the divine godhead—a union that, in Śaivite theology, is also a matter of recognition after forgetting, specifically recognition of divinity (see Pandit *Mirror* chapter 4 and throughout; Śaivism is that branch of Hinduism that takes Śiva to be the supreme deity).

Finally, structural necessitation also figures importantly in Kālidāsa's play. Indeed, there are several relevant patterns, differing in extent and detail. I will mention two. The first concerns the reworking of what is most often a tragic plot of the separation of lovers. Śakuntalā's assumption into the heavens, while it is by no means a death, operates as a sort of substitute for death. It is as if the assumption functioned to hint at and at the same time avoid the tragic episode of death. Similarly, the misery of Duṣyanta, his doting on a painting of his first meeting with Śakuntalā, his general melancholy, the forbidding of the rites of spring, and the associated distress of nature (208–209), all suggest death and mourning, though there has only been temporary separation. Finally, the spiritualized reunion of the lovers in a heavenly *āśrama* (or retreat) following a battle could easily be post mortem. In this way, the actual events of the drama hint at another series of events that are both closely connected and tragic: the death of the (rejected) woman, the mourning of the man, the death of the man (in battle), and the reunion of the lovers in heaven. (Indeed, Kālidāsa's tale of Aja and Indumatī, in *Raghuvaṃśa*, proceeds along these general lines.) Thus it derives a part of its unity from these events, while at the same time denying them and transforming them into comedy.

A second structural pattern is to be found in the relation of this story to that of Rāma and Sītā, a pattern of detailed connections manifest in part through inversions of the sort isolated and examined by Claude Lévi-Strauss. In outline, the major parallels are the following. Śakuntalā and Sītā are the children of divine or superhuman beings but are abandoned in infancy and raised by mortal foster parents. Specifically, Śakuntalā, the daughter of a heavenly *apsaras*, or nymph, is found by a hermit on a river bank, while Sītā, the daughter of the earth, is found by the king in a furrow in the ground. Each marries a king who abandons her in a forest when she is pregnant. In response to this mistreatment, each calls out to the earth to open and receive her and each is, in consequence, removed from the human world and received by her mother—Sītā entering the earth, Śakuntalā entering the heavens. Years after rejecting Śakuntalā, Duṣyanta goes to battle, then meets his initially unrecognized son in an *āśrama* on a mountain. Likewise, years after abandoning Sītā, Rāma performs the (martial) *aśvemedha* rite, meeting his initially unrecognized sons from an *āśrama* in the forest.

This parallel with inversions is quite close to that concerning death. Indeed, the story of Sītā and Rāma is in many ways a tragedy of the sort implied and deferred by *Śakuntalā*. In this way, the force of each parallel is increased by the operation of the other. The suggestion of the tragic structure of life, separation, and death, and the suggestion of the sacred story of Sītā and Rāma contribute to a feeling of "rightness" about the events of the play—and hence to a feeling of unity and necessity for the play as a whole. At the same time, the inversions of the Sītā/Rāma story may have political significance as a tacit criticism of Rāma, akin to the explicit criticism that Kālidāsa set out in the *Raghuvaṃśa*; if so, this would further tighten the structure of the play by giving thematic point to those sections that are causally dubious and that deviate from the prototypes we have been considering—most particularly, those sections surrounding Duṣyanta's forgetting and recollection of Śakuntalā and his ultimate reunion with her.

We have treated only two plays here—and two of the best. But the same principles hold for other Sanskrit dramas and other Indian literary works, in much the way they hold for Western literary works. Like a belief in the peculiar Westernness of literary innovation—and like a belief in the peculiar Westernness of logic, empirical investigation, adjudication by simplicity criteria, etc. (a belief that writers such as Frits Staal have shown to be absurd)—a belief in the peculiar Westernness of rigorous literary structure is entirely unfounded.

Toward a New Comparative Literature: Literary Reconstruction and Aesthetic Universals

Once one clears one's mind of the Kiplingesque cliché quoted at the outset, once one frees oneself from the baseless view of the mutual absolute Otherness of East and West, a whole new field of potential investigation opens up, especially in the realm of aesthetics. There are two broad areas of inquiry that are immediately apparent in this general field. Both address nonrandom similarities across literatures. The first concerns monogenesis, or common origin. The second concerns polygenesis. The first involves the reconstruction of a sort of regional "protopoetics." The second involves the isolation of literary universals, the search for what Paul Kiparsky refers to as "a 'universal poetics' analogous to and closely related to universal grammar" ("On Theory and Interpretation" 192), a poetics based upon the view that "all literary traditions . . . utilize the same elements" ("Role" 11).[10]

The paradigm case of monogenetic study is, of course, the well-known work of Georges Dumézil and his followers dealing with the reconstruction of proto-Indo-European myth (for an overview of this research, see Puhvel). Along similar lines, writers such as Jaan Puhvel, Udo Strutynski, and Scott Littleton have examined the recurrence and transformation of Indo-European motifs in nonmythic literary works. There is still a great deal to be done in this area, but the relevant comparatist research is clearly underway and has already led to noteworthy and plausible reconstructive hypotheses.

Moreover, beyond myth and motif, historical reconstruction has proven valuable with respect to a range of structural, rhetorical, and other features. The isolation of ring-composition is one obvious example. As Calvert Watkins explains, "Ring-composition is the beginning and the ending of a discourse or complex utterance higher than the sentence level, with the same or equivalent word, phrase, or even sound" ("Aspects" 109–10)—a pattern to be found in a number of Indo-European literatures. Metrics also has benefited from reconstructive work, though the attempts to define a specific, standard proto-Indo-European meter have been unsuccessful for reasons discussed by Kurylowicz. Similarly, researchers such as Watkins have been able to reconstruct certain proto-Indo-European poetic formulae, some more general principles governing the generation of sets of formulae, and some formula-related associative complexes important to aesthetical intent and experience ("Aspects"). Watkins has also been able to reconstruct a few "meta-poetic" principles, such as the imperative of obscurity and the judgment that obscure poetic language is in some way associated with divinity, at the very least in its opposition to ordinary human speech ("Language").

Clearly, there are many possibilities for future work in this area. However, equally clearly, such work is bound by strict historical and cultural limits. In this respect, the study of universals is of even greater interest and importance. Before considering what it might mean to seek specifically literary universals, however, it is important to say a few things about the use of the term "universal" in the present context, and about some of the types of universals, in this sense of the term. I am using "universal" in the very broad sense in which it is employed by linguists to cover statistically significant tendencies of languages—or, here, literatures—either as an undifferentiated group or according to type (see Comrie). More exactly, we may distinguish the following categories of universal: (1) Statistical universals are simply broad tendencies that occur across (genetically unrelated) languages, literatures, etc. more frequently than would be predicted by chance. (2) Disjunctive universals comprise series of principles, at least one of which must apply to any given language, literature, etc. If the disjunction is "inclusive," then more than one of the properties may apply in any given case; if it is "exclusive," then only one can apply. (3) Implicational universals are principles defining either necessary or sufficient conditions for the instantiation of a given principle, or in some cases simply formalizing a statistically significant correlation. Thus, though all literatures may not employ technique q, it still may be possible to determine that *if* a literature has property p *then* it will employ technique q; or, for necessary rather than sufficient conditions, if a literature does not have property p, then it will not employ technique q; or, for statistical correlations, if a literature has property p, then it is more likely to employ technique q than if it does not have property p.[11] And finally, (4) absolute universals are principles shared by all languages, literatures, etc.

A nice example of a statistical universal may be found in the preference of most cultures for verse lines of no less than eight and no more than twelve syllables (see Kurylowicz 421; for a discussion and possible explanation of this preference and of various exceptions, see Hogan "Possibility"). Along the same lines, there is a broad, cross-cultural preference for repetitive sequences involving no more than three elements; as Kiparsky points out, "the pattern *abcdabcd,* for example, is rarely used either as a rhyme schema, or as a pattern of parallelism" ("Roles" 12).

An obvious candidate for a disjunctive universal would be the division of systems of versification into syllabic, accentual, and quantitative—plus accentual-syllabic, if this is considered distinct from accentual, and/or tonal (see Lotz), if this is not reducible to quantitative and accentual (see Jakobson 360–61). There has been some controversy as to the precise nature of this disjunction, but in any case it is clear that the number of systems of versification is very limited and the vast majority of conceptually possible systems simply do not exist; for example, there do not appear to be any systems based on number of linguistic sounds.

An example of a possible implicational universal may be found in Mircea Eliade's typology of myth systems based on cosmogony, where various genetically unrelated myths of origin are linked categorially (26–40). Another candidate for an implicational universal would be some form of the "sociological thesis," discussed by Arnold Hauser (49). This posits a presumably statistical link between the degree of market freedom in a given period and the degree of realism during that period. Hauser also suggests that when there is a patterned combination of naturalistic and formalistic elements in art or literature, the formalistic elements are invariably associated with persons highest in the social hierarchy (47–48). Analyses such as those of Lord concerning orality fall into this category as well, in that they claim that certain properties (e.g., the extensive use of formulae and epithets) inhere in a subset of literature, specifically that which is orally composed (for an overview of the research in this area, see Ong). Kiparsky has made some fascinating suggestions that fit here also; for example, "Alliteration . . . seems to be found as an obligatory formal element only in languages where the stress regularly falls on the same syllable in the word, which then must be the alliterating syllable" ("Role" 9), and "Most richly inflected languages do not use rhyme, and those that do, like Russian, tend to avoid rhymes that depend on grammatical endings" (10). No doubt the best known case of literary typology is Northrop Frye's *Anatomy of Criticism.* While primarily confined to Western literature, Frye's important work provides one possible framework from which more broadly comparatist research in typological universals might set out.

Finally, candidates for absolute universals might include the aesthetic valuation of structural unity in plot, and perhaps its higher valuation with respect to tragic events than with respect to comic events; the use and nature of aesthetic metaphor and related phenomena, such as imagery; the use of unifying rhetorical techniques of some sort, and even the use of specific techniques such as foreshadowing and circularity; the use of parallelism at a number of levels, from sound to phrasing to plot structure; the aesthetic valorization of pattern with unpredicted but recognizable variation at a number of levels, beginning with sound, pitch, and rhythm (perhaps involving the more specific properties of assonance, alliteration, etc.); the presence of an "aesthetic" and associative attitude—or *dhvani* attitude, to employ the Sanskrit concept (on the notion of a *dhvani* attitude, see Amaladass 117)—an attitude that is characteristic of anyone's approach to both artistic and natural beauty; the existence of fictional narrative itself and the operation of aesthetic identification (or empathy) in narrative; the presence of certain themes, such as conflict over love, separation and reunion of lovers or relatives, etc.; the preference for certain image correlations over others (e.g., the preference for associating lovers with birds, rather than fish or land animals; or the preference for associating love with flowers rather than grains or legumes); and so on. (For discussion and examples of various of these possible universals, see Hogan, "Shakespeare" and "Possibility.")

There is a sort of continuum across the various foci of comparative study, from political, social, and cultural history through monogenetic reconstruction, through the various grades of universals. All are important. The first is no doubt more important for analyzing individual works and, along with the second, it is necessary for comprehending broad social trends and cultural differences. The third, however, is absolutely crucial for our understanding of the nature and operation of the human mind. Again, non-European literature, such as that of India, is virtually absent from comparatist study today. Moreover, the work of Indologists has focused on social and cultural history, along with some reconstruction, to the exclusion of universal poetics. Indeed, as we have seen, Indologists frequently emphasize Indian/European differences quite as much, and often in the same terms, as earlier imperialist writers who had very different aims. Certainly, it is important to understand the differences between cultures. But it is also important to understand the superficiality of these differences and not to be led into affirming false oppositions on the basis of ideological clichés.

As Edwin Gerow notes in his overview of Indian poetics, Sanskrit literary theorists did not emphasize historical particularity or any other sort of difference. Rather, they were "concerned . . . with the form of poetic utterance in its generality" (231). Perhaps as Indian and other non-Western literatures are more thoroughly incorporated into comparatist study, the Eurocentric stress on cultural/historical difference will decrease. Perhaps the integration of comparative literature—which today, might justifiably be called "Occidentalism"—with the various strands of Orientalism will render both disciplines more Indian in this respect, bringing workers in each field closer to such universalists as Ānandavardhana and Abhinavagupta; perhaps it will make writers on India less prone to ideological determination, less likely to repeat the dichotomistic errors of earlier generations; and perhaps it will even create an environment in which comparatist research may begin to contribute to a real understanding of the nature and function of beauty in the human mind and in human society, of aesthetic feeling and literary cognition, as well as of the ideologies that distort each of these.[12]

Notes

1. Of course, Dimock's aim here is to avoid superficial evaluations of Indian literature by superficial criteria. But it is still relevant that he, like many other Indologists, chooses to emphasize the irrelevance of these criteria without indicating or, evidently, recognizing their superficiality—or, more importantly, the possibility that there may be more universal principles that are less superficial.
2. There are, of course, important exceptions to this tendency amongst Orientalists. The most obvious is Sir William Jones. A good recent example of nondichotomous analysis may be found in Jeffrey Moussaieff Masson's discussion of the opposition between advocates of poetic craft and advocates of poetic inspiration (6–7). Masson does not falsely identify one position with the West and one with the East, but is careful to give examples of each position from both regions—an eminently reasonable approach, which should be unremarkable.
3. Such judgments also cannot be based upon the supposed "representativeness" of the views expressed by individual Indians, women, and so on. It is rarely supposed that individual white men are representative of white men as a group. However, it seems frequently to be supposed that individual women, Indians, and other "subalterns" may be called upon to present not merely their own views, not merely "one

woman's perspective" or "one Indian's perspective," but "*the* woman's perspective" or "*the* Indian perspective." I cannot think of any reasons other than sexism and racism that would cause people to think that there is any less individual diversity (or any less fallibility) amongst women, Indians, and so on than amongst white men.

4. Occasionally, such alterations are to be found in medieval Western literature, for example, in the bizarre and fascinating *Genesis A*. (I am grateful to Robert Hasenfratz for pointing out this text to me.) However, works of this sort are extremely uncommon and hardly central to the canon (unlike Bhavabhūti's very canonical play). Indeed, the sanctity of religious plot at this time is indicated, for example, in Frederick Biggs's analysis of the Old English *Andreas*. Biggs points out that the Anglo-Saxon author's "strict adherence to the narrative progression" of the source—the apocryphal "Acts of Andrew and Matthias"—counts as evidence that he or she "considered the tale itself to be historically accurate and orthodox" (427), and thus inalterable in basic narrative structure.
5. This is not to say that the play has no standard or type characters. It does indeed. For example, the relationship between the lovers is in part mediated by Śakuntalā's two friends, Anasūyā and Priyaṁvadā, the standard female confidant characters of Sanskrit drama; comic relief is provided by the usual male confidant/buffoon character, and so on. However, the presence of such standard or type characters hardly supports the thesis that Indian literature is more tradition-bound than Western literature, for the character typology of Greek and Roman New Comedy is, it seems clear, at least as determinative as that of Indian comedy. Indeed, Terence himself at various points pokes fun at this typology. For example, in the prologue to *The Self-Tormentor*, he presents the following catalogue: "a scurrying servant, an irate oldster,/a gluttonous parasite, both smarmy and impudent,/a miser" (120; 11.37–39; my translation here and below). And in the prologue to *The Eunuch*, Terence runs through the lengthier list: "a scurrying servant . . . goodly matrons . . . evil harlots,/a gluttonous parasite, a braggart soldier,/a substituted boy, a servant-swindled oldster" (238; 11.36–39).
6. While in these last cases the unity in question is defined in affective rather than structural terms, they are not irrelevant. Though it will not be a major concern in the following pages, it is important to recall that Indian theorists are not alone in conceiving of poetic unity at least in part in terms of emotional effect. Even Aristotle at times places such effect above structure, at one point going so far as to say that "any 'impossibility' may be defended by reference to the poetic effect" (111; XXV.26).
7. A student of mine once asked if it is true that Easterners really do rejoice when loved ones die. At the time, I was appalled by the total dehumanization of Asians that this statement implied and hardly ex-

pected to find much the same understanding of Asian people in the work of major contemporary Orientalists. Indeed, this view is especially disturbing because of the brutal way in which it was deployed during the Vietnam War when the high number of Vietnamese casualties—roughly two million (Jhally, Lewis, and Morgan 52)—was repeatedly explained not by reference to our historically unprecedented and criminal bombardments, but rather by reference to the Asian view of life (see Herman 73). More recently, Marlin Fitzwater and others have cited the Iraqi indifference to death as a major factor in the tens of thousands of casualties inflicted by allied bombing (see Hitchens 294).

8. Moreover, tragedy is by no means merely Indo-European. See Kuan and Chikamatsu for, respectively, Chinese and Japanese instances. For a discussion of Japanese drama and tragedy, see Gerstle. I would also argue that not all the Sanskrit comedies are as straightforward as is frequently assumed. For example, *The Signet Ring of Rakshasa* may be understood as a problem comedy, disturbing in the way some comedies by Terence or Shakespeare are disturbing. Recall, for example, that in this play the ultimate victor is a man who brags, "Did I not take the vow to obliterate the Nandas from the face of the earth? Look at the burnt-out cities, the vultures, the desolate fires, the dead bodies of the Nandas carried in procession to the burial places! Who did that?" (Vishakadatta 223). In this way, it, too, is a play that violates the common conception of Sanskrit drama as pleasant romantic comedy.
9. It is worth noting that this is a good example of how the study of universal principles does not exclude but complement the recognition of cultural differences. It is often asserted that the search for universals or invariants involves a denial or loss or ignorance of particulars or variants. But nothing could be further from the truth. Certainly the discovery of universal principles indicates the relative superficiality of cultural differences. But it is only through a knowledge of those differences that we can recognize the universals—just as it is only through a concentration on universals that we can isolate and recognize the function of significant differences. Thus, without an understanding of the mythic or folkloric significance of *cakravāka* birds, we cannot see that reference to them constitutes a form of foreshadowing—just as we will not see any point in exploring and explicating the (culturally specific) reference to *cakravāka* birds if we are not aware of the structural unity of Sanskrit drama, the use of foreshadowing, etc. In a similar way, our understanding of the causal unity of Sanskrit literature does not prevent us from understanding, for example, the non-Western notion of karma, but rather in part depends upon that knowledge.
10. There is also the comparative study of poetic theory, which can be enormously valuable as well. There have been many fine theoreticians in many cultures and none of them was able to say all that there is to say on the topics of literary response, narrative structure, etc. For ex-

ample, Abhinavagupta's account of aesthetic feeling neatly complements Aristotelian analyses in a way that is clarifying for both theories. On the other hand, it should be kept in mind that comparative poetic theory cannot be substituted for comparative poetics. Specifically, theories about the literature of one's own culture are just as hypothetical as theories about the literature of another culture. We should not assume that the claims of a culture's poetic theories are true of that culture's literature any more than we should assume that a culture's medical theories are true of the physiologies of the people in that culture. Wendy Doniger O'Flaherty makes a similar point when she argues that indigenous interpretations of myths should be approached with the same critical attitude as nonindigenous interpretations (8) and when she points out that much that we consider typically Indian concerns not Indian thought and action, but Indian theory of thought and action (59). In more general terms, this is a commonplace of much sociological theory (see, for example, Marx's discussion in *A Contribution to the Critique of Political Economy* in Marx and Engels 85).

11. Obviously, statistical universals should if possible be developed into disjunctive universals, and disjunctive universals should if possible be developed into implicational universals. Moreover, implicational universals should if possible be coordinated into typologies. (Here and below, I treat typologies as a special case of implicational universals.)
12. I am grateful to Lalita Pandit, Jim Scully, and Barbara Stoler Miller for comments on and criticisms of earlier drafts of this essay.

Bibliography

Abhinavagupta. *The Aesthetic Experience According to Abhinavagupta*. 2d ed. Ed. and trans. Raniero Gnoli. Varanasi: Chowkhamba Sanskrit Series, 1968.

———. "Locana." In *The* Dhvanyālokā *of Ānandavardhana with the* Locana *of Abhinavagupta*. Trans. Daniel Ingalls, Jeffrey Masson, and M. V. Patwardhan. Ed. Daniel Ingalls. Cambridge: Harvard University Press, 1990.

Amaladass, Anand. *Philosophical Implications of Dhvani: Experience of Symbol Language in Indian Aesthetics*. Vienna: De Nobili Research Library, 1984.

Ānandavardhana. *The Dhvanyālokā of Ānandavardhana with the Locana of Abhinavagupta*. Trans. Daniel Ingalls, Jeffrey Masson, and M. V. Patwardhan. Ed. Daniel Ingalls. Cambridge: Harvard University Press, 1990.

Apte, V. S., et al. *Sanskrit-English Dictionary*. Poona: Prasad Prakashan, 1958.

Aristotle. "The Poetics." Trans. W. Hamilton Fyfe. In *Aristotle: The Poetics; "Longinus": On the Sublime; Demetrius: On Style*, ed. E. Capps, T. E. Page, and W. H. D. Rouse. New York: G. P. Putnam's Sons, 1927.

Bate, W. Jackson. *The Burden of the Past and the English Poet*. Cambridge: Harvard University Press, 1970.

Bhabha, Homi K. "The Other Question. . . ." *Screen* 24: (1983), 18–36.

Bharata-muni. *The Nāṭyaśāstra*. Trans. Manomohan Ghosh. Calcutta: Manisha Granthalaya, 1967.

Bhartrihari. In Bhartrihari and Bilhana. *The Hermit and the Love Thief*. Ed. and trans. Barbara S. Miller. NY: Viking, 1991.

Bhat, G. K. *Tragedy and Sanskrit Drama*. Bombay: Popular Prakashan, 1974.

Biggs, Frederick M. "The Passion of Andreas; *Andreas* 1398–1491." *Studies in Philology* LXXXV, no. 4. (Fall 1988).

Butcher, S. H. *Aristotle's Theory of Poetry and Fine Art*. 4th ed. New York: Dover, 1951.

Chikamatsu Monzaemon. *The Courier for Hell*. Trans. Donald Keene. In *Masterpieces of the Orient*, ed. G. L. Anderson. New York: W. W. Norton and Co., 1977.

Cixous, Hélène. "The Laugh of the Medusa." In *New French Feminisms*, ed. Elaine Marks and Isabelle de Courtivron. New York: Schocken, 1980.

Comrie, Bernard. *Language Universals and Linguistic Typology: Syntax and Morphology*. Chicago: University of Chicago Press, 1981.

Coulson, Michael, ed. and trans. *Śakuntalā*. In *Three Sanskrit Plays*. New York: Penguin, 1981.

Dave, K. N. *Birds in Sanskrit Literature*. Delhi: Motilal Banarsidass, 1985.

Dimock, E., E. Gerow, C. Naim, A. Ramanujan, G. Roadarmel, and J. van Buitenen. *The Literatures of India: An Introduction*. Chicago: University of Chicago Press, 1978.

Droit, Roger-Pol. "*Victor Cousin, La Bhagavad Gita et l'ombre de Hegel*." In *L'Inde et l'imaginaire/India in Western Imagination*, ed. Catherine Weinberger-Thomas. Paris: Éditions de l'École des Hautes Études en Sciences Sociales, 1988. (Collection Purusartha, 11).

Eco, Umberto. *The Limits of Interpretation*. Bloomington: Indiana University Press, 1990.

Eliade, Mircea. "Myths and Mythical Thought." In *The Universal Myths: Heroes, Gods, Tricksters and Others*, ed. Alexander Eliot. New York: New American Library, 1990.

Eliot, T. S. "The Music of Poetry." In *On Poetry and Poets*. New York: Farrar, Straus, and Giroux, 1979.

Epstein, Cynthia Fuchs. *Deceptive Distinctions: Sex, Gender, and the Social Order*. New Haven: Yale University Press, and New York: Russell Sage Foundation, 1988.

Faludi, Susan. *Backlash: The Undeclared War against American Women*. New York: Crown Publishers, 1991.

Fanon, Frantz. *Black Skin, White Masks*. Trans. Charles Lam Markmann. New York: Grove Press, 1967.

Fausto-Sterling, Anne. *Myths of Gender: Biological Theories about Women and Men*. New York: Basic Books, 1985.

Frye, Northrop. *Anatomy of Criticism: Four Essays*. Princeton: Princeton University Press, 1957.

Gardner, Helen. "*As You Like It*." In *As You Like It*, ed. Albert Gilman. New York: New American Library, 1963.

Gerbrands, A. A. "The Anthropological Approach." In *Main Trends in Aesthetics and the Sciences of Art*, ed. Mikel Dufrenne. New York: Holmes and Meier Publishers, 1979.

Gerow, Edwin. *Indian Poetics*. Wiesbaden: Otto Harrassowits.

———. "Plot Structure and the Development of *Rasa* in the Śakuntalā. Part I." *Journal of the American Oriental Society* 99, no. 4 (October-December 1979): 559–72.

———. "Sanskrit Dramatic Theory and Kālidāsa's Plays." In *Theater of Memory: The Plays of Kālidāsa*, ed. Barbara Stoler Miller. New York: Columbia University Press, 1984, 42–62.

———. "Bhāsa's Ūrubhanga and Indian Poetics." *Journal of the American Oriental Society* 105, no. 3 (July-September 1985): 405–12.

Gerstle, C. Andrew. "The Concept of Tragedy in Japanese Drama." *Japan Review* 1 (1990): 49–72.

Gilman, Sander L. "Black Bodies, White Bodies: Toward an Iconography of Female Sexuality in Late Nineteenth-Century Art, Medicine, and Literature." *Critical Inquiry* 12, no. 1 (Autumn 1985): 204–42.

Hart, George. *The Poems of Ancient Tamil*. Berkeley: University of California Press, 1975.

Hauser, Arnold. *The Social History of Art (Volume I): Prehistoric, Ancient-Oriental, Greece and Rome; Middle Ages*. Trans. Stanley Godman. New York: Vintage Books, 1957.

Hegel, G. W. F. *Aesthetics: Lectures on Fine Art*. 2 vols. Trans. T. M. Knox. Oxford: Clarendon Press, 1975.

Herman, Edward. "Mere Arabs." *Z Magazine*, February 1991, 72–73.

Hitchens, Christopher. "Minority Report." *The Nation*, 11 March, 1991, 294.

Hogan, Patrick Colm. *The Politics of Interpretation: Ideology, Professionalism, and the Study of Literature*. New York: Oxford University Press, 1990.

———. "The Possibility of Aesthetics." *The British Journal of Aesthetics* 34.4 (1994): 337–49.

———. "Shakespeare, Eastern Theatre, and Literary Universals: Drama in the Context of Cognitive Science." In *Shakespeare East and West*, ed. Minoru Fujita. Tokyo: Japan Library, forthcoming.

———. "Some Prolegomena to the Study of Literary Difference." *Poetics* 22 (1994): 243–61.

Horkheimer, Max, and Theodor Adorno. *Dialectic of Enlightenment*. Trans. John Cumming. New York: Continuum, 1986.

Hulin, Jean-Paul. *"L'Inde dans les premiers écrits de Kipling: Orthodoxie et Deviance."* In *L'Inde et l'imaginaire/India in Western Imagination*, ed. Catherine Weinberger-Thomas. Paris: Éditions de l'École des Hautes Études en Sciences Sociales, 1988. (Collection Purusartha, 11).

Jakobson, Roman. "Closing Statement: Linguistics and Poetics." In *Style in Language*, ed. Thomas Sebeok. Cambridge: The MIT Press, 1960.

Jhally, Sut, Justin Lewis, and Michael Morgan. "Amherst University Knowledge Poll." *Propaganda Review* 8 (Fall 1991): 14–15, 50–53.

Jussawalla, Adil, ed. *New Writing in India*. Baltimore: Penguin Books, 1974.

Kailasapathy, K. *Tamil Heroic Poetry*. Oxford: Clarendon Press, 1968.

Kale, M. R., ed. and trans. *The Abhijñānaśākuntalam of Kālidāsa*. 10th ed. Delhi: Motilal Banarsidass, 1969.

Kiparsky, Paul. "The role of linguistics in a theory of poetry." In *Essays in Modern Stylistics*, ed. Donald C. Freeman. New York: Methuen, 1981.

———. "Roman Jakobson and the Grammar of Poetry." In *A Tribute to Roman Jakobson 1896–1982*, ed. Morris Halle. New York: Mouton, 1983.

———. "On Theory and Interpretation." In *The Linguistics of Writing: Arguments Between Language and Literature*, ed. Nigel Fabb, Derek Attridge, Alan Durant, and Colin MacCabe. New York: Methuen, 1987.

Klemenz-Belgardt, Edith. 1981. "American Research on Response to Literature: The Empirical Studies." *Poetics*. Vol. 10, 357–80.

Kuan Han-ch'ing. *The Injustice Done to Tou Ngo*. In *Six Yuan Plays*, trans. Liu Jung-en. New York: Penguin Books, 1972.

Kuntaka. *The Vakrokti-Jīvita of Kuntaka*. Ed. and trans. K. Krishnamoorthy. Dharwad: Karnatak University, 1977.

Kurylowicz, Jerzy. "The Quantitative Meter of Indo-European." *Indo-European and Indo-Europeans*, ed. George Cardona, Henry M. Hoenigswald, and Alfred Senn. Philadelphia: University of Pennsylvania Press, 1970.

Lal, P., ed. and trans. *Great Sanskrit Plays in Modern Translation*. New York: New Directions, 1957.

Langer, Susanne. *Feeling and Form*. New York: Charles Scribner's Sons, 1953.

Littleton, C. Scott. "Some Possible Indo-European Themes in the 'Iliad.'" In *Myth and Law Among the Indo-Europeans: Studies in Indo-European Comparative Mythology*, ed. Jaan Puhvel. Berkeley: University of California Press, 1970.

Lord, Albert. *The Singer of Tales*. New York: Atheneum, 1976.

Lotz, John. "Elements of Versification." In *Versification Major Language Types*, ed. W. K. Wimsatt. New York: New York University Press, 1972.

Mammaṭa. *The Kāvyaprakāśa of Mammaṭa: First, Second, Third & Tenth Ul-*

lasas. Ed. and trans. A. B. Gajendragadkar. 3rd ed., revised by S. N. Gajendragadkar. Bombay: Popular Prakashan, 1970.

Marx, Karl and Frederick Engels. *On Literature and Art*. Ed. Lee Baxandall and Stefan Morawski. New York: International General, 1974.

Masson, J. Moussaieff. "Introduction." In *The Peacock's Egg: Love Poems from Ancient India*. ed. and trans. W. S. Merwin and J. Mousaieff Masson, NY: Columbia University Press, 1977.

Miller, Barbara Stoler. "Kālidāsa's World and His Plays." In *Theater of Memory: The Plays of Kālidāsa*, ed. Barbara Stoler Miller. New York: Columbia University Press, 1984.

Miner, Earl. *Comparative Poetics: An Intercultural Essay on Theories of Literature*. Princeton: Princeton University Press, 1990.

Mukherjee, S. N. *Sir William Jones: A Study in Eighteenth-Century British Attitudes to India*. Cambridge: Cambridge University Press, 1968.

Nandy, Ashis. *The Intimate Enemy: Loss and Recovery of Self under Colonialism*. Delhi: Oxford University Press, 1983.

O'Flaherty, Wendy Doniger. *Women, Androgynes, and Other Mythical Beasts*. Chicago: The University of Chicago Press, 1980.

Ong, Walter J. *Orality and Literacy: The Technologizing of the Word*. New York: Methuen, 1982.

Pandit, B. N. *The Mirror of Self-Supremacy or Svātantrya-Darpaṇa*. New Delhi: Munshiram Manoharlal Publishers, 1993.

Pathak, R. S. *Vakrokti and Stylistic Concepts*. New Delhi: Bahri Publishers, 1988.

Pope, Alexander. "An Essay on Criticism." In *Literary Criticism of Alexander Pope*. Ed. B. Goldgar. Lincoln: University of Nebraska, 1965.

Puhvel, Jaan. *Comparative Mythology*. Baltimore: Johns Hopkins University Press, 1987.

Rajan, Chandra. Ed. and trans. *Kālidāsa: The Loom of Time*. NY: Penguin, 1991.

Rajamannar, P. V. *Aesthetic Experience: Sir George Stanley Endowment Lectures*. Madras: University of Madras, 1960/61.

Ramanujan, A. K., ed. and trans. *Poems of Love and War from the Eight Anthologies and the Ten Long Poems of Classical Tamil*. New York: Columbia University Press, 1985.

Richman, Paula, ed. *Many Rāmāyaṇas: The Diversity of a Narrative Tradition in South Asia*. Berkeley: University of California Press, 1991.

Said, Edward. *Orientalism*. NY: Vintage, 1974.

Shakespeare, William. *The Tragedy of Romeo and Juliet*. Ed. J. Bryant. NY: New American Library, 1987.

Staal, Frits. *Universals: Studies in Indian Logic and Linguistics*. Chicago: University of Chicago Press, 1988.

Strutynski, Udo. "The Three Functions of Indo-European Tradition in the 'Eumenides' of Aeschylus." In *Myth and Law among the Indo-Europeans: Studies in Indo-European Comparative Mythology*, ed. Jaan Puhvel. Berkeley: University of California Press, 1970.

Sukla, Ananta Charana. *The Concept of Imitation in Greek and Indian Aesthetics*. Allahabad: Rupa and Co., 1977.

Terence. *Terence (Vol. I): The Lady of Andros; The Self-Tormentor; The Eunuch.* Cambridge: Harvard University Press. 1986.

Thapar, Romila. *A History of India (Vol. I): From the Discovery of India to 1526*. New York: Penguin, 1966.

Venkatesananda, Swami. *The Concise Rāmāyaṇa of Vālmīki*. Albany: State University of New York Press, 1988.

Vishakadatta. "The Signet Ring of Rakshasa." In Lal.

Watkins, Calvert. "Language of Gods and Language of Men: Remarks on Some Indo-European Metalinguistic Traditions." In *Myth and Law Among the Indo-Europeans: Studies in Indo-European Comparative Mythology*, ed. Jaan Puhvel. Berkeley: University of California Press, 1970.

———. "Aspects of Indo-European Poetics." In *The Indo-Europeans in the Fourth and Third Millennia*, ed. Edgar Palomé. Ann Arbor: Karoma Publishers, 1982.

Weinberger-Thomas, Catherine. "*Introduction: Les Yeux fertiles de la mémoire. Exotisme indien et representations occidentales.*" In *L'Inde et l'imaginaire/India in Western Imagination*, ed. Catherine Weinberger-Thomas. Paris: Éditions de l'École des Hautes Études en Sciences Sociales, 1988. (Collection Purusartha, 11).

Part II

Theorizing Cultural Difference and Cross-Cultural Invariance: Authors, Readers, and Literary Language

2

The Question of Authorship in Indian Literature

Jeffrey Ebbesen

Films sometimes clarify historic cultural misconceptions. A case in point is Caleb Deschanel's revisionist film *Crusoe*. It offers both a cinematic deconstruction of Defoe's eighteenth-century classic *Robinson Crusoe* and a timely illustration of common critical misconceptions. Deschanel's Crusoe, like Defoe's, plies the slave trade, is shipwrecked, and attempts to "civilize" a "native." But unlike Defoe's imperialist, the updated Crusoe finds his "enlightened" attempts to "civilize" utterly ineffectual. Instead, he finds himself admiring the obstinate native, whose language and culture appear so different from his own. Before sincere cultural exchange comes to fruition, a passing research vessel rescues one (Crusoe) and imprisons the other (the native). On board ship the lead scientist states his intention to sell the native to a "research institute" as a showpiece. A second scientist concurs in his decision: "These tribes are a single mass. They don't think of themselves as individuals." The next morning Crusoe unlocks the native's cage, allowing him to escape.

Like Deschanel's scientists, numerous critics fail to grasp what Crusoe certainly understood. Namely, they inviolably delimit the continuum of observable cultural difference. This predilection often results in a metaphysical edict, an edict proclaiming "Eastern" and "Western" mind structurally disparate. In a correlate move, some critics, like Deschanel's researcher, conclude that Indians possess diminished individuality, perhaps no sense of self. For example, the prominent Indologist Edwin Gerow has maintained that, in Indian culture, "The status we call 'individual' is, insofar as can be determined, simply a defective condition, requiring remedy, and is not in itself significant, apart from its treatment."[1]

While differences certainly exist between cultures, and therefore also between the arts reflecting those cultures, it seems at best hasty to conclude that these are differences in kind rather than degree. Barbara Johnson voices a similar concern, pointing to our habitual disregard for the defects incurred at moments of opposition formation. The reading of any text or culture in a binary manner (e.g., East/West) necessarily involves a certain blindness: "The problem of difference can thus be seen both as an uncertainty over separability and as a drifting apart within identity. . . . The starting point is often a binary difference that is subsequently shown to be an illusion created by the workings of differences much harder to pin down. The differences *between* entities (prose and poetry, man and woman, literature and theory, guilt and innocence) are shown to be based on a repression of differences *within* entities, ways in which an entity differs from itself."[2] This is an important observation, and it poses weighty problems for any theory asserting binary oppositions between cultures.

In connection with this, I should like to focus in the following pages on the literatures of Greece and India, addressing the specific issue of authority and authorial pride in these literatures. Questions of authority and authorial pride are of special concern since they so often appear as critical *"points de capiton"*—to borrow a Lacanian metaphor—in our opposition formations between Eastern and Western literatures. Specifically, it is critically/culturally commonplace to assume that pride of authorship exists only in the West; in the more social East, the concept is supposed to be virtually nonexistent.[3] In the following pages, I should like to examine and dispute this claim.

In his book *Dissemination*, Jacques Derrida discusses the educational methods propounded by Plato and his teacher Socrates. Derrida observes that the Socratic/Platonic school utilized a dialectical teaching method whereby all knowledge was imparted to students through direct contact with the teacher's voice. It follows then that "Central to this handing-down of tradition is the idea of philosophy as an access to truths whose authority derives from that privileged relationship between teacher and good, receptive student."[4] It also seems clear that writing necessarily assumed a secondary and inferior position in relation to teaching.

Not surprisingly, a similar method of teaching existed in early India. Like the Socratic model, its methods were "catechetical, the pupil asking questions and the teacher discoursing at length on the topics referred to him."[5] The similarities regarding pedagogy do not end here. The Indians shared a mutual concern for the commanding power and authority of the spoken word. "Not out of manuscripts or books does one learn the texts, but from the mouth of the teacher. . . . The written text can at most be used as an aid to learning, as a support to the memory, but no authority is attributed to it. Authority is possessed only by the spoken word of the teacher."[6] It even appears that some teacher(s) required a devotion from their students bordering on worship, as is demonstrated in a line from the final address of teacher to student: "Adore your teacher like a god."[7]

This data supports a theory affirming eminence of individual Brahmans and their works. An emphasis on the *singular* utterance of a teacher certainly suggests more than the simple desire to impart truth. Surely issues of "origin" and "authority" are also at stake. Could it be that both dialectical traditions reflect the teacher's desire to preserve his/her own power over the text, along with the prominence accompanying that power? Perhaps these Indian examples even demonstrate Foucault's maxim of author as principle of thrift? If so, Indian literature would seem a far cry from the "Other" idealized by many scholars.

Some might object to this line of inquiry on the grounds that it fails to consider elements of oral transmission present in ancient Indian literature. However, this objection seems immaterial to the question at hand, since Greece also possesses a lengthy tradition of orally transmitted literature—two obvious examples being the *Iliad* and the *Odyssey*. Additional data concerning the nature of orality lend support to the contention that authorial pride may have had a real and significant place in ancient Indian literature. As Walter Ong has indicated, the Greek poet owned an extensive vocabulary of "hexameterized phrases" enabling him to "fabricate correct metrical lines without end, so long as he was dealing with traditional materials."[8] This vocabulary amounted to rough formulae (e.g., "The swift footed Achilles") whereby the poet constructed the general story. In short, epics were not memorized verbatim, but were instead composed of a storehouse of flexible phrases. Having been formulated in this fashion, it is unlikely that any of these works was ever repeated in precisely the same manner. Indian epic poetry (e.g., the *Mahābhārata*) is similarly oral in provenance.[9]

Though necessarily conservative, the oral method of transmission allowed space for improvisation and artistic expression. No doubt, the various manipulations of stock phrases would often yield a kind of signature, for no two poets ever recited in precisely the same fashion. This being the case, some narrators must have been better than others; and certainly the better tellers in the community were praised over the worse. It is hard to imagine that this was a matter of complete indifference to the poets. Certainly the burden of proof is on those who would claim otherwise.

Examples of ornate poetry (*Kāvya*) and *Praśāsti* ("praises of Kings") illustrate further parallels between East and West. Both embody Foucault's notion of death transcendence through "narrative." This is particularly clear in the case of *Kāvya*, where, as Winternitz puts it, "Panegyrics . . . afforded just as much incentive to ingenuity of form as erotics. When poets glorified in song the heroic deeds of the princes at whose courts they lived, the more elaborate these poems, the better were they appreciated by the princes as a mark of esteem."[10] Velcheru Narayana Rao's comments on the Telugu *Kāvya*s of the Vijayanagar period (1300–1600) would seem to support Winternitz's argument as well. As Rao observes, "The opening and concluding verses of each chapter of a *Kāvya* were utilized by poets to elaborate on the idealized personal qualities of the royal patron"[11] In addition, such chapters contained more Sanskrit than the body of the work, a textual strategy making them not only unintelligible to the average person, but also supportive of the text's claims to legitimacy and preeminence. For as Rao indicates, "In a paradoxical way, its unintelligibility and sacred status were connected. A language, to be ritually powerful, had to be beyond normal intelligibility."[12] What appears most striking here is the degree to which the poet actively *creates* an ideal image of the patron, one that is clearly intended for public adoration as well as posterity.

From these observations we may justly infer that *Kāvya* and *Praśāsti*, like their Greek counterparts, seem "intended to perpetuate the immortality of the hero: if he was willing to die young, it was so that his life, consecrated and magnified by death, might pass into immortality; the narrative then redeemed this accepted death."[13] If Indian kings were unconcerned with themselves as individuals, how do we explain the desire for aggrandizement on the part of these same kings?

Kāvya, *Praśāsti*, and dramatic poetry also illuminate issues of patronage and authorial pride on the part of bards and Brahmans. As the Brahmans were competing against one another, and against the lower ranking bards (*Sūtas*), they were most likely dependent on royal patronage and the generosity of the public for their welfare.[14] It seems reasonable to infer from this that the poet's self-interest was an operative factor during the construction of any *Kāvya*. After all, the laudable poet was the one who most flattered the court while also achieving greatest use of ornamental forms.[15] It would not be surprising then to find poets competing for the affections of kings, whose patronage could provide them with both notoriety and comfortable circumstances. Assuredly this competition for patronage created intense rivalries[16], as is indicated by Sidhanta's remarks on competing Brahmans: "Sometimes there was great rivalry between prominent sages, the Vasisth-Viśvāmitra strife . . . being the most famous instance of such rivalry. Perhaps some of these quarrels originated in a desire for the exclusive patronage of some powerful king, of obtaining him as a disciple . . . and the priest was generally a prominent figure in the court."[17] Commenting on the elegant *Praśāsties* of the Gupta kings (350–550 A.D.), Winternitz makes much the same observation: "Even in those days there was rivalry, as is proved by these inscriptions, not only among the ornate poets themselves, but also between the princes and their court poets."[18]

These rivalries—especially the ones between poets and princes—suggest the high esteem accorded the poet and his poetic act. Obviously, if princes were contending with poets for the accolades of court and public, there was something special about being a poet, about being an *author*. An instance illustrative of this royal pride of authorship is found on a coin dedicated to King Candragupta II,[19] which bears the epithet "rūpakṛtin" ("composer of dramas"), indicating his reputed gift for poesy.[20]

While it is certainly the case that some patron kings composed poetry themselves, many achieved authorial distinction through the simple act of usurpation. This usurpation could be accomplished in several ways. For example, a king might elevate his reputation by interpolating one or more famous poets into his circle of patronized bards or Brahmans. This convention can be noted in the Indian text *Jyotirvidābharana*, which alleges a close affiliation between Vikramāditya and Kālidāsa.[21] The ancient verse tells of a King Vikramāditya in whose court "lived nine 'jewels', namely the scholars and poets Dhanvantari, Kṣapaṇaka, Amarasiṃha, Śanku, Vetālabhaṭṭa, Ghaṭakarpara, Kālidāsa, Varāhamihira and Vararuci."[22] As Winternitz observes, the only truly renowned names on the list are Varāhamihra, Amarasiṃha, Vararuci, and finally Kālidāsa. He further asserts that the presence of all of these poets in Vikramāditya's court is an impossibility, since historical evidence indicates the acclaimed poets lived at different times (except in the cases of Vararuci, Kṣapṇaka, and the versifier Ghaṭakarpara, whose specific dates are unknown). Winternitz reasonably concludes that "the sole purpose of the verse was to enhance the fame of some Vikramāditya or other, by transferring poets and scholars of various periods all into his reign."[23]

A different sort of usurpation is visible in ancient apocryphal literary works attributed to Indian royalty. For example, native tradition attributed authorship of *The Clay Cart* to King Śūdraka. However, some modern scholars believe the king did not create the piece, that it is in fact a product of some anonymous court poet.[24] A similar instance is the *Bhāvaśataka*, a collection of riddles dealing with courtly love life. Though credited to Nāgarāja, a king in the "Rajput dynasty of the Tākas",[25] additional evidence suggests that the real author was a court poet working under the auspices of the monarch. In both cases, the true authors enjoyed royal patronage, albeit at the expense of remaining in the king's shadow.[26] The vital point here is that this usurpation was a common royal practice, its purpose being the acquisition of *praise* for the patron as *author*.

Undoubtedly, India's history of patronage differs from the West's[27]—an example of which is the evidently greater frequency of author attribution to kings/patrons in India. However, the frequency of this occurrence appears again, not so much as a difference in kind as in degree. For example, Arnold Hauser has noted that it was common practice in the European Middle Ages to disregard the author of a statue or building (i.e., artist or architect) and bestow credit elsewhere. Speaking on this convention, Hauser states, "One must not forget . . . that often where, in the medieval style, the predicate 'fecit' is added to a name in an inscription, it is the person who commissioned the work that is meant and not the artist who did the work, and that the bishops, abbots, and other clerical gentlemen to whom the buildings were ascribed in this way were in most cases merely the chairmen of the building committee and neither the actual architects nor the supervisors of building operations."[28] The parallel between Western authorial attribution to patrons in art and Indian authorial attribution to patrons in poetics seems clear. In any case, these facts appear to support the view that there was the same sort of individual pride in authorship in India as there was in the West.

But concern with authorship was not confined to the circle of the royal court. Understandably, the public also venerated the poet, some individuals going so far as to seek a slice of the poet's acclaim. (This is particularly evident in Indian *Bhakti* poetry, as will be indicated shortly.) Ancient Indian anthologies offer voluminous examples of the praises accorded poets. One sings the accolades of the distinguished poet and grammarian Pānini: "Hail to Pānini, who by the grace of Rudra first composed the grammar and then the poem Jāmbavatīvijaya!"[29] Another anthology speaks of the poet Kālidāsa's consummate versifying powers: "When formerly people used to count the poets, they gave the little finger to Kalidasa, and even down to the present day the finger next to it is called 'the nameless' (*anāmika*), because no poet arose who could equal Kālidāsa."[30] Even the legend of Kālidāsa's name figures prominently in Indian literature. He is well known as the fool who, through his reverence to the goddess Kālī, received brilliance. For this reason, it is said, he became known as Kālidāsa—servant of Kālī.[31]

A concern with individual authorship becomes even more apparent when one looks in more detail at particular forms of poetry, such as *Bhakti*. It is well known that bhakti (devotion), as expressed in the *Pad*,[32] gives favored status to the signature of the poet. In fact, the genre of the *Pad* requires that the "poet's name appear in the last one or two lines as a sort of oral signature."[33] Even so, the *Pad* is not a singular case as regards the use of authorial markings in Indian literature. The Hindi *Dohā* (the rhymed couplet) also frequently displays the poet's name in the first two lines, and Bengali *Caryā* poetry exhibits the author's name in the conclusion though it does not appear requisite in either of these cases.[34] And the fact that a genre requires a signature lends credence to a hypothesis asserting importance of individual authorship. For, in all of these cases, the signature appears both as a mark of individual distinction, and as a sign of authority. Nonetheless, the significance of the former point has been virtually dismissed. John Stratton Hawley's article addressing the life and work of *Pad* poet Ravidās (fifteenth century) serves as a splendid illustration of this point.[35] In this otherwise thoughtful piece, Hawley indicates the reverence accorded Ravidās by members of his own Untouchable caste.[36] Not surprisingly, much of Ravidās's work is directed toward the members of his own class and is expressive of profound empathy. In one such *Pad* (13), Ravidās assumes the persona of an Untouchable little girl. Here we see the tremendous veneration accorded the poet/guru, along with the requisite authorial markings:

Mother, she asks, with what can I worship?
All the pure is impure. Can I offer milk?
. . . Everything's tainted—candles, incense, rice—
But still I can worship with my body and my mind
and I have the guru's grace to find the formless Lord.
Rituals and offerings—I can't do any of these.
What, says Ravidās, will you do with me?[37]

Hawley is certainly correct in his belief that the *Pad* has a double meaning, as Ravidās is himself an Untouchable; undoubtedly thoughts of his "untouchability" necessarily accompany any reading of the poem. Still further, Hawley seems just in asserting that *Pads* exhibit reverence to gurus while also designating authority. Even so, Hawley always affirms the necessity for closure of meaning. He exhibits the classical essentialist turn of mind, which would limit all of *Bhakti* poetry (not simply that of Ravidās) by seeking ultimate reference in "authority" and idealized religion. From this point of view, individual authorship is only of minimal consequence.[38] Instead, all significance must be found in the far-reaching religious implications of the name "Ravidās" (i.e., Ravidās as guru, Ravidās's teacher as guru, and finally satguru [God]). As Hawley states of Ravidās, "His authorship is only secondarily relevant . . . it is his authority that counts."[39]

While the authority presupposed by "Ravidās" cannot be disputed, the implication that authorship is necessarily of lesser importance seems problematic on several counts. For one thing, the accumulated mythology pertaining to Ravidās (much of which is cited by Hawley himself) would seem to contradict this idealized view of the guru figure.[40] This plethora of mythology functions to solidify conceptions of character rather than to dismiss them. In addition, although many of the legends surrounding Ravidās involve religious themes, they clearly celebrate the author as an individual, much like tales recounted in the West. For example, legend has portrayed the youthful and beautiful Sophocles as dancing "in the chorus which celebrated the victory of Salamis, where Aeschylus had fought as a soldier."[41] The myriad legends surrounding the life of the Greek Cynic Diogenes of Sinope serve as further Western examples. Indeed, in both cases, religious themes are involved as well. Insofar as Ravidās has been celebrated as a class hero (i.e., as a hero from the Untouchable caste), other analogies come to mind. For example, the case of Robert Burns is not entirely dissimilar. Burns's arduous existence as a farmer and his accomplishments as a poet[42] have rendered him symbolic of the Scottish spirit, along with the spirit of a certain class. Even today his name evokes a particular feeling of pride and solidarity among the Scottish people.

Still other counts against a claim of perforce difference between Eastern and Western conceptions of authorship are to be found in texts such as the *Gurū Ravidās Granth.* Hawley himself indicates surprise at hearing an anomalous reading of the *Gurū Ravidās Granth* text while in a temple at Sri Govardhanpur.[43] According to Hawley, such interpolations are due to a traditional Indian literary practice in which poets would sign the name of a great lyricist to their own work, thereby intensifying the authority of that work. Other *Pads* provide supplementary evidence supportive of this contention. For example, the name "Sūr" has probably been utilized by many different Indian poets besides the original Sūr (who was himself a great versifier surrounded by a certain degree of mythology).[44] Though outside of the *Pad* genre, Kālidāsa makes an excellent example. Many other writers imitated his style as well. Some even went so far as to sign the moniker "New Kālidāsa" to their poetic works. Hawley is certainly right to insist that, through supplementing the Ravidās text (or by signing "Ravidās"), different poets increased their level of authority while also elevating the level of reverence accorded the individual man named Ravidās. Hawley goes on to claim that this supports the view that individual authorship is meaningless in Indian literature. This claim seems problematic, however, since similar cases have occurred in the West. Here I will cite but a few Western instances similar to Indian examples already stated, though a lengthy catalog could no doubt be formulated. A noteworthy example is the play *Rhesus,* which was spuriously attributed to the Greek playwright Euripides.[45] An instance of Greek interpellation may also be observed in the surviving corpus of the elegiac poet Theognis. Although the entire corpus has been attributed to him, numerous poems are not in fact Theognidean. Certain dating techniques have indicated that the poems were actually created by many versifiers over a great expanse of time.[46] Longinus's classic *On The Sublime* is a further instance. Although authorship has customarily been ascribed to a certain Cassius Longinus (third century A.D.) and various men named Dionysius (e.g., Dionysius of Halicarnassus, Aelius Dionysius of Halicarnassus), scholars today generally agree the work was composed in the first century (around 50 A.D.) by an unknown author.[47] As a final illustration, we may look to the *Homeric Hymns.*

Authorship has traditionally been attributed solely to Homer, but now it is recognized that many hymns were composed by poets mimicking Homer's style and phraseology (e.g. Hymn XXVII, to Artemis).[48] While accident or poor scholarship may account for many such cases of erroneous authorial attribution, some instances are likely the result of younger poets attempting to cash in on names and reputations of established versifiers.

If what has preceded is not enough to persuade us of the importance of authorship in Indian literature, we may also consult primary texts in Indian aesthetics. Here, I speak of Rājānaka Ānandavardhana's *Dhvanyāloka* (ninth century A.D.) and Abhinavagupta's *Locana* (A.D. 1000). The latter text is a commentary on the former, but, as Daniel Ingalls reminds us, both "texts have proven over the centuries to be the most influential works of India on the theory and practice of literary criticism."[49] With this in mind, we should perhaps regard with greater appreciation Abhinavagupta's explanation of Ānandavardhana's comments on authorship and its importance. In his commentary, Abhinavagupta observes that people usually pursue only those activities (e.g., learning) that offer the possibility of success. He also remarks that an individual's belief in the possibility of success is directly related to the reputation of that person's informant or teacher, and that "the confidence in such a possibility arises from hearing the name [of his informant] and his consequent memory of the qualities for which the informant was well known: his conduct, his knowledge of poetry, etc."[50] Hence, if the author's role is that of informant, we must agree that designation of authorship is essential, for the act of naming carries with it important associations, which serve to legitimize or elevate texts.[51] On a practical level it seems clear, then, that if people wish to achieve their desired goals (e.g., enlightenment, knowledge), then they must be made aware of certain works. Indeed, this is precisely what Abhinavagupta declares. This being the case, he explicates the meaning behind Ānandavardhana's authorizing signature of the *Dhvanyāloka*: "So the authors of books mention their names as part of an effort to bring their audience, whom they would help, to take up the book. It is with this intention that our author gives his name, Ānandavardhana. The word 'far-famed' conveys just this: that while the hearing of his name may turn some readers away, that may be ascribed to the working of their jealousy and is a matter of no account. For on hearing that the purpose of a book is salvation, if some man of passion should turn away from it, what of it? We certainly cannot say that the purpose of the book has been rendered void. So it stands proved that a famous name is part of winning over those who are seeking [the goal which an author has to offer]."[52]

In conclusion, it appears noteworthy that the factuality of authorship has itself never been disputed. Certainly works lacking some distinguishing paraph have been duly designated frauds; but the reality of authorship, origin, and authority has never been questioned by either Indian or Indologist. So, for instance, Kālidāsa and Ravidās retain intrinsic relations to certain works that originated within their creative genius. This fact holds even if works were inspired by divine sources. But as Derrida has indicated, the very notion of signature or authorship implies certain metaphysical preconceptions. Namely, "a written signature implies the actual or empirical nonpresence of the signer. But, it will be said, it also marks and retains his having-been present in a past now, which will remain a future now, and therefore in a now in general, in the transcendental form of nowness (*maintenance*) . . . For the attachment to the source to occur, the absolute singularity of an event of the signature and of a form of the signature must be retained: the pure reproducibility of a pure event."[53] Paradoxically, however, such purity cannot be maintained, since signatures depend on iterability: "The condition of possibility for these effects is simultaneously, once again, the condition of their impossibility, of the impossibility of their rigorous purity. In order to function, that is, in order to be legible, a signature must have a repeatable, iterable, imitable form; it must be able to detach itself from the present and singular intention of its production. It is its sameness which, in altering its identity and singularity, divides the seal."[54]

For Derrida, this paradox reflects the "logocentrism" of metaphysics, that philosophical tendency that seeks foundation in the self-presence of "thought, truth, reason, logic, [and] the Word."[55] Of particular interest to Derrida is the logocentric privileging of speech over writing, a privileging he finds firmly ensconced in the thinking of Plato and Rousseau and which he deconstructs in some detail.[56] In both instances, Derrida finds Plato and Rousseau according speech unique access to primary or originary "presence," while assigning writing the role of mere derivative.

What appears strikingly relevant to the issue at hand is Derrida's further pronouncement that logocentrism lurks beneath the veneer of Western metaphysics in general. Interestingly, his declaration seems equally applicable to Indian thought, since it also insists on the irreconcilably present signature and the originary vocalization of the teacher. To draw this conclusion is to equate everyday Indian metaphysical preconceptions with those of the West. And that is truly a "sameness" in thought, albeit a sameness in difference.

Notes

1. Edwin Gerow, "Bhāsa's Ūrubhaṅga and Indian Poetics," *Journal of the American Oriental Society*, V105 (July/Sept. 1985), p. 411.
2. Barbara Johnson, *The Critical Difference: Essays in the Contemporary Rhetoric of Reading* (Baltimore: Johns Hopkins University Press, 1980), p. X.
3. For a mild version of this thesis, see Edward C. Dimock, Jr. *The Literatures of India: An Introduction* (Chicago: University of Chicago Press, 1974), pp. 39–40.
4. Christopher Norris, *Derrida* (Cambridge: Harvard University Press, 1987), p. 30.
5. Krishna Chaitanya, *A New History of Sanskrit Literature* (New York: Agla Publishing House, 1962), p. 48.
6. M. Winternitz, *A History of Indian Literature: Vol. I, Part I* (Calcutta: University of Calcutta, 1962), p. 29.
7. Chaitanya, p. 48.
8. Walter Ong, *Orality and Literacy: The Technologizing of the Word* (London: Methuen 1982), p. 58.
9. N.K. Sidhanta, *The Heroic Age of India: A Comparative Study* (London: Knopf, 1930), p. 60.
10. M. Winternitz, *History of Indian Literature Vol. III, Part I* (Calcutta: University of Calcutta 1959), p. 5.
11. Velcheru Narayana Rao's afterword in Hank Heifetz and Velcheru Narayana Rao trans. and introduction. *For the Lord of the Animals—Poems from the Telugu* (Berkeley: University of California Press, 1987), p. 141.
12. Heifetz and Rao, p. 141.
13. Michel Foucault, "What is an Author" in *The Foucault Reader* (New York: Pantheon Books, 1984), p. 102.
14. This competition is interesting in itself, since one could speculate that the later monopolization by the more "articulate" Brahmans, to the exclusion of the less "articulate" bards (who in early times sang the praises of kings and accompanied them into battle), constitutes a further cultivation of self-praise. A noteworthy parallel in later Greek history is the rise to prominence of Rhetoricians (Sophists), whose

brand of persuasive and articulate argumentation appeared in politics as well as art—much to the chagrin of traditionalists like Aristophanes. The wiles of Sophistic method can be observed in both Helen's defense in *The Trojan Woman* and the nurse's speech to Phaedra in *Hippolytus*. See Werner Jaeger, *Paideia: Ideals of Greek Culture Vol. I, bks. 1 & 2* (Oxford, Oxford University Press, 1939), p. 344.

On the livelihood of Brahmans, see Sidhanta, p. 127.

15. Winternitz, *Vol. III, Part I*, p. 6.
16. Undoubtedly, this situation was somewhat different in Greece, given its contrasting political system. However, rivalries certainly existed between Greek playwrights at the Great Dionysia or City Dionysia dramatic festival, held annually in Athens. As Jaeger has indicated, "The competitive element which was implicit in all forms of Greek poetic activity grew in proportion as art became the centre of public life and the expression of the whole political and intellectual outlook of the age. Accordingly, it reached its highest point in drama. That is the only possible explanation of the huge numbers of second- and third-rate poets who took part in the Dionysiac competitions." (Jaeger, p. 265.)
17. Sidhanta, p. 127.
18. Winternitz, *Vol. III, Part I*, p. 16.
19. He is also known by the title "Vikramāditya." See Barbara Stoler Miller, *Theater of Memory* (New York: Columbia University Press, 1984), p. 11.
20. Winternitz, *Vol. III, Part I*, p. 14.

    For a lengthy analysis of Gupta coins and their relationship to issues of patronage, see Barbara Stoler Miller's essay "A Dynasty of Patrons: The Representation of Gupta Royalty in Coins and Literature" in her book *The Powers of Art: Patronage in Indian Culture* (N.Y.: Oxford University Press, 1992). Miller's book is an unparalleled source of information on a wide range of issues concerning patronage in India. It provides a number of cogent arguments on the subject, while also furnishing historical examinations of patronage from its earliest manifestations up to its more recent configurations under British imperialism.
21. This text has been erroneously attributed to Kalidasa and was probably not transcribed until the sixteenth Century. (Winternitz, *Vol. III, Part I*, p. 20.)
22. Winternitz, *Vol. III, Part I*, p. 20.
23. Winternitz, *Vol. III, Part 1*, p. 20.
24. Chaitanya, p. 307.
25. Winternitz, *History Vol. III, Part I*, p. 156.
26. E.P. Horowitz, *The Indian Theatre* (New York: B. Blom, 1967), p. 78.
27. I feel obliged here to recognize Velcheru Narayana Rao's comments on the development of the poet-patron relationship in India. In specific, I refer to Rao's brief but informative afterword to Heifetz and Rao pp. 131–166. His afterword supports (though perhaps unintentionally) many points in this essay regarding usurpation, competition, and ado-

ration of poetic creativity. In addition, however, Rao discusses the historical development of poet-patron relations, which obviously involve issues of authorship and authority. In this context, Rao examines the three primary modes of poet-patron affiliation in Telugu literature (specifically in the *"mārga,"* or "mainstream" branch). While space does not permit a full examination of Rao's three historical modes, they may be sketched briefly.

(1) Poet as Guru, and King as Disciple: In this mode the poet is spiritually superior, possessing wisdom and purity. The king/patron desires this wisdom and purity, which would connect him with the illustrious "heros of sacred history" (133). Association with a poet therefore provides this connection, and its accompanying status, for the king/patron.

(2) Poet and King as Friends: In this mode, conventional descriptions remain similar, but the poet is no longer superior to the king/patron. Here, patronage is especially ubiquitous, as is ornamental language, since the king/patron seeks not spiritual advancement, but fame and entertainment. It will also be noted that the poetic functions of both 1 and 2 provide support for the king's sovereignty, and thus his power.

(3) Temple Poets: Though this mode has a variety of configurations, it is primarily associated with the poet who is independent of human patronage. In this case, the poet serves only the god/patron of the individual temple. Here, the king is not equal to god, but merely an aspect of god. Therefore, the poet provides less support for the king's sovereignty. Rao further observes that many temple poets were ideologically opposed to court poets, considering them "whores" to the king's (or patron's) court, who merely pursued enjoyment of worldly pleasures and fame.

As Rao opposes the temple poets to those of the court, he also registers important differences in aesthetics. In particular, he comments on the regimentation of literary convention in court poetry, setting it against temple poetry's relative lack of such restrictions (e.g., the *sataka* genre). Given this lack of convention, Rao postulates that the *sataka* genre in particular functioned as a form of active resistance against the idealized poetic code of court poetry.

For a slightly altered version of this argument, see Rao's later essay "Kings, Gods and Poets: Ideologies of Patronage in Medieval Andhra" in Miller *The Powers of Art.*

28. Arnold Hauser, *The Social History of Art, Vol. I* (New York: Vintage Books, 1959), p. 175.
29. Winternitz, *Vol. III, Part I,* p. 6. There is some controversy as to whether Pānini the grammarian and Pānini the poet are the same person.
30. Winternitz, *Vol. III, Part I,* p. 36.
31. Miller, p. 5.

32. *Pads* are generally defined as "rhymed lyric compositions of about six or eight lines in length . . . that center on religious themes . . . and [are] intended to be sung." John Stratton Hawley, "Author and Authority in the Bhakti Poetry of North India," *Journal of Asian Studies*, Vol. 47 No. 2. (May 1988), p. 269.
33. Hawley, p. 270.
34. Hawley, p. 270.
35. Hawley, pp. 269–289.
36. Even today, Ravidās is highly revered; the numerous temples and institutions that bear his name testify to the fact. A mission has even been founded to discover more about his life and work (Hawley, p. 270).
37. Hawley, p. 283.
38. A somewhat similar criticism can be leveled at Velcheru Narayana Rao in his discussion of the *śataka* genre (texts containing roughly 108 poems addressed either to persons or deities). Rao affirms that numerous "*śatakas* . . . have a concluding poem recording the name of the author as well as other information, such as the date of composition." Yet he also remarks that "Authors of *śatakas* did not aspire to literary recognition" (Rao's afterword to Heifetz and Rao pp. 163–164). While it is not my intention to engage in semantic hair-splitting, it seems obvious that such authors "aspired" to some sort of "recognition." If not, why record the author's name at all? This objection appears especially valid since, by Rao's own admission, *śataka*s were intended not for public, but rather private consumption (164). Why would a particular person's name need to be attached to such works if not for some sort of recognition?
39. Hawley, p. 272.
40. Hawley gives an example of this mythology. "There is a tree in Sri Govardhanpur that is believed to possess remarkable properties and is associated in local legend with an unnamed Untouchable wonder-worker. . . . Great yogi though he was, Gorakhnāth suffered from the heat, so Ravidās took a twig from a pile of sticks that had been gathered for firewood and plunged it into the ground near where Gorakhnāth sat. Miraculously, a shade tree sprang up to shelter the yogi. . ." (Hawley, p. 271).
41. Jaeger, p. 271.
42. Burns achieved literary fame, despite the fact that his writings were primarily composed in his own patois of Lowland Scots. See *The Reader's Companion to World Literature*, ed. Lillian Herlands Hornstein et al. (N.Y.: New American Library 1956), pp. 64–65. For further references see *The Concise Cambridge History of English Literature*, George Sampson, N.Y.: Macmillan 1946), Chapter X.
43. "I found a text totally at variance with anything I had been led to expect. As far as I am able to determine, it contains not one of the lyrics of Ravidās that appear in the *Granth Sāhib*" (Hawley, p. 271).

44. Hawley cites as evidence the difference between the old and new Sūrsāgar manuscripts. The older Sūrsāgar manuscripts contain only a few hundred poems by Sūr, while the updated manuscripts (i.e., nineteenth century) contain thousands (Hawley, p. 274).
45. Diana Bowder, *Who Was Who in the Greek World*. New York: Washington Square Press, pp. 229–232.
46. Bowder, pp. 451–452.
47. See *The Princeton Encyclopedia of Poetry and Poetics*, ed. Alex Preminger (Princeton: Princeton University Press 1974), p. 819. For other references see *Longinus On the Sublime*, by W. Rhys Roberts (Cambridge: Cambridge University Press, 1907).
48. See *Homer and the Oral Tradition*, G.S. Kirk (Cambridge: Cambridge University Press, 1976), chapter 8. For other references see *The Homeric Hymns*, Translation and Introduction by Apostolos N. Athanassakis (Baltimore: Johns Hopkins University Press, 1976), pp. X–XIII.
49. Daniel Ingalls, Jeffrey Moussaieff Masson, and M.V. Patwardhan trans., *The* Dhvanyaloka *of Ānandavardhana with the* Locana *of Abhinavagupta*, ed. with introduction by Daniel Ingalls (Cambridge: Harvard University Press, 1990), p. 1.
50. Ingalls, Masson, and Patwardhan, p. 725.
51. Of course, the opposite is equally true. That is to say, some names might carry associations that delegitimize or impugn a text.
52. Ingalls, Masson, and Patwardhan, p. 725.
53. Jacques Derrida, "Signature Event Context" in *Margins of Philosophy* trans. Alan Bass (Chicago: University of Chicago Press, 1982), p. 328.
54. Derrida, "Signature" pp. 328–329.
55. Jonathan Culler, *On Deconstruction: Theory and Criticism after Structuralism* (Ithaca: Cornell University Press, 1982), p. 92.
56. For an analysis of Jean-Jacques Rousseau, see Jacques Derrida, *Of Grammatology*, trans. Gayatri Chakravorty Spivak (Baltimore: Johns Hopkins University Press, 1976).

3

The Genre Theory in Sanskrit Poetics

V. K. Chari

In this paper, I propose to review the genre theory in Sanskrit and to provide an assessment of the place it occupied in that critical tradition. Several generic classifications are attempted in the Sanskrit theory, although some of them are thought to affect the aesthetic character of literary compositions not in a vital way, but only in a formal or peripheral way. A given generic form could, for instance, make some difference in the structuring of the poetic material, but it would not alter the essential nature of the work or affect its evaluation. Both in their theory and practical criticism, the Sanskrit critics were, by and large, guided by the essential, defining properties of literature as a type of discourse and applied to works criteria of evaluation generated by such properties. There were, however, many different definitions of literature, and the critics were divided into schools.

At any rate, it may safely be asserted that literary criticism in Sanskrit is not predominantly a genre-oriented criticism, in spite of the recognition by critics of many formal divisions of literature. There is nothing in it like a continuing debate on the question of literary kinds, such as we find in Western criticism from the Renaissance down to our own century, nor the kind of speculative endeavor to build systems of genres that we have witnessed in our own time.[1] It would appear on the whole that the kinds that these critics were familiar with, with a few exceptions, meant no more to them than a convenient means of labeling works of different formal sorts. The genre concept did not serve as an important critical instrument.

A discussion of the genre theory naturally involves consideration of the larger question of defining the scope of the term "literature," the question of literature itself as a genre. For, before we start classifying works into species, we must have some conception of their common nature or genus. The Sanskrit equivalent of "literature" is *kāvya*. But this term, like its equivalent in Western criticism, came to be applied widely to writings of diverse kinds. It encompassed a great variety of things, including historical and gnomic/didactic writing, in addition to drama, epic, lyric, and romance—some in prose and some in verse, and others in mixed form. Included were even kinds of writing in which the purpose was to expound some technical or scientific principles, not to evoke an aesthetic response in the reader. There was the type called *kāvya-śāstra*, whose aim was at once the inculcation of the principles of some scientific discipline and the treatment of a story or some other poetic material, that is, *Bhaṭṭikāvya*, which is a book on grammar and rhetoric, but which also tells a story about the killing of the demon king Rāvaṇa. There was also *śāstra-kāvya*, which dealt with a technical subject, such as ethics or erotics, but gave it a poetic treatment employing a language embellished with figures and other stylistic devices. In addition, there was the didactic fable, allegory, or parable, that is, *Pañcatantra* and *Śukasaptati*. Scriptural and canonical literature, and purely scientific and technical treatises, which were invariably in the form of sūtras or aphorisms, or in verse, were of course not included. However, in the critical tradition of Bharata and the early rhetoricians (Bhāmaha, Daṇḍin, Vāmana, and others) only the long narrative poem, the stray verse, drama, lyric, and prose romance were accorded the status of *kāvya*. The test of a *kāvya* was taken to be the quality of delight or emotional thrill (*camatkāra*) that poetry communicates.

The definition of the nature of *kāvya* varied from school to school, but the criteria adopted fall roughly into three categories. First, literature is defined by some speciality or deviancy in its use of the linguistic medium, whether it is figurative expression, or stylistic patterning, or foregrounding of some sort. The *alaṃkāra* or figurationist view espoused by Bhāmaha, Udbhaṭa, and Rudraṭa, the theory of *rīti* or style of Vāmana, and the theory of deviant expression (*vakrokti*) of Kuntaka—all emphasized the formal linguistic peculiarities of literary expression.

The second type of definition was one based on the claim for a special poetic semantics consisting in oblique or implicative expression, as opposed to the literal manner. This was the theory of *dhvani*, or suggestion, propounded by Ānandavardhana in his work *Dhvanyāloka*. Suggestion was the secret of poetic speech, according to this school, rather than figurativeness or stylistic structuring. That in poetry the linguistic medium is the focus of interest rather than the meaning or message, or that poetic language involves a special semantic function is also a widely held view in modern criticism.[2]

The third major definition to be offered was a view that was based on the quality of the meaning itself, which in poetry is emotive meaning, or *rasa*—this term being understood not as the affective response of the reader but as the cognitive content of the work itself, determined contextually by the presented situation or thought and by the type of discourse that the work purports to be. Literature is emotive discourse or a discourse having for its end the evocation of emotions (of which there are a definite number: the tragic, the comic, the heroic, the erotic, etc.)—through the presentation of their objective situational factors. Every work, poem or play, establishes a dominant tone for itself through an orchestration of various major and minor emotional strands and comes to be identified as a tragedy, comedy, heroic poem, love poem, and so forth. The implications of this view for the genre theory will be reserved for the end.

It may be noted that the distinction between prose and verse never enters into any of the definitional proposals offered by the Sanskrit critics. Although, right from the Vedic times, verse had been the predominant vehicle of poetic as well as scriptural expression and a great sanctity attached to meter (*chandas*), the Sanskrit critics seem to have realized that this distinction could not be a seminal distinction affecting the essential nature of literature. No one today seriously entertains the idea that this distinction has any significance except from the generic point of view. It has been recognized since the days of antiquity that verse itself does not make "poetry" (in the wider Aristotelian sense). The existence of versified scientific treatises led Aristotle to seek the principle of definition in imitation. The same consideration weighed with the Sanskrit theorists in their definitions. However, they do make the distinction for taxonomical purposes, without at the same time making that distinction the basis for differentiating the literary from the nonliterary. Thus *kāvya* could occur both in verse (*padya*) and prose (*gadya*). *Gadya* is simply "poem in prose" or poetry without verse.

It will be useful at this point to list the major genres and subgenres in Sanskrit to see how fundamental they are for the appreciation of literature. Works in Sanskrit were grouped in different ways according to different taxonomical principles. Four such principles may be discerned. The first is the distinction based on the mode of representation—between literature that is meant to be read or heard (*śravya*) and that meant to be enacted (*dṛśya*)—which corresponds to Plato's and Aristotle's distinction between the narrative and drama according to the manner of imitation. The second is the distinction between verse and prose; the third, based on the magnitude of the composition—short or long; and the fourth, based on the consideration whether the subject is fictitious or drawn from a historical or legendary source. However, these divisions were not all deemed to be of the same importance.

The broadest classification of literature was into *dṛśya* (spectacle, drama) and *śravya* (audible), or *abhineya* (actable, performable) and *anabhineya* (not actable, only readable). This distinction was thought to be the most significant aesthetically, since it involves a difference in the medium of presentation. A stage drama, by its very nature, is, in terms of Bharata's dramaturgy, something to be enacted and involves all the four types of *abhinaya* (expression)—the physical, the verbal, the psychic (inner psychic reactions, such as horripilation, tears, sweating, change of facial color, and so on—which are of course manifested on the stage visibly as physical reactions and hence may be included under the physical), and finally, make-up, ornaments, costume, and stage decor (expressive of the character's disposition and state of mind). Although Bharata gives first attention to the verbal expression (*vācika*) of the dramatic emotions (the *rasas*) through their objects and other concomitant conditions, for him, speech itself, whether the poet himself is the speaker or a character created by him, is a form of action/enactment, a mode in which people express their reactions to whatever situations they are involved in. But speech is not the only form in which people act, although it is an important part; much is also expressed through nonverbal forms of behavior: looks, motions, and dress can all be expressive gestures or attitudes. A dramatic work is thus, according to Bharata, presented for sight as well as for hearing; it offers a complete, integrated experience of the eye and ear. All that happens on the stage is for him dramatic expression or gesture and integral to drama. Unlike Aristotle, who gave primacy to the words of the play and considered the spectacle the least vital aspect of the theatrical act,[3] Bharata attached equal importance to the verbal composition and to the kinaesthetic aspects of stage production. It is for this reason that dṛśya-śravya was regarded as the most important generic distinction.

The distinction between the dramatic and the nondramatic is therefore not a purely formal one, in terms of Bharata's dramaturgy, but a more substantive one involving a difference in the medium adopted. The narrative is presented through the verbal medium alone, whereas stage drama employs both the verbal and visual mediums. The dialogic structure is of course what distinguishes drama from the narrative formally and what makes enactment possible. But Bharata seems to imply that, since dialogue is conceived of as a mode of performative or gestic behavior, it is inseparable from the physical exhibitions that accompany stage action invariably. Bharata gives a great deal of attention to the structure of the dramatic plot, enumerating various stages of its development, to characterization according to character types (the noble-minded hero, the blustering arrogant type, the sportive, and so on), and to speech in accordance with the character's disposition and mood. And he would agree with Aristotle in his emphasis on the primacy of plot. But he conceives of drama holistically, as a total act, rather than simply as a particular "manner" of verbal representation.

It may also be remarked that the mere presence of the dialogue does not make a material difference in the reading experience. "A play read," as Dr. Johnson said, "affects the mind like a play acted."[4] It is the sequence of events and the character reactions and interactions, by which the drama is constituted, that the reader follows, whether the presentational mode is wholly narrative, wholly dramatic, or mixed (as in the novel or epic). Character interactions are anyway apprehended by the reader "scenically," in the dialogic form as direct speech, even though they are only reported or described as indirect speech. In actual literary practice, too, we know that the narrative and dialogue modes are convertible into each other; that is, a drama can be rewritten as a novel, and vice versa.

As many as 28 dramatic species were known to the ancients, of which 10 were considered to be of the first order, and the rest of the second order.[5] The divisions among these varieties were not always sharp, but, in general, they were based on a combination of factors: the high or low, divine or human status of the personages, the fictitious or historical/mythological derivation of the fable, the prevailing emotion of the theme (usually love, mirth, heroism, or pathos), the number of characters, and so forth. There was no pure tragedy in Sanskrit, and calamitous endings were averted through the intervention of gods or sages, and reconciliation was effected. There was also the intermingling of comic scenes in serious dramas; but the pathetic *rasa* was fully exploited. The tragic, the comic, the romantic or erotic, and the heroic were the most popular sentiments treated in the dramas, and they accounted for the major dramatic genres.

The next major classification of *kāvya* was into prose, verse, and mixed. The mixed variety was called *caṃpū*; it used metrical and nonmetrical language with more or less equal prominence.[6] The verse poem, in turn, had many subvarieties depending on magnitude. Thus, there was the single stray verse (*muktaka*) or short poem containing a single thought, emotional expression, or description of any sort; the single unit of two or more stanzas in the same meter (*paryāya-bandha*); the long narrative poem (*sarga-bandha* or *mahākāvya*) bound into cantos with tight sequential ordering of the story into junctures (*saṃdhis*) in the manner of the drama or *rūpaka* (e.g., the *Raghuvaṃśa* and *Kumārasaṃbhava* of Kālidāsa, Māgha's *Śisúpālavadha*, and Śrīharṣa's *Naiṣadhakāvya*); and the long poem (*khaṇḍa-kāvya*), also called *saṃghāta*, or a constellation of verses treating a continuous theme, but without a narrative sequence (e.g., *Meghadūta* of Kālidāsa). The prose *kāvya* was, in turn, classified into *kathā* or romantic novel (e.g., Bāṇa's *Kādaṃbarī*, Daṇḍin's *Daśakumāra-carita*, Subandhu's *Vāsavadatta*), and *ākhyāyikā* or historical novel recounting the deeds of kings and heroes of old (e.g., Bāṇa's *Harṣacarita*).[7] The *kathā* is again of two types: the complete story (*sakala-kathā*) and description of an episode from a story (*ekadeśa-varṇanā*, called *khaṇḍa-kathā*).

The third genre, *caṃpū*, was a narrative in mixed prose and verse, of which there are numerous examples, the most famous being *Nalacaṃpu* of Trivikrama and Bhoja's *Rāmāyaṇacaṃpū* and *Bhojaprabandha*, and *Bhāgavatacaṃpū* of Abhinavakālidāsa. In this kind, the alteration of prose and verse seems to have served no special purpose except that it afforded the poet greater ease of expression and also provided a richer variety by the mingling of the prose and verse rhythms.[8] Nearly the same stylistic effects may be seen to be achieved through the verse or prose medium. And a subject treated in a prose romance could also be done in the *caṃpū* form; that is, *Vāsavadatta* of Subandhu is in prose, but a mixed form of this story *Vāsavadatta-campū* was also known to the ancients. The *campū* was usually a full-fledged composition of epic proportions, in the so-called *prabandha* or ornate style and divided into parts. There was, however, another kind called *birudam* or eulogy addressed to a king, which also mingled prose and verse.[9] But eulogies were also written in verse, and they could be in a single stanza or a number of stanzas. Yet another class of prose compositions, called *vṛtta-gandhī* (having the flavor or traces of meter), employed measured, rhythmical sentences closely approximating metrical structures.[10]

The mingling of prose and verse was not, however, an exclusive feature of the *campū*, for both the romantic and historical novel used verses in particular meters for introductory or commendatory purposes, or for the purpose of summarizing the context of the story, or to lend point to some idea in the narrative. Sanskrit drama, too, employed a mixture of prose and verse in its dialogues, the prose dialogues often designed to exhibit character interactions, and verse to give lyrical elaboration to a poetic idea or sentiment (e.g., Kālidāsa's *Śākuntalam*).

In addition to these, there were other classifications of *kāvya*, into those treating "invented" or imaginary themes (*utpādya/kalpita*) and those treating themes derived from well-known sources, such as history (*itihāsa*) and legend (Purāṇas); and again, into stray verse (*anibaddha, muktaka*) and the well-structured long poem (*nibaddha, prabandha, sargabandha*). The first division applies equally to compositions in verse, prose, or mixed verse and prose.

The longer compositions, prose, verse, or mixed, also share a few other common features. They all treat a unified theme and develop it in all its fullness in terms of the various junctures (*saṃdhis*) or stages of developing action, with a proper causal sequencing of events. In this, they partake of the structure of the drama. These stages are: (1) *mukha* (exposition), corresponding to the protasis of the Greek drama; (2) *pratimukha* (epitasis or metabasis) in which the initial action is further complicated, promoted, or impeded by a further event; (3) *garbha* (catatasis), representing the height and full growth of the drama, where the initial pursuit is continued against all odds; (4) *avamarśa* (peripeteia or reversal); and (5) *nirvahaṇa* (apodosis or catastrophe) in which the dramatic plot is unraveled. It is obvious that any plot structure—epic or novel—must progress through these stages if it is to sustain the interest of the reader. In this respect, therefore, it is similar to the drama.

Furthermore, the language of all the three types of long composition is heightened by poetic figures. They all contain descriptions of natural scenery, and evocative elaborations of the poetic emotions (the nine basic *rasas* with their accompanying transitory emotions), and other features necessary for a vivid presentation of the human situation being recounted. All the features, except for the meter, found in the great verse narrative (*mahākāvya*) are also found in the long prose narrative, including the most essential elements of plot (*itivṛtta*), *rasa*, and figurative language (*alaṃkāra*).[11] All these elements are discussed by Bharata as they are the common features of the verbal text of the drama (*pāthya*). The critic Vāmana goes so far as to say that the prose narrative (historical or romantic novel) is but a derivative of the drama.[12]

The above outline of the Sanskrit genres may be shown in a tabular form as follows:

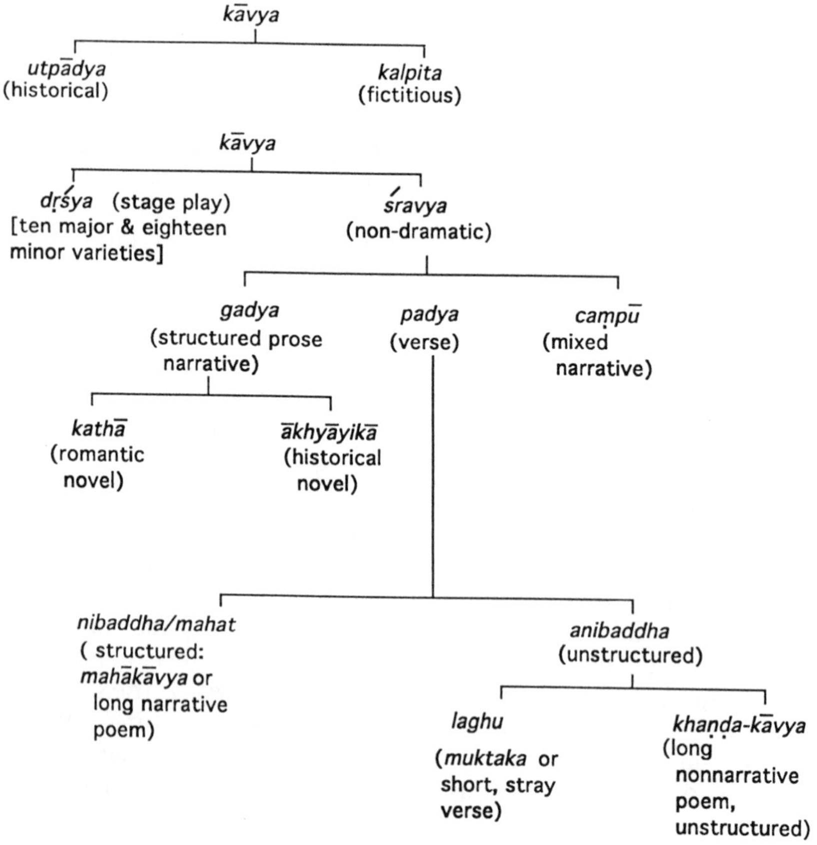

Of these groupings, as we have already seen, the dramatic-nondramatic distinction was held to be the most significant aesthetically. The distinction between structured/narrative and unstructured/nonnarrative also, no doubt, appears important for purposes of description and analysis. But the structured narrative in prose or verse is thought to be an extension of the drama, since it is constructed on the same principles as drama—it derives its most important element, namely, plot structure, from the drama and shares with it some common thematic and stylistic elements as well. Even in terms of its aesthetic effect, as a composition in the verbal medium, it is not essentially different from the verbal text of the drama. As for the kinds in the verse medium, the Sanskrit theory has no names, in fact, no clear definitions, for the epic and the lyric. The five famous "great poems" (*mahākāvyas*) in Sanskrit, which include Kālidāsa's *Raghuvaṃśa* and *Kumārasaṃbhava*, Bhāravi's *Kirātārjunīya*, Māgha's *Śiśupālavadha*, and Śrīharṣa's *Naiṣadha*, are long poems constructed on an ample scale and treating of historical or mythological themes. Some of these share features traditionally associated with the epic; they deal with momentous actions and superhuman deeds of valor and are centered on a heroic figure or figures. But the heroic element is by no means a constant, as the first of these, *Raghuvaṃśa* is a dynastic history and extremely varied in theme, and the last mentioned poem, *Naiṣadha*, is a romantic love poem. Its only distinguishing mark is thus its size.

The Sanskrit short poem (*muktaka*), too, is similarly ill-defined, and although it is customary to equate it with the lyric, it has only its size to entitle it to that designation. It need not, for one thing, always be an expression of subjective thought or feeling, which is what we generally understand by that term. A short poem in Sanskrit could be, indifferently, a description of nature, a vignette, an expression of a state of mind or a posture of affairs, a hymn, or a eulogy addressed to a king or a god. It does not occupy the same generically significant position that the lyric does in the Western theory, in the triadic division of drama, epic, and lyric.

The distinction of fictitious and nonfictitious/historical, too, is not a fundamental generic distinction, for, in terms of the Sanskrit theory of poetic truth, the very question of the historicity or otherwise of the presented persons or events is irrelevant to the reader's apprehension of poetic meaning. In poetic apprehension, there is an imaginative identification with the presented person or situation, in its universal or representative aspect, regardless of its precise ontological status. As Ānandavardhana states, any inquiry into the logical truth or falsity of poetic statements would be ridiculous because this question does not alter out apprehension of the poem as a delectable object.[13] Given this position, then, the Sanskrit critic would not attach much importance to this generic division.

It is of course recognized that the magnitude of a poem will make a difference for its stylistic texture. Thus, in a short one-stanza poem, describing an emotion, only a simple syntactic construction would be proper. But, where there are more than one stanzas, the syntactic structure could be more involved. In prose narratives, in which lengthy descriptions of natural scenery and the like are common, a style consisting of big words, long epithets, and ponderous periodic structures will be in order. In the drama, which normally requires a speech-based language, on the other hand, such a style would be out of place. According to the *rasa* theorist, the decorum of the emotions (*rasaucitya* or propriety with regard to the delineation of emotions) is the governing principle in the choice of diction and style. There is also of course the consideration of the character of the speaker, the nature of the meaning conveyed, and the context of the utterance, which has an effect on such a choice. But, as Ānandavardhana observes, the propriety dictated by the literary form has also sometimes to be taken into account.[14]

As for the prose-verse distinction, the foregoing analysis has revealed that it is not a distinction based either on the manner of presentation (dramatic or narrative) or on the nature of the subject. A grand heroic theme could be treated in a dramatic form (e.g., *Veṇīsaṃhāra* of Bhaṭṭa Nārāyaṇa), in verse, in prose, or in the mixed form. Literary language, too, whether in a short lyric, or in a long poem or prose narrative, was distinguished by the presence of the poetic figures, by stylistic features, and finally by the invariable presence of *rasa* or *rasadhvani* (evocativeness), which, according to many, was the necessary condition of all literature.

Thus, although there is not much theoretical significance attaching to the prose-verse distinction in Sanskrit criticism, an examination of the practice of the writers would indicate that the distinction was still an important one in some ways. For one thing, the Sanskrit writers were well aware of the difference between the movement of the metrical foot and the rhythmic stride of prose syntax, which achieves a different kind of effect than that of verse, depending as it does on the principle of balance or equilibrium of parallel eurhythmic structures of phrasal or sentential units rather than on metrical regularity. Many of the verbal figures, like alliteration, could also no doubt be displayed within the bounds of prose syntax, even as in verse. But the prose composition calls for a different kind of patterning and a different kind of skill, and its management was considered to be the touchstone of poetic art.[15] Metrical and nonmetrical languages offered two different kinds of advantages. Verse, with its compact form, its capacity for concision, and above all its prosodic and stanzaic structure was used primarily as a rhetorical aid, for highlighting an idea or for making a pithy statement. The sound structure of the verse could also of course serve an evocative purpose. But, according to the *rasa* theory, rhyming and versing do not become evocative apart from meaning; *rasa* is solely the outcome of the complex of emotive factors. But it is recognized that, where such a context of meaning is present, the sound structures of words can reinforce the evocation, although their use is by no means confined to the expression of feelings alone. For instance, verse was used also for gnomic/didactic purposes, or for summarizing a story told in prose (*kathā-saṃgraha-ślokas*). Bhoja distinguishes between kinds of gaits (*gatis*)—quick, slow, quick-slow, and so on—which become efficacious according to the nature of the situation.[16] But these gaits apply equally to prose and verse movement. However, since the time of Vedic poetry, writers have found verse to be a more adequate vehicle of the emotions.

On the other hand, prose, with its more leisurely and unconstrained gait, afforded an opportunity not only for the display of the poet's descriptive powers, but for elaboration in style. Naturally, then, the prose work was marked by elaborate descriptions of nature, of battle scenes and the exploits of heroes, of the beauty of the heroines, etc. and by all kinds of rhetorical embellishments, including figures, long rolling compounds, and polysyllabic and sesquipedalian words. Literary prose in Sanskrit was a rhythmic prose such as was cultivated by the English prose writers and orators before the Royal Society promulgated its ideal of a plain mathematical style.

The *campū*, as a generic form, combines the separate advantages of prose and verse. The most powerful utterances in any *campū* and its most dramatic moments are generally recorded in verse, whereas the narrative and descriptive parts are reserved for prose. And the prose, too, as in the prose narrative, is a highly ornate rhythmic prose. The *campū* does not attempt a fusion of prose and poetry in the manner of the modern prose poem.[17] It simply cultivates the two forms as alternate vehicles of expression.

From the foregoing analysis, it is clear that the Sanskrit critics were fully aware that formal differences, such as those between short poem and long poem, prose and verse, and narrative and nonnarrative imply certain entailments for the structure and style of compositions. The distinction based upon the presentational mode, namely, that between drama and narrative, is not, as in Greek theory, one stemming from the role played by the poet—the poet speaking in his person as narrator or speaking through his characters, as in drama. Generally, there is little attention paid in Sanskrit criticism to the poet's formal role in his work (and this may account for the fact that there is no conception of the lyric as a subjective form of expression). Significantly, the drama is called "*rūpaka*" (etymologically, a metaphorical representation), because, in it, the identity of the character is attributed to the actor. It is also called a "*nāṭya*" as it is an enactment by an actor. Hence its characterization as "visible" (*dṛśya*) or "actable" (*nāṭya* or *abhineya*).[18] The real distinction of drama is, then, in its being a theatrical act, rather than its dialogue form. The principles of construction in both drama and narrative are the same, and they are, as in Aristotle, derived from the model of the dramatic plot.

While classification of the literary kinds thus has a place in Sanskrit criticism and many genres and subgenres are distinguished, one gathers the impression, in taking an overview of the critical texts, that the emphasis of the critics, in their analysis of texts and of illustrative passages, rests heavily on their general literary properties, such as figures, style qualities, and the *rasas* (which cut across generic boundaries), rather than on their specific generic features. The genre concept itself was not applied as a general criterion of evaluation. There is no rigorous application of the criteria appropriate to each genre, no evaluation of the work as being "good of its kind." In their theoretical excursions as well, the overriding concern of these critics is with their respective doctrinal standpoints—figuration, style, suggestion, deviant expression, *rasa*, and so forth—in terms of which they sought to define the nature of literature. From this, one might hazard the conclusion that the theory of genres or formal categories did not play a crucial role in the Sanskrit theory of literature, as it did in Western criticism.

But this is not to say that the Sanskrit critics entirely discarded the notion of literary classification, that they were content only with an anonymous literariness of works. As some recent critics have pointed out, questions of genre are central to interpretation and evaluation.[19] According to Hirsch, all linguistic meaning is genre-bound; an utterance can be made sense of only as belonging to a particular type.[20] In fact, generic thinking is part of our perception; an individual is identified and named only as the member of a class. At any rate, no critical appreciation of a literary work would be possible unless we are able to identify its specific aesthetic character. Determining the nature of a work as a piece of literature is of course the unavoidable first step in the critical procedure. But it does not yet give us any notion of the distinct pleasure that it communicates, or, more accurately, of the meaning components that communicate that pleasure. Hence a further discrimination of its aesthetic quality will be required. However, this quality can be best identified only by means of the criteria that we apply in determining the nature of literature itself as a type of discourse. That is to say that whatever generic distinctions we make—distinctions that will account for the distinct pleasure the work engenders—must be relevant to the criteria that made the work a piece of literature in the first place, its essential aesthetic properties.

Now the criteria based on the language concept, namely, figurativeness, stylistic structure, semantic deviancy, suggestion, and so forth, cannot serve as the sole differentia of literature, since these features are found equally in nonliterary speech and since literary speech, too, can sometimes be quite literal or prosaic, as in some types of emotional and descriptive writing. Neither can they be, as we have noticed, the basis for generic differentiation, since they are common to most literary forms. Formal categorization by the means of presentation (whether the work is to be staged or recited) is no doubt a fundamental generic distinction. But it takes us beyond the strict verbal limits of literature. Other formal distinctions, such as long and short, and prose and verse, do not significantly affect the aesthetic character of the work, although they make some difference for its organization. It is also significant that Sanskrit theory does not make a clear differentiation between the epic and the lyric modes except in terms of long and short, and narrative and nonnarrative. But the latter distinction, namely, narrative-descriptive/nonnarrative is significant for the structure of the aesthetic effect and remains the only basic generic division.

However, of the various theories of literature advanced by the Sanskrit critics, the *rasa* doctrine seems to offer not only the best definition of the literary art, but a more satisfactory basis for distinguishing between kinds of aesthetic effects and consequently for generic distinctions. "*Rasa*" is not of course employed as a genre term; it is not a type of literature, being, according to its protagonists, the necessary condition of all literature. But *rasa* is not also simply a nameless emotional quality of the meaning; it does admit of a number of distinct tones and subtones, each yielding a different kind of pleasure and hence forming a genuine generic type. Thus there is the tragic tone, the comic, erotic, heroic, marvellous, and so forth, which do not depend on any particular formal organization or "manner" of representation, such as dramatic, narrative, and lyric. For instance, a tragic theme can be treated in a drama, in a prose or verse narrative, or in a short lyrical poem. And it is its tragic quality, rather than its form, that will identity its aesthetic character and distinguish it as a type of composition different from other types. Aristotle's definition of tragedy and comedy is fundamentally of this nature inasmuch as it rests upon the distinction between the serious and the ludicrous, although they both are for him dramatic forms, and he also uses moral criteria (higher or lower types of characters) in defining their difference. Aristotle also does not show any substantive difference between tragedy and the epic, the only difference being formal (the epic is a narrative and is less unified than tragedy).[21]

But the *rasa* theory would provide for a sharper distinction between the tragic and the epic in terms of the predominant tone of each, regardless of their form. That is to say that if something is to be called an epic, in contradistinction to tragedy, then the only ground for doing so would be its heroic theme and tone. This is not of course to say that a tragedy cannot admit the heroic element or that the epic cannot admit the pathetic. There are heroic tragedies, and the *Iliad* contains tragic scenes. Works may often contain a mixture of emotional themes according to their mutual affinities. But it is the prevailing tone of the work—which one determines by weighing the various motifs in the work and their respective prominences, including such features as the beginning and the concluding notes—that allows us to name it as a tragedy or epic. The Indian poem *Rāmāyaṇa* (a so-called epic) is predominantly pathetic but also develops the heroic *rasa* as a subsidiary theme. The *Mahābhārata* (also called an epic) is predominantly heroic but also contains some sorrowful scenes.

An objection to this view may be that even such genres as tragedy, comedy, and the heroic epic are difficult to define, as there are extreme variations within any given category and modulations of its form. And there are all kinds of literary hybrids. One tragedy may not be like another tragedy. The disparities between *Oedipus at Colonus* and *Hamlet*, and those between *Hamlet* and a modern tragedy like *Death of a Salesman* are more noticeable than the common features that they share. Also witness the mutations that the epic underwent from Homer to Milton, and the mixture of romance and epic elements in Spenser's *Faerie Queene*. Such considerations have led some recent theorists to question the very usefulness of the genre concept as an interpretative or evaluative tool and to allow for it only a certain pedagogical or purely taxonomical role in criticism.[22] Or again, there is the view, popular since the Romantic theorists that the genre theory plays no part in the actual creative process and that each artistic creation is unitary in its aesthetic essence and not amenable to generic classification.[23]

But one suspects that the opposition to the genre theory arises from the traditional conception that it is the form that fixes the genre. When formal criteria are employed, generic categories will be seen to be fluid and unidentifiable, because formal differences are infinite and every art object may have its own form. But when more essential, aesthetically relevant criteria are applied, it is possible to distinguish between literary kinds that correspond to the more basic laws of human nature and that will therefore account for the essential differences existing between literary works and for their underlying unities as well.[24] Thus, although there may be different kinds of tragedies according to formal differences or differences in content (Greek tragedy, Shakespearean tragedy, heroic tragedy, revenge tragedy, and so on), it is easy to perceive that, although they vary in formal embodiment, they are all tragedies in some essential sense, which makes them distinct from comedies, epics, romances, and so on.

The *rasa* theory, with its elaborate typology of nine basic emotions (erotic love, the heroic spirit, sorrow, wonder, comic laughter, fear, aversion or disgust, rage, and quietude or serenity), which are fundamental psychological stereotypes, each with its own distinct tone or flavor, and several other (31 or so) lesser or subsidiary emotions (e.g., jubilation, dejection, agitation, debility, weariness, indolence, and so forth)—which have no independent existence apart from the basic emotions into which they dissolve themselves in any given composition—offers a more viable basis for literary classification than the other criteria do. This conclusion is not directly stated by the Sanskrit critics but may be drawn as an implication from their detailed analysis of different *rasa* types and the emphasis they lay on fixing the tone of individual poems in terms of those types, and also from the common practice of designating works in terms of their dominant *rasa*, as love poems, comic farces, tragedies, and so on.[25]

Notes

1. See Alaister Fowler, *Kinds of Literature: An Introduction to the Theory of Genres and Modes* (Cambridge: Harvard University Press, 1982), ch. 13, "Systems of Genres."
2. For Roman Jakobson, poetry is "focused upon sign, and pragmatical prose upon referent" (Roman Jakobson and Claude Lévi-Strauss, *Fundamentals of Language*, The Hague: Mouton, 1956, pp. 81–82). For Michael Riffaterre, the basic law of poetry is that it "says one thing and signifies something else." It is a form of "catachresis." See "The Prose Poem's Formal Features," in Mary Ann Caws and Hermine Riffaterre, eds., *The Prose Poem in France: Theory and Practice* (New York: Columbia University Press, 1983), p. 118.
3. *Poetics*, VI, 1450 b.
4. Bertrand H. Bronson ed., "Preface to Shakespeare," in *Samuel Johnson: Rasselas, Poems and Selected Prose*, (New York: Holt, Rinehart & Winston, 1965), p. 256.
5. For a fuller discussion of these and other species, which also included musical dramas and dance dramas, and for the definition of the terms involved see V. Raghavan, *Sanskrit Drama: Its Aesthetics and Production* (Madras, 1993), pp. 163–200.
6. "*padya-prācuryam gadya-sama-kakṣatayā apekṣyate*": Daṇḍin, *Kāvyādarśa* (Poona: Bhandarkar Oriental Research Institute, 1970), editor's commentary, 31.
7. A distinction rejected by Daṇḍin, *Kāvyādarśa*, pp. 25–30.
8. See A. B. Keith, *A History of Sanskrit Literature* (London: Oxford University Press, 1966), p. 332; and M. Krishnamachariar, *History of Classical Sanskrit Literature* (Varanasi: Motilal Banarsidass, 1970), p. 496.
9. "*gadya-padya-mayī rājastutiḥ*": *Sāhityadarpaṇa*, 6.337.
10. Vāmana, *Kāvyālaṁkāra-sūtrāṇi*, 1.3.23.
11. "*rasānurūpa-sandarbhatvam, sadalaṃkāravākyatvam*": Hemacandra, *Kāvyānuśāsanam* (Bombay: Nirnayasagar Press, 1934), p. 404.
12. "*daśarūpaksyaiva hīdaṃ sarvaṃ vilasitam*": Vāmana, 1.3.32.
13. *Dhvanyāloka* (Bombay: Nirnayasagar Press, 1935. Reprint. New Delhi: Munshiram Manoharlal, 1983), pp. 253–54.
14. *Dhvanyāloka*, III, 6–9 and gloss.
15. Vāmana, 1.3.21.
16. Raghavan, *Bhoja's Śṛṅgāra Prakāśa* (Madras, 1963), p. 356.
17. For a discussion of the prose poem, see Caws and Riffaterre (see n.2); and Jonathan Monroe, *A Poverty of Objects: The Prose Poem and the Politics of Genre* (Ithaca: Cornell University Press, 1987).
18. Dhanaṃjaya, *Daśarūpaka* (Madras: Adyar Library, 1969), 1.7., pp. 6–7.
19. Fowler, *Kinds of Literature*, ch. 14.
20. E. D. Hirsch, *Validity in Interpretation* (New Haven: Yale University Press, 1967), ch. 3.

21. *Poetics*, II, V.
22. John Reichert, "More Than Kin and Less Than Kind: The Limits of Genre Theory," in Joseph P. Strelka, ed., *Theories of Literary Genre* (University Park and London: Pennsylvania State University Press, 1978); Allan Rodway, "Generic Criticism: The Approach through Type, Mode and Kind," in Stratford-Upon-Avon Studies, 12: *Contemporary Criticism* (London: Edward Arnold, 1970).
23. Adrian Marino, "Toward a Definition of Literary Genres," in Strelka, *Theories of Literary Genre* (see n.22).
24. Cf. Northrop Frye, "The Archetypes of Literature," in *The Fables of Identity: Studies in Poetic Mythology* (New York: Harcourt Brace, 1963). Frye's classification of literature into four "generic plots" or mythoi—the romantic, the tragic, the comic, and the satiric/ironic—is, no doubt, based on a different principle than that of the *rasa* theory. But inasmuch as his archetypes do imply emotions or experiential states corresponding to each ("romance" = celebration and rhapsodic joy, "tragedy" = death and elegiac mourning, and so on), there may be no essential disagreement between the two, even as there is no essential disagreement with Aristotle's formal division. *Rasa* would no doubt be interested in the emotional quality or tone of the expression, whatever the thematic type or form of that expression may be.
25. For example, *Prahasana* (comic farce) is the name of a dramatic kind. *Śṛṅgāra-naiṣadha* is the title of a long poem (in Telugu) treating the erotic *rasa*; Bhavabhūti's *Uttararāma-carita* is a drama in which the pathetic *rasa* is the reigning emotion.

4

THE YOLK IN THE PEA-HEN'S EGG
Language as the Ultimate Reality

W. P. Lehmann

Language and the Absolute

Concern with language makes up most of Raja Rao's short foreword to his first novel, *Kanthapura*. Having decided to "tell" the story in English, he reports that "the telling has not been easy . . . We cannot write like the English. We should not. We cannot write only as Indians. We have grown to look at the large world as part of us" (vii). It is remarkable that a young writer publishing his first novel should be so concerned with language. It is more remarkable that he links the type of language he is fashioning with the "world" as India embraced it. But in making that link, Rao continues the long Indian view of language as integrally related to the world around it, to the ideas it represents. Usually expressed with reference to "words," this basic view of Indian thought assumes an intimate relationship between a "word" and its meaning.

The contrast with the Western linguistic tradition, certainly its dominant position today, could scarcely be greater. As "first principle," Saussure's highly influential theoretical work on language proclaims the "arbitrariness" of the sign (word). Accordingly there is no "internal connection between the idea 'sister' and the French signal for it: *s-ö-r*. Moreover, the meaning 'ox' is signaled by *b-ö-f* in one region, by *o-k-s* (Ochs) in another" (Saussure 100), and so on through individual languages. By Western tradition, the "word" expressing a specific meaning is a result of historical events. If Charlemagne's son had left his empire to only one of his sons instead of dividing it among three, most speakers of western Europe today would be using the same word for the animal—presumably "Ochs" if Ludwig the German had been the sole heir, but "*boeuf*" if Charles the Bald had been favored. Or if Caesar had not invaded Gaul, a reflex of the Gaulish word may have prevailed, with no more inherent relationship to the animal by Saussure's view than the German or the French word. And rather than "ox", the animal might be designated by the word "steer" or some other sequence of sounds with no relation whatsoever to the meaning. By the position of Western linguistics, history has led to the set of signs, to the words, we happen to use.

The contrasting Indian view makes Rao's concern clear. For if words are related to the meanings they signify in the world as recognized by its users, the form of that world will determine the method of expressing it among those users.

This concern of a current literary artist is not new or novel in Indian thought. Kalidasa begins one of his major works, his *Raghuvaṃsa*, with a statement on language, in which *vāc*, "word," is the first item. His first verse may be translated

> Like language and meaning tightly bound—
> to understand that language-meaning union
> I invoke Earth's parents, so too united,
> Parvati and the Supreme Lord.

For Homer, by contrast, "wrath" is the first word in one epic, "man" in the other, each disclosing the central topic of its poem. And in possibly the most intense concern with the "word" in a major Western literary work, Goethe has his Faust reinterpret the passage in Western tradition that has elicited and continues to elicit the greatest comment in efforts at interpretation. Unable to value *lógos* of John 1:1 so highly as to translate the passage: "In the beginning was the word," Faust shifts to "meaning," then "force," and finally to "act, action" (*Faust* 1224–37) so that the translation would read "In the beginning was the action." For Goethe and many others in our tradition, the word is a symbol, in Saussure's term a "sign," that cannot be inherently related to a specific meaning, let alone equated with the eternal spirit that created the world.

By contrast, in Indian tradition the word is eternal; the world is a transformation of language. Unlike Genesis 1, the world is not first created and its components then named. Nor after God has provided the central names would Indian views on language accept expansion by man, as in Genesis 2:19–20, where Adam assigns names to animals. For Indian thought, language is equivalent to the ultimate reality. Like "the yolk in the pea-hen's egg, which has all the variety and picturesqueness of the colors of the fully-grown peacock already in it . . . the expressive word with the thing expressed are present as one and undifferentiated in the speaker" (Iyer *Bhartṛhari* :153; somewhat rephrased). They are there as a unit because the individual is one with Brahman and the universe. As for Rao, the word is determined by the world in which individuals find themselves.

Background of the Indian Linguistic Tradition

This brief introduction represents only one view of language in a long tradition of intense concern with it. Indian society was established in such a way that a select group, the Brahmins, were totally supported by the other castes so that they could preserve the doctrines of the past with absolute maintenance of every sound, word, and sentence. Credit or responsibility for interpreting the sacred texts was not entrusted solely to theologians. The precise expressions used in the sacred texts had to be maintained so carefully that linguists as well were intimately involved. Their discipline was in fact a means for its specialists to attain salvation. But as in Western concern with language, those specialists varied in their view of language, developing several schools. Yet tenets of these differ so greatly and consistently from those of the West that only the central tradition in India, as represented from the Vedas through eminent literary figures of the early period to its major novelist today, is sketched in this essay.

The Indian grammatical tradition received its classical formulation by Panini, the early Indian linguist who has become so thoroughly embraced by the West that his name is included in desk dictionaries—and to the discomfort of pedants, without the diacritics that accurate transliteration would demand. The American linguist, Leonard Bloomfield, is reported to have kept a copy of Paṇini's grammar at his bedside; in his handbook, *Language*, he referred to the grammer as "one of the greatest monuments of human intelligence" (11). The grammar is now available, fortunately, in the admirable translation by the eminent scholar, Sumitra Katre, *Aṣṭādhyāyī of Pāṇini.*

Producing his grammer in the preliterate period, Panini formulated it through sutras—"threads" or rules tightly constructed, and compacted even more by brief formulae for grammatical categories and lexical classes. Centuries later, Patanjali's commentary expanded on Panini's rules. And the "grammarian Bhartrihari," as the principal character in Raja Rao's *The Chestmaster and his Moves* recalls him (5), somewhat later produced a classical commentary, especially for literary scholars.

Indian attention to language has then been more intense and disciplined than was Western concern. Moreover, it was closely allied to religious tradition in contrast with ours, which originated in and has maintained close ties with philosophical discussion, as incidentally Indian linguistics has also. Plato's dialogue *Cratylus* is the first major treatise on language in our tradition that has come down to us. Curiously enough, it deals with a topic also of concern in Indian linguistics, that is, whether or not there is an inherent relationship between a word and the item it signifies. Using descriptive compounds, like *blackbird*, Cratylus, the participant in the dialogue for whom it is named, asserts that such a relationship exists, that words were fashioned originally with such a relationship in view. His opponents in the argument are given ample room to present their position, and Socrates as the moderator remains neutral. Yet in the subsequent centuries, the position represented by Cratylus prevailed. Efforts to determine the original basis of words were pursued so vigorously, also among the Romans, that absurd attempts at explanation were produced. The most widely cited such "explanation"—*lucus a non lucendo* "a forest is called a *lucus* because it is not light"—has been maintained as a stigma to be imposed on illogical utterances. But its fate today illustrates that Cratylus ultimately lost, as Saussure's first principle emphatically indicates.

The central Indian view of linguistics, maintained rigorously in Vedanta philosophy, is based on the *Rigveda*, notably hymn 125 of book 10, in which the "word" is a goddess *Vāc*, a direct cognate with Latin *vōx*, which through French has become our word "voice," among other reflexes in the Indo-European languages like Greek *épos*. A song of praise, the hymn discusses her powers; among these, she "carries" the gods and brings riches to men. Originating in the waters, she gives birth to her father and extends throughout the worlds, encompassing all of them beyond this earth and heaven. Other hymns provide their own characterization. Hymn 114, line 8, of book 10, for example, makes *vāc* coextensive with Brahman.

Whether deified or not, *vāc* "speech" is characterized as possessing an existence also outside human speakers. Within them, she is inborn. But we learn in hymn 164, line 45 of book 1 that only one of her four parts is expressed by them. What these four parts are is left vague.

The status of "speech" as equivalent to Brahman and its role with respect to other powers is the basis for subsequent attention paid it. As is amply known, the sacred writings in Indian tradition were to be maintained in their original form, not merely through written transmission like the Western Bible, but with the original sounds, intonation, and forms intact. Brahmins entrusted with their portion of the purportedly inspired text memorized that portion in such a way that its accents were maintained for millennia, as well as sounds that disappeared before writing was introduced into India. The original presence of these lost sounds has been corroborated by comparative study and by the fortunate maintenance of related forms of them in Hittite, as recorded early in the second millennium B.C. It is this devotion to the original language that led to its thorough description, in standard form by Panini, followed by commentaries. The prestige accorded the original language also led to a concern with it that was far more intensive than linguistic study in the West. Bhartrihari's treatise leaves no doubt on the extent of analysis and classification.

The Sentence (*vākya*) and the Word (*pada*) According to Bhartrihari

Producing his treatise on language, the *Vākyapadīya,* about a thousand years after Panini, Bhartrihari enjoyed the benefit of an established tradition as well as the privilege of elaborating on it in accordance with the central school of Indian thought. A Vedantist of the *advaita* school, he interpreted Panini's highly formalized grammer in accordance with his theology, by which the world is undivided (*a,* "not," *dvā,* "two," followed by the adjectival suffix *-ita*). Brahman, the Universal, is the only reality. There is no distinction between the individual (ātman) and the absolute (Brahman); the possible appearance of separate existence for individuals is an illusion. Accordingly, the essence of language—*śabda-tattva,* which Joyce might have defined as the speechness of speech—is equivalent to Brahman. Words represent eternal universals. Since other philosophies had arisen that promoted contrasting views, like those of Buddhism, which considered language a convention as we do in Western tradition, it was important to formulate the standard position precisely. Bhartrihari does so with the thoroughness and elegance cultivated by generations of Brahmins.

Before examining his formulation, we may note that it is not simply a scientific treatise like the increasingly numerous books in our tradition entitled *Language*. Because śabda-tattva cannot be separated from Brahman, knowledge of grammar and precise use of language is one of the roads to paradise, or *mokṣa*—"release" from temporal existence and union with Brahman.

Bhartrihari, his predecessors, and his students, were well aware of the multiplicity of languages. Moreover, although they recognized Sanskrit as sacred, they also knew that it has undergone change. Besides differences in the Classical Sanskrit of their day from Vedic Sanskrit, they were aware of even further differences in the subsequent languages of everyday use, the Prakrits; like other classical poets, Kalidāsa, put Prakrits in the mouths of his women and servants, while men, whether human or divine, used Sanskrit. Accordingly, even Classical Sanskrit does not represent śabda-tattva. For the understanding of language that leads to mokṣa, the actual situation had to be determined and stated.

In his approach to such understanding, Bhartrihari accounts for language under eight topics, four sets of pairs. The sets consist of forms, meanings, relationships, and results.

The two items in the pair of forms are the linguistic elements that need to be explained and the elements used in their explanation. Indian linguistics would then reserve terms like "passive," "subject," and "case" for the second set, unlike many Western linguists, who use such terms in their general sense as well as the technical, often leading to confusion. And the actual forms are merely external manifestations of the abstract language stored internally. This internal language itself is but an intermediate stage to the eternal language. The external manifestations then can take various guises—English, Hindi, and Sanskrit among thousands. From any of these, the writer seeks the manifestation that is closest to the eternal language.

The pair of meanings consists of those that are fixed and those obtained by analysis. The pair of relations consist of those that are fit to provide the meaning and those that are causative. Causative relations involve the will of the speaker and accordingly represent the participation of speaker and hearer in communication.

In this way, the first three sets correspond at least in part to the three constituents of communication as portrayed by Charles Sanders Peirce, and now widely held under the rubric "semiotics." Peirce singled out three items in communication: the sign, the referent or concept referred to, and the individuals involved in communication. Linguistics then includes three large components: lexicon and grammar, which Peirce called syntactics, that is, signs and the relations among them; semantics, the relations between signs and referents; and pragmatics, the relations between signs and speakers. In this respect, the framework of a semiotic approach to language is not unlike much of the apparatus that Bhartrihari saw in language.

But at this point Peirce stopped, as have Western linguists. Bhartrihari, however, continued with an additional pair that represent the results of language. The first of these is proper understanding of meaning, which might be subsumed under pragmatics. But the second member of the last pair is totally outside any Western concern with language; that item is dharma, "spiritual merit," which as noted above is acquired through proper use of language. At best in our tradition, skillful use of language brings esteem and applause, whether to an author or in daily use, such as effective repartee. But even our greatest devotee of language would refrain from stating that its mastery would make straight the way to heaven. And though we may not assume such a view among all members in the Indian tradition, the use of language, especially among authors, involves much more responsibility, much greater care, than does that of even superb stylists in the West. In this way, we can account for the approach that we have noted of Raja Rao when he set out to produce a national novel in the language of the rulers of his country, a language that would make his work much more widely accessible than his native Kannada.

Language as One with Brahman

Rao's adoption of English may seem strange when we recall the position of an *advaita* Brahmin concerning equivalence of the word with Brahman. Though also of the Indo-European family, English is by no means the language closest to Sanskrit that Rao might have selected; many languages of India are current forms of the spoken languages equivalent to Sanskrit in the first millennium B.C. and earlier. A language need not therefore be sacred, or descended from a sacred language, to enjoy such a relationship with Brahman. In a conference of Indian authors arranged by the eminent critic, Narasimhaiah, Rao may have answered the question, telling his fellow authors "unless you, the writer, could go back to the changeless in yourself, you could not truly communicate with the reader." Further, "unless the author becomes an *upasaka* (devotee) and enjoys himself in himself, the eternality of the sound (*Śabda*) will not manifest itself" ("The Writer" 230). It is then the individual in union with Brahman who achieves communication, whatever the natural language may be. Apparently such a devoted individual can overcome the requirement that "Unless word becomes *mantra* no writer is a writer, and no reader a reader" (231). English or any other language may therefore be selected for communication.

Bhartrihari's view of language, reflecting Panini's, provides a key to the apparent paradox that language is one with Brahman even though as many as 7,500 different languages have been identified as in use today, any of them potentially acceptable for the kind of communication Rao has in mind. Each of those different languages is merely a manifestation of the eternal language.

The view of language as made up of a surface manifestation and an abstract structure is now general among linguists, though differing from that of Indian tradition and also varying among several groups of current linguists. It owes a great deal to Baudouin de Courtenay and his student Kruszewski, who introduced it with reference to the sound system. We may contrast briefly three variants of the view, by which the essential language is regarded as a social, or as a psychological, or, as in India, a spiritual entity.

The social view was maintained by Saussure, for whom the actual language of the individual, parole, is a manifestation of a social convention, langue. As the speech of the individual, parole may be idiosyncratic, even ungrammatical; nonetheless, it is a reflection of the language that a given society maintains. The social set of conventions called "langue" is a general form to which we relate parole and by which we interpret utterances. In view of Saussure's great prestige as the "father of modern linguistics," his conception of language has been widely adopted. On the other hand, for mentalists, such as Sapir, the real language is a psychological entity. Linguists may maintain one or the other of these views; after Chomsky, a mentalist, the psychological entity has displaced among many the Saussurean approach. By both of these positions, actual speech is imperfect, with possible lapses, grammatical errors, dialect variants, and the like.

Since parole, or the output of the surface structure in generative grammar, is manifested, it is a part of the role of language in our lives that we automatically relate the often imperfect speech used by ourselves and others with the abstract language without suffering obloquy or lack of understanding because of our less than perfect command of it. That is to say, we have no moral compulsion to move toward a superior type of language. By Indian tradition, on the other hand, striving for the perfect language is highly important; by achieving it, even segments of it, one gains merit. Even the humblest outcaste may be accorded a distinctive mantra. For the eminent literary figure, as we have noted from Raja Rao's statement, every word must be a mantra.

To illustrate further the considerable difference between the traditional view of language in the West and that of India, we may note briefly the difference in presentation of the forms, especially the noun forms. Nouns in our tradition are said to be inflected for cases, which are labeled like those illustrated below. Latin nouns are said to have six cases, using as example the word for friend:

Nominative	*amīcus*	"friend"
Genitive	*amīcī*	"of a friend"
Dative	*amīcō*	"to, for a friend"
Accusative	*amīcum*	"friend"
Ablative	*amīcō*	"from a friend
Vocative	*amīce*	"oh friend"

In our treatment of the language, we use the same names for the actual forms and for the classes, that is, the abstract forms; accordingly, in the Latin second declension, the form *amīcus* is labeled "nominative," and the nominative is also specified as the abstract form required for the subject. On the other hand, in Indian grammar, already in Panini's, the actual case forms are listed in accordance with the most economical order and simply named by their sequence: first, second, etc. Thereupon, classes are identified, and the actual forms are equated with them.

For example, in treatment of the abstract class "actor" (Sanskrit *kartṛ*), we find that the Indian first case, comparable to the Latin nominative, is equated with it, but also the third, comparable to an instrumental case, so that two different inflected forms may fill the role of *kartṛ*, as in "*My brother* gave me the book" but also "The book was given me by *my brother*." An approximation to the Indian approach to grammar has been introduced, known as "case grammar." Case grammar includes abstract classes like "agent," which corresponds to Panini's *kartṛ*. For Panini and the other grammarians, abstract sounds, words, and grammar constitute the real language, which then is expressed by actual speech. The physical sounds and forms of speech are therefore only manifestations of the real language.

Whether Western linguists today view the "real" language as an abstract structure of a social kind or a psychological kind, they deal with language in a comparable way. The essential elements of language are not the physical manifestations that can be recorded and analyzed by procedures of acoustic physics, but rather classes determined largely by relationships. In this way, our conception of language is comparable to that of Panini and many other Indian grammarians, though, at least for *advaita* Brahmins, their abstract language has a spiritual basis.

A comprehensive comparison of the Western and Indian approaches would be extensive, as would further presentation of the Indian treatment of language. As the many accounts of Indian linguistics indicate, their treatment was detailed and presented with multifold terminology (cf. Katre). Here only a general characterization can be given, while basic differences may be indicated beforehand by several general statements.

Indian linguists like Bhartrihari set out to link spoken language to thought, identifying key points in the process. By contrast, in Western attention to communication, linguistics concerns itself with language, leaving the problem of its relation to thought for psychologists and philosophers.

For Bhartrihari, as noted above, there are three stages of language, from the concrete manifestation, through an inner stage in which form and meaning are distinct, to a stage in which they are one—and further to the thought-image itself. This image Bhartrihari labels *sphoṭa*. While of great interest, I leave details on *sphoṭa* theory, and especially the labels and their characterization, to individuals who may wish to pursue them further. The extensive commentary on Bhartrihari's grammar by Iyer serves as an admirable source.

Besides these stages by which phenomena are related to abstract images, in our practice, whether linguistic or elsewhere in academic areas, we distinguish between theoretical and practical approaches. Engineering, for example, is the applied form of physics, chemistry, and other sciences. Less developed fields like linguistics simply divide specializations between theoretical attention and application; for example, students of the meanings of words may specialize in theory, that is, lexicology, on the one hand, or in practice, that is, lexicography, on the other. An applied linguist may set out to teach languages, while a theoretical linguist concentrates on patterns or structures with no attempt to make them especially transparent to language learners. In Indian practice, as noted in the preceding paragraph, the distinction is not made, at least intellectually; a linguist would consider the practical side of a discipline as much a part of the field as the theoretical.

Further, disciplines that are separate for us are closely linked to one another in Indian approaches. Because language is considered in relation to thought, the field of psychology is closely related to language study by Indian view. And like it, there is a close link between what we treat as theoretical and applied areas of psychology. The term for the general field of psychology is "yoga." It is often discussed in Western concern, generally with reference to application. Yet the aim of such applied yoga is comparable to that of careful cultivation of language; one seeks to obtain salvation, or *mokṣa*. *Sphoṭa* theory then is pertinent for psychology as well as for linguistics. Both disciplines are avenues to understanding the absolute and to the ultimate merger of the individual (ātman) with Brahman.

Language to the Teller of Tales: Bhoja and Poetics

Still another field that we treat separately falls under *sphoṭa* theory: aesthetics. For Bhartrihari, language includes a further dimension that he referred to as *dhvani*. Difficult to interpret or label precisely, it may be characterized as poetic suggestion. For the perceptive user of language, its elements, whether sounds, forms, sentences, or other patterns, may occasion special effects, such as approval or objection or elevation. The experience resulting in this way is known as *rasa*.

Indian aesthetics has been treated as extensively as has its linguistics. The ideals of literature have been thoroughly examined, classified, and named. In probably the most highly esteemed treatise on poetics, that by Bhoja, the two basic elements of language—*śabda*, "form, word, speech," and *artha*, "meaning"—are considered essential, as they are in linguistic study; but for literary effect the essential is taken to be their union, or combination: *sāhitya*. As Patrick Hogan reminds me, one recalls Pope's maxim that "the sound must seem an echo to the sense" (1.365) Equated also with the notion of "harmony," the term *sāhitya* has come to mean "rhetoric, poetry" (cf. Raghavan).

Bhoja's treatise deals initially with grammatical relations, elaborating those with special effects. The most important of these is *rasa,* which he treats after three others: *doṣa,* "deficiencies," *guṇa* "stylistic elegance"; and *alaṁkara,* "poetic ornament." Like other Indian technical terms, *rasa* is generally given with its literal meaning, "juice," and then with its technical adaptations, which are expounded differently among literary scholars. Central to such definitions is the notion that the juice of a fruit is its best part; in literary discourse, *rasa* then refers to the outstanding elements of a literary work. Among numerous *rasas,* are love, heroism, anger, and pity. In Bhoja's treatise, *rasa* is treated at great length, with attention to it making up over half of the chapters. For our purposes, we wish primarily to provide some notion of the extensive background in literary theory on which current Indian writers may draw.

Since Indian literature of the past was largely oral, the aesthetic principles and critical attention dealt with lyric and dramatic forms. In adopting the novel as a literary form, however, these principles were also adapted to this Western form. When applied by Rao and other writers following the ancient tradition, and when sanctioned by rigorous critics like Narasimhaiah, the results represent a composite of the Western tradition with the Indian. Prose works in the Indian tradition are not, then, produced primarily for entertainment or for other types of amusement such as the pursuit of mysterious situations, as in a detective story. While it may be something of an exaggeration to state that they are designed to provide a way to attain *mokṣa,* novels produced by such writers might be labeled, as by Rao, philosophical.

According to the widely esteemed writer, R. K. Narayan, the ancient tradition was also maintained by storytellers who are "part and parcel of the Indian village community." According to him, such a storyteller "has no doubt whatever that the *Vedas* were created out of the breath of God, and contain within them all that a man needs for his salvation at every level." A knowledge of the Vedas is therefore essential to understand "the significance of any story"; for the stories are "interrelated [with] scriptures, ethics, philosophy, grammar, astrology, astronomy, semantics, mysticism, and moral codes" (cf. Narasimhaiah *Fiction* 232–39). The everyday stories, told by individuals comparable to the bards in ancient cultures, then, are complex accounts with didactic, moral, spiritual, and intellectual aims presented in cultivated, poetic language.

In his monograph on Raja Rao, Narasimhaiah finds a similar complexity in his third novel, *The Cat and Shakespeare.* And he wonders whether "the average reader of fiction" will appreciate the "richness that underlies its several layers . . . unless he has a true appreciation of the term Kavya in Sanskrit poetics and makes no distinction between prose and verse." For the novel requires "knowledge of many disciplines . . . with words becoming images, images fusing into myths, myths manifesting as symbols . . . [since] a variety of devices have been employed by the novelist to explore his concepts" (130–31). The novelist by this view is a *kavi*—sage or poet—wise, inspired, in control of poetic language, open to prophetic imagination, the source of *kāvyam* for his audience. If a village storyteller is steeped in the ancient traditions and "has precise knowledge of Sanskrit grammar, syllabification, meaning of words" (Narayan "The World" 234), a dedicated writer could scarcely "recapture the magnificent mythical imagination of Indian antiquity" (Narasimhaiah xii) without more cultivated attention to literary traditions and broader knowledge of them, including the work of theoreticians like Bhartrihari and Bhoja. All the variety and colors of the peacock may already be in the pea-hen's egg, but they may also be visible largely through the help of seers (*kavi*s) and scholars who have constructed increasingly thorough methods of observation and presentation through thousands of years.

As these references may suggest, concern with language, as well as its study, in India is founded on venerated authorities and has also been more intense than is that of the West. There, according to many, linguistics is the science of sciences. The disciplines touched on above, as well as others, rely heavily on linguistics as their basis. If indeed language is one with Brahman, understanding of the absolute, of the Supreme Lord, is available to the individual through a property possessed by every human being. Appropriate attention to language then opens the way to *mokṣa*, revealing also the other intellectual capabilities and disciplines, such as functioning of the mind in psychology, pursuit of logic in philosophy, and appreciation of beauty in aesthetics. Like Bhoja, one first masters the situation in language and then proceeds to clarification of the principles in these and other disciplines with the aim of achieving understanding of the absolute.

Reflections in the West of the View that Language and Its Referents Are Interrelated

As we have noted at the beginning of this essay, linguists today strongly hold to the position that there is no relationship between words and their referent. They recognize onomatopoetic words, as for animal cries, but point out that even these are stereotyped approximations, as illustrated by *cock-a-doodle-do* in English, *kikeriki* in German, and so on in other languages and in attempts at reproducing cries of other animals in a language. Saussure's first principle on the arbitrariness of the sign is a major tenet in subsequent linguistics.

The popular view, however, often differs. A relationship is often felt between names and their referents, as indicated by changes in the name. Because of widespread aversion to Germany and German names in World War I, many names were changed or modified, such as Eisenhower from Eisenhauer. And after World War II in communist countries, favorable names like Karl-Marx-Stadt displaced previous geographical names, as have also names of countries, especially in Africa. Moreover, we have seen a succession of changes of names for racial groups, such as Afro-Asiatic for Black for Negro, and similarly for Mexican-American, which itself has different evaluations in different areas of our country. Major social movements may also relate names and things, as has feminism. Designations like "chairman", "postman," and so on have been rejected as sexist, their second component replaced by the less offensive "person." Many such associations are maintained strongly, either taken as favorable, as "Palestine" is by one group, or rejected, as it is by another group. In short, Saussure's first principle may be one of the major tenets on which his linguistic theory was based as well as subsequent theory; but for many speakers, the associations between words and their referents are anything but arbitrary.

When such popular views prevail, the words selected for modification are generally limited to small, obvious sets, and the effects superficial. Yet occasional linguists have proposed a deeper and wider interrelationship among language, thought, and reality. The most generally recognized among them is the late American Benjamin Lee Whorf, whose papers were published under that title. Linked in this view with Edward Sapir, Whorf is credited with the hypothesis that a language affects its speaker's views of the world. The interrelationship then is not eternal, like that of the Indian sábda-tattva; rather, by the Sapir-Whorf hypothesis, every language governs its speakers' views of reality.

The Sapir-Whorf hypothesis is generally illustrated by actual incidents that reputedly led Whorf to his position. An insurance executive, he was struck by fires that smokers started in the neighborhood of gasoline drums labeled "empty." After investigation, he concluded that the smokers failed to realize that empty gasoline drums were actually more dangerous than full ones in that the remaining fumes would more readily ignite. The word "empty" led speakers to think that a container was harmless; in the real world, emptiness was taken as not disposed to danger. In much the same way a word selected to encourage care—"inflammable," where "in" means "highly" as in "intense"—had the contrary effect because it was interpreted instead to mean "not," as in "insane." To change behavior, Whorf advocated modifying the word often found on gasoline trucks and other containers of materials that readily burn to "flammable."

After some initial acceptance, the Sapir-Whorf hypothesis has been gradually neglected, or even discredited. Yet recently a proponent, George W. Grace, has again argued strongly in its favor, in a book entitled *The Linguistic Construction of Reality*. Grace's position may be indicated by listing the two views of language he assumes: a mapping and a reality-construction view. The designations clearly indicate the two positions. While the first applies to the standard Western view, Grace favors the second, which he equates with that of Whorf. He proceeds to define the reality-construction view with ten assumptions, only the seventh of which is cited here: "That it is misleading to talk without proper qualification of human beings as all living in a common objectively given world; that each language-culture system must to some extent have its own conceptual world that is the product of its own history—a world that has been created continuously by its speakers throughout that history" (11). His position, and Whorf's as he interprets it, is then comparable to the Indian view in closely relating language and culture, but, for Grace, language helps in fashioning the world as conceived by speakers of a given language. By the Indian view presented here, language as equivalent to Brahman constitutes actuality, and world as we see it is at least in part illusion.

A position closer to this view is demonstrable more clearly among generalists. In accepting the Peace Prize of the German Booksellers Association, Václav Havel, the Czech playwright and later president of the country, devoted his address to the "power of the word." In the translated version by A. G. Brain, Havel makes statements about language that might be approved by a Vedantist, such as: "words can be said to be the very source of our being, and in fact the very substance of the cosmic life-form we call Man. Spirit, the human soul, our self-awareness, our ability to generalize and think in concepts, to perceive the world as the world . . . surely all these are mediated or actually created by words." While discussing the potentially "harmful" effect of words more extensively than have Indian writers, Havel nonetheless concludes by stating that "responsibility for and towards words is a task which is intrinsically ethical. As such, however, it is situated beyond the horizon of the visible world, in that realm wherein dwells the Word that was in the beginning and is not the word of Man" (5). Having started his essay by referring to John 1:1, Havel clearly does not agree with Goethe's Faust.

The position Havel proposes is very much like Whorf's in the final paper of his unfortunately short life (Carroll 246–70). Here Whorf proposes that the Western world, while making advances in controlling the physical world—as in harnessing electronics for wireless communication—has failed to recognize the power inherent in language, let alone to control that power. Through the "mantric" art of India, which recognizes the "inner affinity of language with the cosmic order," on the other hand, the "mantram . . . can SET the human organ to transmit, control, and amplify a thousandfold forms which that organism normally transmits only at observably low intensities" (249). Like electronic equipment that achieves its power only when "loose magnets" and "loose wires" are arrayed in the "PROPER PATTERN," so "mantric and yogic use of language [is linked] with the configuration or pattern aspect which is so basic in language" (250). And the "type of patterned relationship found in language may well be but the wavering and distorted, pale substanceless reflection of a CAUSAL WORLD" (269), that is, the world as it is disclosed by investigations conducted by physical scientists; yet for the scientist, Whorf, the configuration of the material world that his colleagues have learned to understand and in part to control may be similarly pale and distorted.

Although Whorf acknowledges repeatedly that this view of language is not recognized in the "modern world," he looks forward to the time of fuller understanding of language comparable to that achieved by Western scientists of the physical world. According to him, such achievement will require far greater insights into language than those gained by the average speaker. For "natural man, whether simpleton or scientist, knows no more of the linguistic forces that bear upon him than the savage knows of gravitational forces" (251). Just as the physical sciences have dispelled some of the ignorance concerning the forces of gravitation, so further knowledge of language will remove what Whorf calls "the illusory necessities of common logic" and "illusory linguistic necessities" (269–70). The illusion, for Whorf, has been "necessitated" by taking the externals of language as the essential in understanding it, and by building on that inadequate understanding Western forms of logic that have also veiled much of the real physical world for scientists as well as savages. After removal of the illusion, Western science will presumably come to understand more fully the real physical world as well as "the bonds between the language and the cosmic order," much as the Vedantists have over the past millennia.

Brahmāṇḍa

According to Puranic tradition, not yet touched on, the universe arose from Brahmāṇḍa, literally the Brahmanic egg. Since "*āṇḍa*" may mean "testicle" as well as "egg," origin of the universe may be taken as asexual. Whether egg, testicle, or a sexually indistinguishable entity, Brahman is the source of what Whorf identifies as the physical world: "an aggregate of quasidiscrete entities (atoms, crystals, living organisms, planets, stars, etc.)" (269). Since the word, as we have noted, is one with Brahman, language is included in that source. It then contains in itself the key to the physical world that emerged from the "egg," just as the yolk of the pea-hen's egg does the colors of the physical bird.

Among tasks of the scientists are exploration of the structure of that physical world, including living organisms like the peacock, and attempts to understand their origin. Literary artists, on the other hand, explore the world of language, seeking to provide an understanding of living organisms, chiefly human, though also planets, stars, crystals, etc., these generally in relation to human beings.

For new insights, Western literary artists concentrate on manipulating the language, inasmuch as it is a separate, independent structure for them as it is for the Western linguist. Their course may vary. Wordsworth and Coleridge considered the language really used by men their source of literary renewal. Others have looked to the classics. By contrast, the Indian writer has the essence of language in himself. His ātman is one with Brahman, who in turn is one with the word. The power of that word may be obtained, and released to an audience, through devotion to a representative of Brahman, much as the mathematician, Ramanujan, who provides such fascination for Rao in the *Chessmaster*, developed new insights in mathematics through devotion to his goddess.

The search for the effective word, then, differs markedly in the Indian and the Western traditions, as does the mission of the writer. For the Indian writer, *voice/vōx/Vāc* is sought within. "Man faces himself when he seeks the word." In doing so, he compounds the "vibrant silence" that is the word "into a momentary act. The act has to be like prayer" (Rao "The Writer" 231). Just as the "Goddess of Namakkal gave all, all" to Ramanujan, "perhaps the greatest mathematician of our age," (*Chessmaster* 118), so the writer secures "the word as pure sound" from Brahman. And that writer, "who like an unquenchable source of a hundred streams is an eloquent father of words resonating in the bosom of his parents, they—heaven and earth—must protect, for his words are true" (*Rigveda* 3.26.9).

Bibliography

Bloomfield, Leonard. *Language*. New York: Holt, 1933.

Carroll, John B. *Language, Thought and Reality*. Selected writings of Benjamin Lee Whorf, ed. John B. Carroll. Cambridge: MIT Press, 1956.

Goethe, Johann Wolfgang. *Faust*, ed. R-M. S. Heffner, Helmut Rehder, and W.F. Twaddell. Boston: Heath, 1954.

Grace, George W. *The Linguistic Construction of Reality*. London: Croom Helm, 1987.

Havel, Václav. "The Power of the Word," trans. A. G. Brain. *New York Review* vol. 36, no. 21–22 (January) 1990, 5.

Iyer, K. A. Subramania. *Vākyapadīya of Bhartṛhari*. Poona: Deccan College, 1966.

———. *Bhartṛhari*. Poona: Deccan College, 1969.

Kalidasa. *Raghuvamsa* Trans. Arthur W. Ryder. London: Dent. Everyman's Library 629, 1912.

Katre, Sumitra. *Aṣṭādhyāyī of Pāṇini*. Austin: University of Texas Press, 1987.

Narasimhaiah, C., ed. *Fiction and the Reading Public in India*. Mysore: University of Mysore, 1967.

———. *Raja Rao*. New Delhi: Arnold-Heinemann, N.d.

Narayan, R.K. "The World of the Storyteller." In *Fiction and the Reading Public in India*, ed. C. D. Narasimhaiah. Mysore: University of Mysore, 1967 232–39.

Peirce, Charles Sanders. "*Elements of Logic*." In Collected Papers, vol. 2., ed. Charles Hartshorne and Paul Weiss. Cambridge: Belknap, 1931.

Pope, Alexander. "An Essay on Criticism." In *Literary Criticism of Alexander Pope*. Ed. B. Goldgar. Lincoln: University of Nebraska Press, 1965.
Raghavan, V. *Bhoja's Sṛṅgara Prakāsa*. Madras: Punarvasu, 1963.
Rao, Raja. *Kanthapura*. New York: New Directions, 1938.
———. *The Cat and Shakespeare*. New York: Macmillan, 1965.
———. "The Writer and the Word," pp. 229–31 in *Fiction and the Reading Public in India*, ed. C. D. Narasimhaiah. Mysore: University of Mysore, 1967.
———. *The Chessmaster and his Moves*. Delhi: Vision Books, 1988.
Rigveda, Die Hymnen des 3d ed. photomechanical reprint. Ed. Th. Aufrecht. Darmstadt: Wissenschaftliche Buchgesellschaft, 1955.
Saussure, Ferdinand de. *Cours de linguistique générale*. Paris: Payot, 1949.

Part III

Interpreting Cultural Difference and Cross-Cultural Invariance: Precolonial, Colonial, and Postcolonial

5

Patriarchy and Paranoia: Imaginary Infidelity in *Uttararāmacarita* and *The Winter's Tale*

Lalita Pandit

Preface

Kālidāsa, Bhāsa, Bhavabhūti, and other Sanskrit playwrights (seventh to tenth century A.D.) wrote tragicomedies that are very similar to the tragicomedy of Shakespeare and his contemporaries. The structural similarities between Shakespeare's and Bhavabhūti's tragicomedies are not indicative of influence, direct or indirect. Instead, the unexpected similarities between the two plays manifest a significant set of aesthetic universals. Both plays draw on earlier works of literature, make innovative use of myth and legend, and mix tragic and comic modes of representation, and construct the sea or large bodies of water (Ganges and other rivers in the Sanskrit play) as regenerative symbols. Both texts constitute a semi-idyllic green world as an alternative to the world of the court. A sprawling time scheme of 12 and 16 years is used by the playwrights to bring about a happy end to a sequence of events that is inherently tragic. In addition, the device of a play within the play is used in both texts to distance the happy ending and, thus, to make it theatrically more plausible.

This is not to suggest that these coincidental similarities are the only basis for the following comparative study of *Uttararā-*

macarita and *The Winter's Tale*. In recent years, postcolonial theory and literatures have received a great deal of attention; however, studies of precolonial traditions of colonized countries are often neglected. The consequence of this neglect is that many academics who teach and write on postcolonial literatures often dissociate these writers from their precolonial past. Therefore, within a framework of academic constitutions of postcoloniality, an insight into the dominant dramatic form of ancient India and its structural affinity with Shakespeare's late romances is a timely project.

As the subsequent discussion will show, Shakespeare's and Bhavabhūti's plays share far more than formal properties. Sita and Hermione, the female protagonists in *Uttararāmacarita* and *The Winter's Tale*, respectively, are suspected of adultery and subjected to extreme forms of punishment. Manifestations of paranoia and mass hysteria over the possible violation of chastity generate tragic action in both plays. In both instances, the supposedly erring women are queens, and the punishing patriarchs are kings. As the prerogative of sovereignty leads to tyranny, the gender-based inequities of legal justice become further perverted.

In *Uttararāmacarita* and *The Winter's Tale*, patriarchal irrationality, hidden in the garb of moralizing "rigor," is invariably associated with tragedy, while retributive justice of another kind is associated with the female agency, which is represented in the Sanskrit play by an anthropomorphic transformation of nature deities. In the following pages, I should like to examine various cultural, aesthetic, and political ramifications of the denigration and reification of the accused women in *Uttararāmacarita* and *The Winter's Tale*.

In both plays, the stigma of adultery forces the female protagonists to spend most of their reproductive lives suspended like ghosts in an underworld, waiting to reclaim their place in family and society. During the waiting period, they are absented as fully realized human subjects and are transformed into aesthetized objects of gaze, turned into memory traces within the mental processes of remorseful remembering (of their husbands). In these contexts, personal memory is not innocent. It is grounded in the larger patterns of reification available in a given culture. Hermione is translated into a memory image, a ghost, and an art object. When she is handed back to her penitent husband at the end, it seems as if Hermione has forgotten her queenly grandeur and has been schooled in the domestic virtues of modesty and reticence. Sita is subjected to similar objectifying constructions. After he banishes her, Rama builds a *Kanchan Sīta*, a golden replica of her, and he remembers her in contexts that emphasize her sensuality and fragility, her kindness to animals, her love of ornamentation, her reticence, her fear of wild beasts, and above all, her dependence on her husband. In all these contexts, the lost wife becomes a wife and daughter of sentiment. The husband's rememoration is shaped by literary/cultural modes of sentimentalization and romanticization of women, especially of women who have become victims of oppression.

I use the term "reification" in the sense in which Lukács has used it in *History and Class Consciousness in Marxist Dialectics* (94). He uses the term to refer to discourse processes in capitalist societies (and this idea can apply to precapitalist feudal societies as easily) that turn human subjects into things and images that elevate, and thus transform into exchange value the humanness of the individual subjects. Lacan has also used this term to speak of the objectified identities of human subjects, identities that are products of various processes of acculturation (*Ecrits* 217). As glorified cultural images and icons, human agents become objectified, and, in that process, their human subjectivity is absorbed by various fetishizing and reificatory agencies of a culture. My assumption is that it is through these agencies that hegemonic systems initiate and sustain forms of oppression. An exploration of imaginary infidelity in Shakespeare's and Bhavabhūti's plays, its causes and consequences, necessitates an inquiry into modes of cultural production that denigrate and reify female sexuality, modes that determine in symbolic terms the exchange value of feminine virtue. Since both texts are to be treated as products of the materialist and symbolic economies of the cultures they are grounded in, the following explorations of gender myths and other marginalizing tendencies of dominant ideologies of the epic and classical periods in India, as well as those found in medieval and Renaissance periods in the West, will help to contextualize the gender politics of imaginary infidelity in *Uttararāmacarita* and *The Winter's Tale*.

Parallel Marginalities of Race and Gender in Bhavabhūti Source Text—Rāmāyaṇa

Oppressive gender ideologies that we find in medieval and Renaissance Europe existed in the Hindu tradition as far back as 750 and 500 B.C. Bhavabhūti's play is based on *Rāmāyaṇa*, which was written around this time. As a great epic, *Rāmāyaṇa* excels in aesthetic transformations of the ideology of dharma, an ideology that politicizes religion and provides moral, spiritual, and mystical justifications for systematic disenfranchisement of women and lower castes. Certainly, there is much more to Indian culture outside of the narrow limits of dharma, and women of these time periods were not any worse off in India than they were elsewhere in the world. However, the specific text we are dealing with in this project is *Rāmāyaṇa,* and this text is different from others in its systematic exposition of the laws of dharma. I do not mean to suggest that *Rāmāyaṇa* is didactic. On the contrary, it is a very beautifully composed epic poem, written in the most lucid and mellifluous Sanskrit, the metrical music of its verse is irresistible, and its narrative structure is extremely sophisticated. However, the aesthetics of the epic poem is grounded in an ideologically constructed value system.

My intention here is not to undermine the more liberatory trends in Indian thought that support individualism and egalitarianism. Many Indologists have recognized that the Purāṇic literature unravels a lost tradition of dominance of woman in Indian culture, while the epics move more toward constructions of patriarchal power structures.[1] This shift is due in part to the development of asceticism in ancient Hindu culture, which "fortified the objectification and marginalization of women and goddesses" (Gatwood 37). Within the living traditions of Rāma worship in India, Sītā is regarded as a multiform of the mother goddess. Yet, in her epic role, she incorporates domestic virtue to such an extreme degree that her divine nature is restricted within the confines of dharma. In contrast, the glorified myth of the divine feminine capitalizes on an attribution of dynamic-creative energy (Śakti) to feminine sexuality. In the most elevated forms, the goddess is freed from the confines of domestic virtue, and she participates fully in the cosmic acts of destruction and creation.

Nevertheless, the common perception that the grandiose myth of the mother goddess empowers women is mistaken in many ways. In terms of social justice and equality, the goddess myths do not do much to empower women. Just as women were not a high-status group in Renaissance and medieval Europe, they were not a high-status group during the epic and classical periods in India. Women and lower castes did not even speak or write in the high-status Aryan language, Sanskrit. Furthermore, even if we grant that the aggrandizing myth, icon, and ritual surrounding the goddess affirms woman power, we must remember that the feminine divine in theology and metaphysics is invariably associated with *Māyā* or *Avidhyā*, the darkening power of illusion (that makes

Brahma's cosmic play of creation and destruction possible). More importantly, the mythic sequences that construct the divinity of the goddess contain twists and turns in them that ultimately constrain various manifestations of the divine feminine within socially defined roles of mother and spouse.[2]

Wendy O'Flaherty's analysis of Śiva mythology shows Pārvatī as one of the goddess prototypes who is given a certain measure of autonomy in accumulating her own *tapas* and *tejas*, in exercising the power it gives her, but whose divinity is ultimately defined and circumscribed by the larger order of Śiva's divinity (*Asceticism*). Even Kāli's fullness and autonomy is eventually compromised, rather than fortified by the Sānkhya abstractions of the divine feminine into *Prakriti*. *Prakriti* is no doubt the energizing principle in creation, but she is also the illusionary seducer who teases creation out of the inert *Puruṣa*. Mythologies often depict Śiva as a more well-rounded figure, the embodiment of erotic desire as well as its suspension in *tapas*, the *yogi* and the *bhogi*, the destroyer and creator, as O'Flaherty's comprehensive analysis of the Śiva lore demonstrates. In Tantric texts, Śakti is attributed great power as divinity, but at the human level, at which the feminine divine provides a blueprint for the ideological constitutions of individualized femininity, the abstract feminine principle is sometimes thought to be the *bhogyā* (the one who becomes the object of erotic consumption) and the male prototype is often the *bhoktā*, the one who eats, consumes, enjoys the object of erotic desire (Pandit 18–23).

Sītā of *Rāmāyaṇa* is certainly more human than divine, yet she is like Pārvatī in many ways. In one of her incarnations, as Daksa Prjāpati's daughter, Pārvatī burns herself alive just as Sītā does. Śiva mourns for Pārvatī and actually dances with her corpse; later, she is born again to be his wife and his fellow divinity. Sītā's living deaths, miraculous survivals and pseudorebirths mirror Pārvatī's actual deaths and reincarnations. What is important is that, in each case, the deaths and rebirths center around the will and desire of the male divinity. Rāma's repudiation of Sītā is more socially and politically grounded, as are her multiple exiles, her self-immolation, and other events in her life.

The sequence of events relevant to *Uttararāmacarita* begins on the day of the epic hero's coronation. On this festive day, instead of being crowned king, he is banished from home, commanded by his father to spend 14 years as a hermit, away from cities and far away from his kingdom. Rāma departs, accompanied by his wife, Sītā, and his younger step brother, Laksmaṇa. Toward the end of their exile, Sītā is kidnapped by Rāvaṇa who enters surreptitiously into Rāma's hermitage and creates the illusion of a bejeweled deer of many hues, tantalizing in its unusual beauty and grace. Sītā desires this illusory deer, and Rāma pursues the fast-moving, ever elusive object. This provides Rāvaṇa access to Sītā, and he takes her away to his opulent pleasure palace in Sri Lankā. Motivated by a sense of personal injury, like Meneleus in the *Iliad*, and empowered by the military resourcefulness similar to that of Agamemnon, Rāma scrambles together a small but loyal army and invades Sri Lankā. His armies defeat Rāvaṇa's forces, and, in a final combat, Rāma kills Rāvaṇa and recovers his lost wife. Many early oral versions of *Rāmāyaṇa* end with the royal couple's happy-ever-after return to Ayodhyā. Even R. K. Narayan's shortened English version of the Tamil *Rāmāyaṇa* leaves out the *Uttar Kanḍa*, because it is, as Narayan maintains, "not popular" (*The Rāmāyaṇa* 171). In this final Kanḍa, Rāma, as the "ideal king" who must stay above reproach, repudiates and banishes Sītā in response to a public scandal inspired by the queen's long stay in Rāvaṇa's pleasure palace.

It may seem odd to Western readers that the king should believe his wife to be innocent, yet punish her. However, the specifically Indian theories of kingship overemphasize the king's obligation to preserve symbolic forms of moral and social order. The people of Ayodhyā do not know that Rāvaṇa tried but failed to seduce Sītā. They do not know, as Rāma does, that Rāvaṇa kept her in a garden behind the palace, where she pined and waited for Rāma—sitting underneath the shadow of an *Aśoka* tree, guarded securely by Rāvaṇa's Rākṣasa women. These details are personal, minor in contrast with the violations of the larger, public form of sexual morality. In taking back his wife who has stayed with another man, Rāma does violence to the public, symbolic form of sexual morality. The laws of dharma, by means of which the family, society, and state are regulated, dictate that the king repudiate his wife, and he does so. At the beginning of what is going to be his glorious *Rāmarājya*, a *Rājya* that he knows will be remembered for thousands of years, will be reified in collective memory through myth, icon, and ritual, Rāma repudiates and marginalizes his wife as woman. Ironically, the glory of his golden rule is in part contingent upon the marginalization of Sītā as wife and woman.

Uttararāmacarita begins at this significant moment in Rāma's career as King, a moment when he has to make difficult choices to manufacture immortal fame for himself and his clan. Vālmiki's Rāma does what he has to do in a hubristic way, a flaw for which the Hindu god-king is never punished because he always cloaks his majesty in pretended humility. Bhavabhūti's Rāma, however, is more genuinely humble and tormented, as a modern tragic protagonist might be. He refers to himself as "the poison tree" whom his wife mistakes for the soft, sheltering *chandan* (scandal) tree. As he hands over Sītā to be left alone in the densest part of the Daṇḍaka woods—where, unprotected, she could become food for the wild beasts—Rāma refers to himself as "an untouchable sinner," a "butcher" who has "handed over to death his *domestic sparrow* [emphasis added]" (*Uttararāmacarita* 1.44—46). Toward the end of the play, when 12 years have passed between the act and its reenactment in memory, Rāma refers to the calumny as the "the poison of a mad dog" that spread within the body politic, grew in time into a "pernicious festering of fate"—"*daiva durvipākah alarkam viṣamiv*" (1.42).

Bhavabhūti's Rāma is not a self-incriminating, raging monarch like King Leontes, who imagines cuckold's horns growing on his head every minute, "inch-thick, knee-deep" (*WT* 1.2 186). When the messenger tells him about the queen's scandal, Rāma simply raises the proverbially long arm of law and retributive justice, the husband's "limb" that the sleeping wife is at the moment resting her head on (1.47). It is through these mildly ironic suggestions of betrayal that the playwright implicates the king. Otherwise, Vālmiki's and Bhavabhūti's texts only hedge around the issue of the king's culpability. In his relatively recent introduction to *Uttararāmacarita*, Bhat applauds Bhavabhūti for exposing "the cruelty of religion" (156). However, what Bhat does not admit is that Rāma *is* the instrument of this cruelty. The woman question in *Uttararāmacarita* cannot be easily dismissed as "cruelty of religion"; it is symptomatic of the marginalizing tendencies of the dharma that Rāma has willingly accepted as his "golden path" to human virtue. Bhavabhūti's aesthetic intention is to depict god as man; the tragic irony underlying this concept is central to Rāma's epic as well as dramatic function.

The Paradox of Deity as Human in *Rāmāyaṇa* and *Uttararāmacarita*

Bhavabhūti's Rāma is, therefore, a god who has chosen to throw away the mantle of divinity to acquaint himself with the human condition in an imperfect and time-bound world; his adjustment to the human condition requires that he conform to the laws of dharma. This qualification circumscribes his divinity, limits his autonomy. The human limitation imposed on Rāma by his acceptance of the law of dharma is thrown into relief when we compare him with Śiva. Both are worshiped with equal rigor by practicing Hindus (Vaiśanavas and Śaivites) in the modern world, yet the extent of their divinity is not identical. In contrast with Rāma, Śiva is a perpetual rebel. Engrossed as he always is in acting out excesses of eroticism and asceticism. Śiva transcends the materialist construct of dharma. The variants of Rāma's story in popular literature, oral narrative, folk and mythic texts, and elite treatises constitute the notion of deity as ideal human as a tragic, ironic, and parodic construct; Bhavabhūti's Rāma incorporates all these contradictions.

Nevertheless, the insufficiency of Rāma's divinity is not a closed book; references to its transformative power are made whenever his actions become ethically problematic. The timeless order of divinity of which he is a part turns up formulae that translate immediate evil into eventual good. As illustration of this phenomenon in *Uttararāmacarita* is the famous episode involving Rāma's murder of Śambūka, a low-caste man who attains great spiritual merit through the rigors of *tapas*. The latter incident provokes the wrath of Rāma's subjects, who see this act as a violation of the laws of caste dharma. After all, the virtue of *tapas* is monopolized by Brahmins and other higher castes. An encroachment of this hegemonic privilege creates such mass hysteria that the Ayodhyā elite attribute the untimely death of a Brahmin boy to the unprecedented event of Śambūka's *tapas*. In order to expedite the *śūdra* ascetic's elimination, they place the corpse at the palace door.

Bhavabhūti's Rāma performs this act doubtfully, remorsefully, and likens it to his banishment of Sītā (2.10). However, in the very instant in which Rāma's hand, the "merciless" and "cursed limb" of the monarch, *Rāmasya gātram*, strikes the blow, the victim of hegemonic terror is miraculously changed into a celestial being (2.10.11). The transformation is seen as a consequence of Śambūka's *tapas*. Rāma's act just opens a door. Death at the hands of a human who is really Indra or Viṣṇu provides instant access to the realms of spiritual merit, the merit that Śambūka aspires to. This transformative, theological reading does not preempt a political reading of this episode. The texts of *Rāmāyaṇa* and *Uttararāmacarita* function at many levels of signification, some of these are mutually compatible, while some cancel each other out. In this instance, Śambūka's compensatory metamorphosis cancels out Rāma's moral culpability—at least it must have done so for Bhavabhūti's immediate audiences and readers.

The deity-turned-human and king does not only transform

śudra ascetics into celestial beings, he kills many supposedly "hermit-killing" *rākṣasa*s in the southern regions. During the early years of their exile, Sītā dissuades Rāma from launching into the southern forests all ready to kill the "demons." The sages in the upper hermitages make the wandering warrior promise that he will enhance the safety of their hermitages by exterminating the *tapas*-destroying "demons." Sītā's opposition shows that the *rākṣasa*s are not really *tapas*-destroyers, and they are not a big threat. She does not want Rāma to reassume the role of a warrior while he is supposed to be an ascetic forest-dweller. "*Kva ca śastra kva ca vanam kva ca kṣyatryam tapah kva ca*," she says to him: "What affinity is there between asceticism and the warrior dharma, between weapons and a hermit's life" (Vālmīki 3.9.27). At this point in the epic narrative, Sītā instructs Rāma in righteousness and warns him about the "subtle ways in which a great man can be led to Adharma" (9.2). Sītā defines *Adharma* as "the terrible evil of killing other people who have not shown hostility and towards whom one bears no justified malice, or grudge. To kill them without provocation is a cruel act performed in ignorance and pride alone—*yadidam roudram paraprāṇabhihinsanam nirvairyam kriyate mohat*" (9.9). She sees this terrible net of ignorance and evil of *Adharma* face her husband ("*samupasthati*") as he enters the southern forests, having been successfully persuaded by the hermits of Daṇḍakāraṇya to kill the *rākṣasa*s (9.10).

Despite Sītā's warnings, Rāma and Laksamaṇa spend several years of their exile in exterminating *rakṣasa*s in Janasthāna and other southern regions. Many translators and commentators have sought to dismiss Sītā's clear perception of Rāma's *Adharma* by reducing the word "*rākṣasah*" to its most literal denominator, "demon." Sītā's legitimate concern about a grave problem of justice, morality, and ethically unsound geopolitical policies is sometimes reduced (by translators) to the kind-hearted Sītā's environmentalist statement about not killing "innocent animals" (*Vālmīki Rāmāyaṇa* 2.666). The Sanskrit words, "*rakṣasah*," "*vānarah*," "*asurah*," "*malechah*," are terms of identification commonly used for individuals from specific races, tribes, clans, and religious orientations. In *Rāmāyaṇa*, these terms rarely refer to real "demons," "monkeys," or "friends." The referent *daśānana rākṣasah*, used often as an epithet for Rāvaṇa, does not mean "a ten-headed monster," as some translations render it. It means the "ten-faced rākṣasa," more often a complimentary term; the ten faces signify the excess of Rāvaṇa's (human) power, not his animality.

As designations for groups, these terms are no doubt abusive and derogatory. India has its share of demonology and animal lore; it also has its own value-laden inventory of terms. Even if we grant that the word "*rākṣasa*" does at times mean "demon" or "monster," as Hopkin's exhaustive catalogue of the spirit lore indicates (Hopkins 43–44), Rāvaṇa and his bad brothers are monsters only in the sense in which Grendel is a monster, the enemy "Other" who threatens the establishment of Hrothgar. Like Grendel and his tribe, Rākṣasas are often refered to as *niśācaras*, the "night wanderers." Thousands of years of reception-aesthetics generated by the text of *Rāmāyaṇa* does not always set up these polarities between the Self and the Other as clear-cut; they are continually created and destroyed, expressed and censored by readers who project into the epic text their own identities and narcissistic investments in terms of caste, gender, region, and other dividing lines.

Racial and Gender Politics of Dharma

Literally speaking, the word "dharma" refers to the "essential nature or quality of a thing." For example, it is the dharma of water to flow, to evaporate under certain atmospheric conditions; it is the dharma of a volcano to remain latent, to erupt, and so forth. This etymological origin adds to the ideological weight of the term, because it suggests that dharma as sacred duty is as unalterable as laws of nature are. Sociologically, dharma functions in the same way in which various political economies do. Perhaps without being fully aware of it, Bhavabhūti represents dharma as it really is, a powerful ideology grounded in the hegemonies of caste, class, race, and gender. Seen in this light, the modes of constitution and propogation of dharma, as evidenced in the text of *Rāmāyaṇa*, are surprisingly consistent with Lukács's critique of ideology. In his critique of ideology, Lukács refers to the "natural laws" of capitalist society that are only laws of chance, but are seen as "eternal iron laws" (*History and Class Consciousness* 101).

According to Lukacs, the belief that society is regulated by 'eternal iron laws' is something that a Marxist critique of capitalist ideology exposes for "what it really is: a pretense" (101). This is not to suggest that the concept of dharma and the capitalist ideologies of industrial Europe are identical. Still, Lukacs's reference to the eternal iron laws of capitalist ideologies fit so well with the Indian notion of the eternal iron laws of dharma. In a purely literary context, dharma supplies conventions of story telling, and various principles of necessity that shape narrative ethos and mythos. One instance of narrative methods derived from the ideology of dharma is the recurrent motif of compensatory resurrection and metamorphosis of victims (of ideological oppression), to which I have referred above. Bhavabhūti resorts to this recurrent motif to evade implicating the king seriously, and the text of *Rāmāyaṇa* includes numerous instances of it; it is often used to defer moral culpability of human agents and to lend an aura of mystery to the ideological uses of power. It is in part this sense of irreversibility of the laws of dharma that makes it possible for Bhavabhūti's Rāma to become, in his own words, his wife's "death-dealing fate."

Rāma's use of monarchical power to marginalize on the basis of caste, gender, race, and region is greatly facilitated by the rarified prerogative of divinity and his general situatedness within the human order. As an epic hero, Rāma emerges as a consummate practitioner of dharma, and the racial politics of *Rāmāyaṇa* is linked with its sexual politics. One instance of this linking is Lakṣamaṇa's mutilation of Śūrpaṇakha, Rāvaṇa's widowed sister. Following Rāma's advice, or command, Lakṣmaṇa cuts the Rākṣasi's nose and ears when she expresses sexual interest in him. Such instances of racially motivated (ascetic) misogyny make Sītā's apprehensions about Rāma's *rākṣasa*-killing campaign more meaningful. As the *Kṣyatriya* (warrior) and protector of dharma, her husband is *her* enemy as much as he is the enemy of the supposedly "priest-killing" *niśācaras* and sexually aggressive *rākṣasis. Bhavabhūti's* Rāma is fully aware of the sinister aspects of the seemingly benevolent order of dharma. In *Uttararāmacarita,* the Śambūka incident is deliberately highlighted and paralleled with the many offenses against Sītā. For example, denouncing Rāma's repudiation of Sītā, Rāma's incognito son—in a verbal battle with his cousin—alludes to Rāma's murder of Tāṭakā, a Yakṣani/Rākṣasi. To Lava, Tāṭaka is fully human. He identifies her as Sunda's wife and he denounces Rāma's murder of her (*Uttararāmacarita* 5.34). When the cousin, Chandraketu, defends Rāma, Lava attributes Rāma's overzealous complicity with the laws of dharma to his relentless pursuit of glory, of undying fame, the grand imperialist design of his *Rājya.*

The opening scene of Bhavabhūti's play sets up a conflict between Rāma's deep love for his wife and his commitment to making history, his designated commitment to inaugurate the radiant dawn of a promised "golden rule." At this crucial moment, Rāma's acceptance of a supposedly defiled woman as his queen shows the fault of uxoriousness. The Ayodhyā elite consider uxoriousness a grave fault, especially in a monarch whose successful wielding of power can be affected by it. The removal of a wife with whom the new king is very much in love clears the path for the opposite virtue of ascetic self-restraint.

The patriarchal tradition consistently glorifies this vice-destroying virtue of Rāma, but a contrary view is introduced into Bhavabhūti's text by Sītā's friend, Vāsantī. She wonders how a king to whom nothing is more important, more desirable than *yaśa* ("fame") could do something so terribly infamous as the repudiation of Sītā. "*Kimayasyo nanu ghoramatah param*"—"What infamy could be worse than this," she says (3.27). Vāsantī's explicitly feminist point of view is shared by other characters in the play, including Rāma's sons, yet it contradicts the mainstream view. Even the female deities have different opinions. Vāsantī and Prithivī consider Rāma's action reprehensible, while Ganges and Tamasā defend it; "The world has to be protected according to Law," Tamasā concludes (*Uttararāmacarita* 3.30). In another country, at another time and place, Shakespeare's play articulates feminist, misogynist, and antimisogynist voices in the context of patriarchal paranoia over imaginary infidelity.

Gender Myths and Marginalities in Medieval and Renaissance England

Like classical Sanskrit drama, most of Renaissance drama also shows a simultaneous collaboration with and deviation from earlier forms of misogyny and sexism. Liberatory as well as repressive gender attitudes and myths, prevalent in Renaissance and medieval Europe (England), that specifically relate to the study of Shakespeare and his contemporaries have been meticulously documented by writers such as Ian Maclean, Eileen Power, Linda Woodbridge, and many others.[3] The medical theories of Galen, for example, assume causal connections between the excessive moisture of the female body and its debilitating effect on mind/brain functions. The physiological theories about the impact of the uterus on the mind generated commonplaces, clichés, and beliefs about the general inferiority of women (Maclean 31–34). In the context of male paranoia about infidelity of wives, the misogynistic cliché of the "congenitally adulterous female" common in the Middle Ages is of specific relevance (Blumstein 19). After the Middle Ages, the more actively disseminative agencies of culture in postmedieval Europe transformed the cliché of the congenitally adulterous female, along with many other clichés of this type, into belief systems. In time, this transformation led to spontaneous asumptions of female guilt in trials for adultery, making possible the use of flimsy evidence at witchcraft trials. As is evidenced during Hermione's trial in *The Winter's Tale* and Desdemona's tragic death in *Othello*, spontaneous assumptions of guilt vastly mimimize the burden of proof. In cases of imaginary infidelity, the idea of a congenitally adulterous female feeds the paranoic, patriarchal frenzy and facilitates miscarriages of justice. Equally relevant to the phenomenon of imaginary infidelity is the allegorical figure of woman as tripartite beast: "part lion (= manhunter), part flame (= desire)" and part devouring dragon (Blumstein 23). Shakespeare's passionately jealous characters' revealing speeches often manifest subliminal presence of this allegorical figure.

However, the gender politics of Shakespeare's *Winter's Tale* is more consistent with Vāsantī's politics in *Uttararāmacarita*. In this play, the culpability of the king is established promptly in the early part of the play. The only character who collaborates and believes in Hermione's guilt is Antigonus. At a time when he is still in doubt, he swears his three daughters will have to pay if the queen is proven guilty. In his paranoid thinking, one woman's adultery incriminates all, even those who are only eleven, nine, and five at the time. These child-women he will "geld," and "fourteen they shall not see/To bring false generations" (2.1.144–148). Thus Antigonus invokes the misogynist cliché of the congenitally adulterous female in connection with Hermione's possible adultery. If the queen is proven guilty, Antigonus will conclude what he had been told was true, that "every inch of woman in the world,/Ay, every dram of woman's flesh is false" (136–137). However, the credibility of this character is immediately undermined because his wife Paulina does not believe the queen has been unfaithful. Moreover, the logic of poetic justice in Shakespeare's play further underscores an antimisogynist aesthetic. Antigonus is expelled from the text of the play by means of a very grotesque stage direction: "Exit pursued by a bear" (3.2.58). One is relieved at this, knowing his little girls won't have to be gelded (castrated like horses).

Camillo and the other lords of Sicilia believe the king is behaving irrationally. None of them reinforce the "bad faith" that would constitute Hermione's crime on the basis of spontaneous assumptions of guilt. The oracle at the temple of Apollo also assumes the queen's innocence. Paulina's role in the play is similar to Vāsantī's in Bhavabhūti. However, while Vāsantī only taunts and chastises Rāma, the widowed and independent Paulina's protracted plan to make the king pay dominates the Sicilian half of *The Winter's Tale.*

The revisionary transformation of ideology is no doubt more thoroughly worked out in Shakespeare's play, yet Hermione (like Sītā) is also subjected to a symbolic death. Once her possible guilt is articulated in legal, religious, and sociomoral discourses, her expulsion from family, society, and the matters of state becomes structurally necessary. Like Sītā, she becomes a nonparticipant in the affairs of the world. She is mysteriously absented after the aborted trial; in this play, it is the infant daughter who is exposed to physical danger. Like Sītā and her unborn infants, the newborn child is abandoned in the woods. Leontes actually orders the supposedly illegitimate daughter to be burned alive. Before his accidental exit and death, Antigonus modifies the extreme form of this punishment. Instructed by a dream-ghost voice of Hermione, he leaves baby Perdita in the woods of Bohemia. In the Bohemian wild of Shakespeare's imagination—or in Robert Greene's Bohemia on whose novella, *Pondosto* (1588), Shakespeare bases his play—there are no hermitages, no sages like the scholarly and nurturing Vālmīki. Instead, in these non-Indian textual worlds, wandering shepherds preserve and nurture abandoned innocents and outcastes. Consequently, Perdita is found by a shepherd minutes before she is to be devoured by the hungry bear, and she grows up in an idyllic world.

However, in *The Winter's Tale*, the repudiated wife's narrative is discounted. Shakespeare's text is uncannily silent about what happens to Hermione while she remains concealed and protected by Paulina. It is as if Hermione's alter ego, Paulina, takes over and makes the queen dispensable as a woman and wife, indispensable as a memory image, as a ghost. Sītā's career in *Rāmāyaṇa* and in *Uttararāmacarita* demonstrates more fully the ideological play of signifiers and the cultural production of a set of values, virtues, and normative ideals associated with the marginalized and absented wife. Hermione is a more abbreviated figure. The prehistory of her epic identity makes Sītā a more comprehensive figure. She combines the grace and humility of Desdemona, the commodified, legendary beauty of Helen, and the endurance of both Cressida and Helen; the last category is mutely suggested by Rāvaṇa's successful seduction of her. The repudiated wife is transformed into a cultural icon that has for centuries assisted in the validation of various ideological forms of oppression (of women). At the same time, modern (Indian) feminisms construct her as an icon and symbol suggesting the need for radical change, articulations of feminist anger, and reconstructive action to correct old habits and errors.

The Repudiated and Reified Wife in *Uttararāmacarita*

Representations of Sītā in Valmiki's epic and in Bhavabhūti *Uttararāmacarita* elaborately demonstrate the virtue- and value-producing potential of what I choose to call the Sītā paradox, an ideological/theological enigma no less powerful than the Rāma paradox. Sītā is attributed infallible virtue and held up as the ideal of womanhood, the *pativratā*, whose only *tapas* is to remain constant to her husband in word, thought, and action. At the same time, she is excluded from family, society, and the state as a defiled woman. She possesses infallible virtue, yet she is branded forever with the stigma of adultery. In their treatment of Sītā, her abduction, and her infallible chastity, both texts simultaneously suggest the possibilities of rape and violation (by Rāvaṇa) as well as the impossibility of such a violation; they suggest Rāma's doubtfulness as well as his constancy and faith in his wife's virtue. The character of Sītā suffers tremendous representational violence at every stage; she is repeatedly annihilated as a human subject and repackaged as a reified icon. Not only is she idealized in terms of feminine virtue, she presents a cosmetically perfected image at all times; no matter how gruesome her situation, the narrator never forgets to describe her "loveliness of limb and attire." In contrast, Shakespeare's Hermione is visibly aged at the end. When she reemerges as the object of his gaze, the first things Leontes notices are her wrinkles. Sītā remains forever youthful, her skin like "molten gold" is always radiant, her hair dark and shiny, her limbs sexy and pleasing to the eye. The flowers in the garland that the mother figure, Arundhatī, gave her when Sītā first became a hermit, are indestructible. They do not fade with time, are not blown by the wind, nor do they burn in the fire.

The enigma of Sītā's infallible virtue, her unwithering beauty, and the unbleachable stain of vice is aptly constituted in a passage in *Rāmāyaṇa* that narrates Rāma's first interview with Sītā in Sri Lankā and the subsequent suicide/fire ordeal of the desolate wife. Because of the stain of suspected sin, Sītā's face "repels" Rāma at this time; he tells her the invasion of Sri Lankā had nothing to do with her. Rāma only wanted to vindicate his honor and seek redress for the injury done to him (Vālmīki 7.115.10–18). *"Kārya-*

masti na me tvayā," he says to the devastated Sītā: "Nevermore will you become the cause of my actions" (18). He points toward the ten spatial directions and advises her to go wherever she pleases. When this episode is retold in *Mahābhārata,* Rāma is quoted as having compared her to "an oblation that has been licked by a dog" (Mahābhārata 3.757), an offering no longer fit for the gods. Focusing on himself, he says his "mind is purified by asceticism" and declares that her sight is as disagreeable to him as light is to someone with sore eyes: "*Dīpo netrāturasyaev pratikūlāsi me ddriḍa*" ("Vālmīki" 7.115.17). Looking at the beautiful but defiled wife has made the ascetic warrior's eyes sore, yet in her resplendent beauty and chastity, she is rather the dazzling light that hurts sore eyes.

In the narration of this episode, the identificatory epithets used for Sītā place her only in the kinship context of her premarital home. She is referred to as *Janakmajā, Vaidehī, Maithilī*—"Janaka's daughter," "the princess of Mithila or Videha"—terms that suggest her claim to the marital home has already become doubtful (Vālmīki 7.116.1–10). The homeless Sītā enters a funeral pyre as Rāma's allies and Rāvaṇa's defeated armies stand around, simply watching the spectacle. However, the Vedic god of fire (Agni) allows a miracle to happen. Agni suspends its heat, the igneous quality; it refuses to ignite Sītā's body and her clothes. Its flames rise only to create an illusion. In a world where humans have submitted their free will to the inexorable laws of dharma, *Agni* is attributed free will; it (he) refuses to participate in the unjust punishment of Sītā, her self-torture. Sītā walks out of the fire as she entered it, unharmed, eternally beautiful, made more resplendent and recycled through the theatrical illusion of the marvellous (Vālmīki 7.116.25–36). Thereafter, she is restored to Rāma not only as a chaste wife, but as a goddess beyond reproach (29–36). Narratively, Sītā's self-immolation after Rāma's repudiation is not at all an impossibility, because Vedavatī, Sītā's double in another incarnation, was actually raped by Rāvaṇa and she did burn herself alive. According to this legend, Sītā *is* supposed to be Vedavatī reborn only to become an instrument of Rāvaṇa's death (Vālmīki 7.17–18).[4] An allusion to a compensatory reincarnation of the sexually violated Vedavatī into Vālmīki's text presents the rape, violation, repudiation, and self-immolation of Sītā as narratively possible. At the same time, it once again underscores Sītā'a paradoxically human-versus-divine status.

In the context of Sītā's banishment from Ayodhyā, one wonders why the news about the miraculous ordeal never reaches Ayodhyā. Why the mythmakers didn't proclaim this miracle in the streets as they sang the praises of the "mighty-armed Rāma of the Ikṣivāku clan." Bhavabhūti's play deals with the latter part of *Uttar Kāṇḍa*, therefore, he does not have to deal with this specific inconsistency in the epic text. In his play, Bhavabhūti absolves Rāma of guilt by emphasizing his vulnerability, his humanity, and by suggesting that, as an inexperienced king, perhaps he overreacted to the public scandal, became paranoid. In this play, Rāma banishes Sītā when his mother and the elders of the clan are not in Ayodhyā. His mother condemns the banishment, as do other members of the royal family of Ikṣivāku. In his grief over his daughter, Sītā's father becomes a hermit, stops eating meat, hates the people of Ayodhyā for ever, refers to Rāma exclusively as "the protector of his people," and remembers his daughter as the child "with a small face, who had budlike teeth and who engaged in faltering, incomprehensible prattle" (*Uttararāmacarita* 141–144). He also remembers her as she who "*Vidhyā Vāgvaiv yamasūt bhavatī*," nostalgically reconstructing the moment of her nativity, when "the goddess of earth gave her birth as speech does to knowledge" (144). Master of the *karuṇa rasa* (pathos) as he is, Bhavabhūti depicts the old and feeble Janaka's loss in a genuinely heart-rending manner.

Nevertheless, the processes of reduction and transformation are evident even in the way Janaka thinks of his daughter. He reduces the adult/wife/queen/mother to a child who has not yet acquired the full power of speech, and he remembers the violated wife in the context of her immaculate nativity. Seeking refuge in these constructs, the noble father of Sītā does not seek to rectify Rāma's error and injustice. In contrast, Rāma's mother takes a stronger stand, something that she does not do in Vālmīki's *Rāmāyaṇa*. To show her dissent, Rāma's mother never returns to what she calls the "Sītā-less Ayodhyā" and vows never to see her son's face (*Uttararāmacarita* 146–150). However, it is interesting to note that the simile Janaka chooses to speak of his daughter's immaculate birth rhetorically reverses his parental paternalism. In the terms of Janaka's figurative comparison, Sītā is knowledge (Vidhyā), and the divine feminine (Prithivī) is speech; the fertility of the ploughed earth (*sītā*) is associated with the generativity of speech (or language) that creates knowledge. The mind/body polarities that are universally used in constructing racist, sexist, and misogynist discourses are reversed here. Within the context of Hindu metaphysics, the idea of divine feminine as *Māyā* is also revised here. In Janaka'a speech, Sītā is associated with the light of knowledge, not the darkness of illusion (*Māyā*). Inexplicitly, Janaka associates Rāma's denigration of Sītā with the denigration of the earth and its fertility, as well as the repudiation of truth, marginalization of the generativity of human mind that invents, accumulates, and disseminates *Vidhyā* (knowledge) and dispels *Avidhyā* (ignorance).

In light of this revulsion that the king's action has aroused in the family members, Bhavabhūti's Rāma comes across as too eager to please his subjects. A more cynical view would indicate that he simply uses their doubts about Sītā's virtue as an excuse to get rid of her. Bhavabhūti rearranges the time sequence in such a way as to introduce ambiguity around the event of the queen's pregnancy. In *Uttararāmacarita*, the queen is visibly pregnant when the couple arrive in Ayodhyā; in *Rāmāyaṇa*, she becomes pregnant much later, long after the coronation and after the couple settle down. Bhavabhūti's rearrangement introduces doubt where the legitimacy of her progeny is concerned. In *Rāmāyaṇa*, too, the suggestions of Rāvaṇa's successful seduction of Sītā are inescapable when we think again of the exquisite golden deer and Sītā's irrepressible desire to have it. It appears in the woods as the fetishized object of desire, the cause of an insatiable hunger. Sītā desires to possess the "golden deer of many hues" and Rāma desires to hunt it down and offer it to his wife. This act causes Rāvaṇa's death and Sītā's lifelong suffering; it results in Rāma's imperialist conquest of Sri Lankā, his perpetual vow of celibacy, and his repeated repudiations if Sītā. Even though Rāma's jealousy remains unarticulated in this truth-eluding text, the narrative sequence of desire, temptation, and seduction that is acted out in the hermitage of the exiled warrior suggests a compelling necessity. The principle of necessity in both texts is indicative of the combined forces of ideology (of dharma), the imperatives of exile and asceticism, the insertion of desire, the attendant suggestion of seduction and fall, and the subsequent redemption sought through the piety of Sītā's perpetual suffering.

Female Virtue and the Female Body: Shakespeare, Burton, and the Semiotics of Jealousy

The significant time marker at the beginning of *The Winter's Tale*, "nine changes of the wat'ry moon," introduces into Shakespeare's play a time-related ambiguity similar to Bhavabhūti's rearrangement of events mentioned above. Leontes's jealousy has literary antecedents in Shakespeare's work, and the king's suspicions are fortified by various theatrical props. The props used in *The Winter's Tale* may not be as tangible as those used in *Othello*, yet they, too, suggest the possibility of infidelity. Polixines has been in Sicilia for nine months, and Hermione delivers her daughter prematurely about 23 days after his departure. In act 2, scene 3, Leontes mentions that the messengers sent to the temple of Apollo have been gone 23 days (2.3.197–198). When Paulina arrives at the prison, Emilia mentions that the queen has delivered "something before her time" (2.2.24). Such accurate calculations of time introduce doubt, provide infallible circumstantial evidence to feed paranoia, though they do not prove anything and eventually serve only to reinforce the king's delusions. He is intrigued by what the sexual body of the queen represents, the body that has "rounded apace" by the weight of advanced pregnancy as she uses her feminine eloquence to make her husband's boyhood friend change his mind and agree to stay longer.

Leontes forgets that the moral virtues of *taciturnitas* and modesty, which would be praiseworthy in a domestic woman, virtues conventionally considered suitable for members of the bourgeoisie or lesser nobility, are unsuitable for a queen. In his discussion of the notion of feminine virtue in the Renaissance and the Middle Ages, Maclean, following Tasso and Castiglione, regards feminine virtue not as an unchanging essence, but necessarily as something that is defined by class origin, class status, social role, and function (see Maclean 62). In *Discorso della virtu feminile e donnesca,* Tasso makes it clear that, because of their royal status and their political and public duties, princesses are not bound by codes of conventional morality. For Tasso, a princess is almost a man by virtue of her birth (62). In his discussion of the status and position of the court lady, Castiglione (book 3 of *Il cortegiano*) considers *taciturnitas* a nonvirtue; instead, wit, eloquence, and flamboyance are the right virtues for a lady of the court (see Maclean 64).

Robert Burton's discussion of the semiosis of sexual jealousy is based on these specific theories of masculine and feminine virtue, as it is defined by social class, status, and role. In *Anatomy of Melancholy,* he explores the nature of psychological disorders that can be generated by inappropriate encounter with behavior patterns that are conventionally associated with the practice of sexual/moral virtues and vices. For example, he considers the atmosphere of royal courts a breeding place for the sexual jealousies of bourgeois men, because courts present a lethal combination of "opportunity and importunity," a combination that might lead to violations of sexual morality. More importantly, courts facilitate impudent deviations from specific manners and gestures that function as reassuring signs of prudence and chastity among the bourgeoisie (*Anatomy* 838–839). Viewed in this light, the phantom of Sītā's infidelity is generated by the feudalist, caste-oriented citizenry of Rāma's city who apply the standards of a limiting, bourgeois appearance of virtue to the royal family. Even in *Rāmāyaṇa*, when Rāma expresses doubt about Sītā's chastity, she accuses him of addressing her like a "common man" and speaking to her as if she were "a common woman" (116.5).

In his further exploration of the "causes of melancholy," Burton connects the structure of this mental disorder with more localized national cultures and their specific modes of behavior. For example, certain behaviors and exchanges (between men and women) may not give rise to suspicion in France and Friesland but may give rise to suspicion in Spain and Italy; "Italy is hell for women," is a cliché that he playfully repeats (827–828). For Hermione, who is the daughter of the "emperor of Russia," Sicilia certainly proves to be hell. In the context of Burton's analysis, it seems appropriate that Sicilia should be the locale for Shakespeare's final play about sexual jealousy. Shakespeare's Hermione assumes a freedom of speech and gesture that she is entitled to as a royal personage, but it is a freedom that the Sicilian king does not wish his wife to exercise.

Upon the occasion when Hermione's invisible "sin" is first constituted in language, she is simultaneously praised for and accused of having "Never, but once" spoken "to better purpose" (1.2. 85–88). She ignores the innuendo and accepts the praise ("our praises are our wages," she says) and wants to know when the other occasion was. Leontes promptly says it was after "Three crabbed months had sour'd themselves to death" and she had opened her white hand and uttered "I am yours for ever" (1.2.101–104). Having constituted a schema of a triangular relationship in which the two instances of his wife's "speaking well" encounter and contradict each other, Leontes assumes that Hermione has wooed and won Polixines as she had once allowed herself to be wooed and won. Her eloquent speech becomes a figure for her sexual body, and Leontes promptly concludes: "my wife is slippery" (1.2.280). This wild leap in logical coherence confirms Burton's claim that the mental schema itself that leads men to believe "all women are slippery" is one of the causes of sexual jealousy (*Anatomy* 830).

Hermione pretends not to recognize the blame hidden in her husband's praise. She hopes her action has been virtuous ("'Tis

Grace indeed") and detects no violation of the codes of sexual morality in having used her virtue of artful utterance first to "win a royal husband" and the second time to win "some while a friend" (105–107). With these words, she exits, royally, hand in Polixenes's hand as her husband stays on stage to envision "paddling palms and pinching fingers," "whispering," "Kissing with inside lip?" "leaning cheek to cheek," "meeting noses," "skulking in corners," and more. Shakespeare's text makes it clear that these incidents are simply distorted versions of friendly exchanges that would be permissible within the codes of courtly decorum.

As a king invested with sovereignty, Leontes merges paranoia with legal justice, the private with the public. Hence, he drags his wife to a public trial in open air right after she has given birth inside the confines of a prison, before she has "got strength of limit," as she puts it. He denies her the sight of "the first-fruit of [her] body," her son, and snatches from "[her] breast" and from "the innocent milk in it" the questionable female infant whom he "Hal'[s] out to murther" (3.2.100–102), accomplishing what Lady Macbeth only brags about being able to do. The conflict between public/political (royal) virtue and domestic (bourgeois) virtue occurs when the passion of jealousy causes Leontes to see the queen only as his wife; he imposes domestic limits to the permissible largesse of her royal behavior.

The queen knows she has become a phantasm ("proclaim'd a strumpet" on "every post") and is willing to be "condemn'd/Upon surmises (all proof sleeping else/But what your jealousies awake" (3.2.110–111). She knows she is being submitted to the procedures of "rigor" (tyranny) and not "law" (3.2.70). "You speak a language that I understand not," she says to Leontes; "My life stands in the level of your dreams . . ." (80–81). To Leontes, "[her] actions" have become "[his] dreams." He is sure that she has "had a bastard with Polixines,/And [he] but dream'd it" (84). Upon the evidence of these "actions" that are constituted by psychotic delusions, he consigns her to the "easiest passage" of his "justice," in which she is advised to look for "no less than death" (91). The miscarriage of justice in this legal proceeding is preferable only to the silently censored and more insidious victimization of Sītā.

Justice and Feminine Revenge in *The Winter's Tale*

In *The Winter's Tale*, Paulina's major asset is her "tongue," which she uses with a freedom that one would expect a gentlewoman of the court to enjoy. Gender-based inequities of the judicial and legal systems were no doubt common in Shakespeare's time. More importantly, women were actively thinking about these inequities. Paulina's character, which Shakespeare invented for this play, is a product of such antimisogynist trends in thinking and awareness at the time. Linda Woodbridge points out that many "women-in-court" scenes in Renaissance drama expose some of these inequities (*Women and the English Renaissance* 246). Specific instances of such dissymmetries and inequities have strong roots in the Greco-Roman tradition as well. For example, the furies (Erinyes) who pursue Orestes for the murder of his mother are bribed into giving up their demand for justice. At Athena's own court, matricide is considered a lesser crime than patricide; Orestes is forgiven and the avenging furies are transformed into "kindly goddesses": the Eumenides. In a strange way, Paulina's character in *The Winter's Tale* incorporates the accumulated function of the furies.

Dorothea Kehler, in "Shakespeare's Emilias and the Politics of Celibacy," has constructed a less furious ancestry for Paulina. Kehler speculates on Paulina's association with Emilia in *The Winter's Tale*. Emilia is an attendant to the queen and speaks to Paulina about Perdita's premature birth. In *The Winter's Tale*, Emilia is a marginal character, but Emilias in Shakespeare's drama are important. They are often widows or semiwidows devoted to the ladies on whom they wait, alienated, disillusioned women, cynical but able to stand up for a cause. The most significant Emilia is of course Desdemona's maid. She unwittingly participates in Desdemona's tragedy and eventually is murdered in the process of uncovering the misogynist crime against her mistress. Kehler thinks Paulina is generically an Emilia-type character, but she is more eloquent and powerful, and she speaks with authority (*In Another Country* 157–159). She is an Emilia empowered by her eloquent and effective speech. In *The Winter's Tale*, Shakespeare seems to celebrate female eloquence and sees it as an instrument of change, justice, and liberation. Hermione is no doubt punished for speaking "too well," yet she conducts herself with a dignified eloquence during the trial and earns a definite moral victory. It is the king who speaks shrewishly and irrationally during the trial. The negative stereotype about female speech in Shakespeare's play is attributed to the paranoid patriarch.

In *The Winter's Tale*, Paulina's intervention, the slow pace of her retributive justice, functions as a corrective to the wrong that is done to Hermione. As I have pointed out, she decides first to "use that tongue [she] has" (2.2.51). She adds, "If I prove honey-mouthed, let my tongue blister/And never to my red-looked anger be/The trumpet anymore" (2.2.34). When Leontes calls her a witch and says he will have her "burn'd," she promptly responds, "It is an heretic that makes the fire,/Not she who burns in't" (2.2.113–115). In the trial scene, she refers to his "jealousies" as "Fancies too weak for boys, too green and idle/For girls of nine" (*WT* 3.4.179–180). In response to the queen's fainting and supposed death, Paulina commands the king to betake himself to "Nothing but despair. A thousand knees,/Ten thousand years together, naked, fasting,/ Upon a barren mountain,/and still winter/In storm perpetual. . . . " (3.2.208–211); *The Winter's Tale* is the tale of such a man, a mirror image of whom we get in Mamilius's ironically suggestive story about a man who "dwelt by the churchyard" (*WT* 2.1.26–28).

Paulina literally has Leontes visit the churchyard every day. She hides Hermione for 16 years and makes the king believe the queen has died, prevents him from remarrying, and haunts him like an unrelenting ghost of vengeance. She demands rigorous repentance and complete celibacy. Having spent 16 years in "nothing but despair" under Paulina's tutelage, the tyrant of the opening scenes seems now to have turned into a feeble-minded, fear-striken victim who has been made to believe that, if he remarries, the dead wife's ghost will haunt him and even drive him to kill his new wife. Strengthening this gothic fiction of a vindictive ghost, Paulina adds, "Were I the ghost that walked, I'd bid you mark/Her eye, and tell me for what dull part in't/You chose her; then I'd shriek, and even your tears/Should rift to hear me, and the words that followed/Should be, 'Remember mine'" (5.1.62–67). She refers to Hermione's ghost and yet presents herself as that ghost as if the two women have merged into one. While Paulina dominates the stage Hermione stays spirited away into the interior of an art gallery. However, it is within this all-female world that the repudiated wife is preserved and from where she is handed back to her penitent husband.

Recuperation of the Lost Wife in *Uttararāmacarita* and *The Winter's Tale*

The rigor of Paulina's silence and secrecy makes this woman's world in *The Winter's Tale* function like the underworld in which Sītā is preserved for 12 years and from which she resurfaces when Rāma returns to the Daṇḍaka woods. As I have mentioned before, in *Rāmāyaṇa,* Sītā stays in Vālmīki's hermitage and watches her children grow. Bhavabhūti changes this part of the story. In his play, Sītā throws herself into the waters of Ganges soon after Lakṣamaṇa leaves. Her twin sons are born while she is drowning. They are miraculously saved by the river deities; Sītā suffers a real and symbolic death. Cutting through the waters of Ganges, she returns to the underworld, the world of her mother (Earth), wishing to be dissolved into her mother's limbs (*"nayatu mamātmanamangeṣu vilayambā"*; 7.262). Having been repudiated for an imaginary sin and absented from Rāma's life, Sītā returns to the mother. The various river and woodland deities (Tamasā, Vāsantī, and others) preserve her in a timeless, all-female world—a world not subject to natural laws or the symbolic (patriarchal) law of dharma. Her children are taken to Vālmīki's hermitage only after they have been weaned. In the *Rāmāyaṇa,* the sage Vālmīki is present at their birth and names them. Bhavabhūti has redistributed part of Vālmīki's function to redefine the gender politics of Sītā's story. By foregrounding the role of the river and woodland deities, Bhavabhūti has made Sītā's affiliations with the mother-world more conclusive.

One does not have to read too much into Bhavabhūti's text to speculate that Sītā suffers a death by drowning and what is left of her is only a shadow image. The theatrical tradition in which Bhavabhūti is working prohibited acting out death and violence on the stage. This constraint commits Bhavabhūti to representational ambiguity. In act 3, the story of Sītā's drowning is retold by one river deity to another. Death is consistently represented in metaphorical terms as Sītā's return to her mother. The myth of her continuity in the timeless womb of death does not contradict the occurrence of physical death. After all, the reiteration of Rāma's remorseful remembering of Sītā and of Vālmīki's reconstruction of the absent wife and mother in his epic—*ślokas* from which Vālmīki's disciples repeatedly recite—all these perpetuate the reified Sītā in collective memory. After 12 years, the river deities bring her back to the hermitage for the 12th birthday of her sons (3.85). She rises from the waters of Ganges as if she were a woodland deity and an art object, "an image of Pathos," (*"Karuṇasya Mūrtiriva"*) and "an incarnate image of *Viraha*" (*"Virahavetheva"*; 3.4).

Texually, she embodies the *vibhāvas* and *anubhāvas* associated with the aesthetic (theatrical) representations of eros and pathos. It is obvious that Sītā returns simply as an object of the gaze, and her return is not fully established as a material fact. In the scenes that reenact Sītā's rising from the waters of death, the reemerged queen remains invisible like a ghost; Rāma feels her touch "smear his body, the interior and the exterior of it." She even revives him when he faints, but he is unable to see her. Even though death is not named, its distance separates the two. This life-in-death and death-in-life situation faces us with another version of the Sītā paradox: She is alive and she is not alive, an objectified construct suspended between the states of being and nonbeing. For 12 years, the river deities have reified Sītā as a figure of sentiment and piety. Hence, in this pseudoreunion scene, she can only be the cause of Rāma's desire, not its satisfaction. The river goddesses gloatingly see the erotic impact of the shadow Sītā on Rāma as he looks at his "trembling, sweating hand" slipping from the "sweating, trembling hand" of the illusionary Sītā (*Uttararāmacarita* 3.41). In the context of the patriarchal laws of dharma, Sītā has to go through the indignities of scandal and repudiation culminating in the final horror of a suicidal death by drowning. At the same time, within the putatively feminine order constituted by the goddess of earth and the river and woodland deities, she is reified in the contexts explored above. However, here she attains a new dignity.

Sītā, Hermione, and Proserpina

It is in this mythic world that Sītā is most like Proserpina, the mythic prototype for Hermione and Perdita in Shakespeare's play. Like Proserpina, Sītā is a fertility goddess. She is not conceived in the womb, but springs miraculously in a furrow in ploughed earth where king Janaka finds her, perhaps during a ritual ploughing at the beginning of spring. In its connection with fertility and agriculture, the Prithivī and Sītā myth is very similar to the Demeter-Proserpina, Ceres-Proserpina, and Kore-Proserpina mythic cycle. There are numerous imagistic parallels, inversions, and associations between the mother-daughter deities in Sanskrit and the better known Greek and Roman variants. For example, Ovid refers to Ceres as "Dame Ceres," who was the "first to breake the Earth with plough the manner found,/She first made corne and stover soft to grow upon the ground" (see Golding *Metamorphoses* 5.435–436).

In Vedic texts, Sītā, like Ceres, is the goddess of ploughmen (Hopkins 12-13). In this context, the phonetic similarity between the names "Ceres" and "Sita" becomes more meaningful. In *Rigveda*, Sītā is associated with ploughed fields. More specifically, she is the line that the plough makes in a furrow (4.57.6–7). The imagistic associations with Proserpina are prompted by the woodland Sītā's flower-gathering moments. In these, she is like the maidenly Proserpina. Bhavabhūti highlights this image of her. When the river deities restore her to the woodlands, she is seen gathering flowers for the birthday rituals of her sons. Sītā's flower-gathering image is more closely associated with Proserpina at the time when Rāvaṇa arrives to take her away. This scene of possible seduction in *Rāmāyaṇa* is similar to the scene where Pluto catches sight of and takes away Proserpina (see Golding 491–495).

However, there is an inversion of the myth in *Rāmāyaṇa*. Sītā's return to the underworld suggests a return to the mother, while Proserpina's journey to the underworld signifies a separation from the mother and ravishment by the king of Hades. The patterns of abduction and possible rape, loss and recuperation, the passage back and froth from the underworld to the surface of the earth, and the motif of the quest are found in both myths. In act 3 of *Uttararāmacarita*, Rāma desperately searches for Sītā in the environs of the woodland, wondering in what region she resides, remembering how easy it was to find her when the warrior Rāvaṇa took her away (3.45). At that time, he understood the warrior's codes of honor, revenge, and valor. Demeter's search for Proserpina is more elaborate, and its sexual politics is different, but it, too, is marked by a similar desperation for finding somebody who has gone under bodies of water, sand, and soil.

For Rāma, the underworld of female deities is as hard to reach as the underworld of Pluto is for Proserpina's mother. Pluto's masculine strength and his clout within the patriarchal order makes the place impregnable. When Zeus is finally asked to intervene, he supports Pluto's claim on Proserpina, a claim strengthened by the girl/wife's eating of the fruit of no return. As a consequence, the wife/daughter figure is divided between mother and husband, the surface of the earth and its entrails, suspended between the regeneration of spring and the sterility of winter, between life and death. In *The Winter's Tale*, Perdita and Hermione are both associated with Proserpina; their reappearance ends the metaphorical winter of despair and of enforced celibacy. Perdita's youthful sensuality, nurtured by the idyllic green world of Bohemia, ends the spiritual and sexual barrenness of Sicilia. In the final scene, Paulina makes Hermione stand in the posture of a sculpted art work. She stages this little play in front of the reassembled cast of Shakespeare's play, demands their suspension of disbelief while the art work moves, breathes, and finally speaks. Like Proserpina and Sītā, Hermione has been stolen from death, and she is implored to "bequeath to death" her "numbness" (5.3.102).

Similarly, when Bhavabhūti's characters finally gather together to watch the shadow Sītā emerge on stage, the audiences are reminded of the golden statue of Sītā and asked to imagine it coming back to life (269). The distancing, abstracting processes of reification weave the figure of Sītā intricately into the tapestry of a beautified culture—its belief systems, complacencies, half-truths, illusions—so that for a reader, too, the human subjectivity of Sītā becomes inaccessible, unrecuperable. As we have seen, Bhavabhūti redefines the sexual politics of Sītā's story; he refuses to offer the unambivalent comfort of her physical return. Yet the politics and the aesthetic of his ending do not recreate Sītā in the same terms as the tragic ending of *Rāmāyaṇa*'s *Uttar Kanḍa* does. The finality of Sītā's refusal to prove her chastity once again, her decision to dissociate herself from Rāma's dharma, leaves behind a more haunting trace of Sītā's subjectivity. While she returns to Prithivī and enters into the "entrails of the earth," the disappearing Sītā signifies a dismal curse, a dissolution of the epic narrative, not its moral/aesthetic resolution. In contrast, Bhavabhūti's play wraps up Sītā's story too well. Perhaps the conventions of classical Sanskrit theater would not have had it any other way. Perhaps Bhavabhūti's Rāma could not be expected to demand another fire ordeal, another proof of chastity, as Vālmīki's Rāma unabashedly does. In any case, Bhavabhūti does not altogether deny the fact of Sītā's disappearance and death; he only hastens it by placing it at the moment of her banishment.

The embedded play in act 7 of *Uttararāmacarita* is enacted by "heavenly nymphs," and the audience includes Rāma, his two sons, and the entire *ikṣivaku* clan. They watch Vālmīki's version of Sītā's disappearance and resurgence. In the embedded play, parts of their own lives are turned into art. At the end, the action does not return to the frame story; the self-referential text of the shadow play and the larger story of Rāma and Sītā are textually merged. Bhavabhūti calls this act the "reunion act" ("*sammelan aṅka*"); but it celebrates only a theatrical reunion of the epic family, the audience's empathic experiencing of "felicitous occurrences" (279). Rāma's final speech, spoken in metrical verse of the *Śardulvikriḍita* variety, emphasizes the sanctity of the epic story, which "purifies from sins" and "captivates the mind like the Mother of Creation" (7.20). Ending with an aesthetic denial of death allows Bhavabhūti to culminate the action of the play with *śanta rasa*, the sentiment of peace and the mental state of tranquility. The return to *śanta rasa* is aesthetically appropriate. In this play, Bhavabhūti uses a range of *rasas*, he takes his audience through the great intensities of pathos (*karuṇa rasa*), tantalizes them with eros (*śringāra rasa*), diminishes anxiety with laughter (*hāsaya rasa*), and restores complacencies and pieties with the dillusional comforts of the marvellous (*adbhuta rasa*).[5]

However, at the end of the play, even as the audiences are

successfully tranquilized by invocations of the sacred, Rāma reasserts his warrior-hero identity. As always, he is the unalterable patriarch. He speaks the final benediction in a metrical verse form that onomatopoetically echoes the sound of the trampling feet of elephants, a meter suitable for the representations of *vīra rasa* (valor). He witnesses the celestial missiles manifesting their mysteries to his graduating sons and takes comfort in this unfailing sign of their legitimate paternity. Vālmīki is firmly established in the so-called reunion scene as the producer and director of the play within the play. The goddess of earth and the woodland and river deities recede into the background. The patriarchal order is firmly reestablished as it is in Shakespeare's play where everybody, young and old, gets married and remarried at the end.

Readers who have never thought of reading Shakespeare along with a Sanskrit dramatist of the eighth or ninth century A.D. might find Bhavabhūti's use of Vedic goddesses, woodland and river deities, and heavenly nymphs as characters a bit odd. The theatrical conventions of his time would have allowed the use of anthropomorphic constructs as characters in the same way in which ghosts and other supernatural beings are used as characters in Shakespearean drama. Insofar as Bhavabhūti's anthropomorphic constructs—Ganges, Prithivī, Vāsantī, Tamasā, and Murlā—function as women, they have the same human status that Paulina, Emilia, Perdita, and Paulina's nameless daughters have in *The Winter's Tale*. Likewise, a more modern instance of James Joyce's aesthetically imagined fusion of the Ana Livia figure with river Liffey in *Finnegans Wake* is surprisingly similar to Sītā's bodily fusion with the Ganges, her parturition, death, and rebirth in the currents of this physical and mythological river, the river associated with the agencies of nature, nurture, and culture, the river of floods and fertility, a timeless icon of present and the past of India.

Notes

1. In *Women, Androgynes, and Other Mythical Beasts*. O'Flaherty has shown that female dominance in Puraṇas is evident in the myths of spouse-devouring deities, myths that show stronger Tamil influence. The myths become less affirmative of female dominance wherever Vedic influences surface. The Śakta texts attribute greater free will, creative energy, and creative potential to the female goddesses. However, male

dominance in mythology and theology serves only to reify woman power. The categories in which this power manifests are always grounded in gender ideologies. Pāravati is appealed to by the gods so that she can marry Siva and produce a demon-killing son. This makes her only a hero-mother in conventional terms and does not really show any significant reversal of gender hierarchies (80–105).

2. Lynn E. Gatwood, in *Devi and the Spouse Goddess* recognizes that "On a theological level, the incipient spousification of Devi" provides "an ideological ground for women's decline in status" (38).
3. Eileen Power, in *Medieval Women,* explores various forms of misogyny as well as oppositions to misogynism in literature and other cultural texts. Linda Woodbridge, in *Women and the English Renaissance: Literature and the Nature of Womankind, 1540–1680* also isolates patterns indicative of misogyny. But more importantly, she speaks of assumption of power and authority by Renaissance women, their search for legal justice and various forms of autonomy, and the scope and limits of their feminist ventures (301–313). Specifically relevant to the subject of imaginary adultery is her discussion of *Swetnam the Woman Hater Arraigned by Women,* a play based on Joseph Swetnam's *Arraignment of Lewd, Idle, Froward and Unconstant Women. Swetnam the Woman Hater* borrows plot elements from Shakespeare's jealousy plays: *Othello, The Winter's Tale,* and *Cymbeline.* In it, the male partner in adultery is exiled, and the female is sentenced to death. This gives rise to women's appeal for justice and their revenge. Woodbride points out that eventually "women's pursuit of justice is blocked by men's appeal to chivalry."
4. After the coronation, the new king is entertained by stories about his defeated enemy Rāvaṇa; the story of Rāvaṇa's rape of Vedavatī and Rambha are among the many exploits of the mighty king of Sri Lanka (Venkatesananda 128).
5. Ingalls et al. *Rasasūtra* states that a "rasa is produced by the combining of determinants (*vibhāvas*), the consequents (*anubhāvas*), and the temporary and transient states of mind (*vayabhicaribhāvas*)." The nine dominant *rasas* are; the erotic (*śringāra*), the comic (*hāsya*), the tragic (*karuṇa*), the furious or cruel (*rauḍra*), the heroic (*vīra*), the fearsome or timorous (*bhayānka*), the gruesome or loathsome (*bībhatsa*), the wondrous (*adbhuta*), and the peaceful (*śanta*) (Ingalls, et al., 16).

Bibliography

Beowulf. In *The Norton Anthology of English Literature.* ED. M. H. Abrams. New York: Norton, 1986.

Bhavabhūti. *Uttararāmacarita*. Trans. G. K. Bhat. Surat: Popular Publishing House, 1956.

Blumstein, Andrée Kahn. *Misogyny and Idealization in the Courtly Romance*. Bonn: Verlag, 1977.

Burton, Robert. *The Anatomy of Melancholy*. Ed. Floyd Dell and Paul Jordan Smith. New York: Tudor Publishing, 1927.

Dumezil, Georges. *Archaic Roman Religion*. Vol. I. Trans. Philip Krapp. Foreward. Mircea Eliade. London: University of Chicago Press. 1966.

Dumezil, Georges. *Archaic Roman Religion*. Vol. 2. Trans. Philip Krapp. London: University of Chicago Press, 1966.

Gatwood. Lynn E. *Devi and the Spouse Goddess: Women, Sexuality and Marriage in India*. Maryland: Riverdale Company, 1985.

Golding, Arthur. *Ovid's Metamorphoses*. Ed. John Frederick Nims. London: Macmillan, 1965.

Greenblatt, Stephen. *Shakespearean Negotiations: Circulations of Social Energy in Renaissance England*. Los Angeles: University of California Press, 1988.

Hopkins, Washburn. E. *Epic Mythology*. Strasburg: Verlag, 1915.

Ingalls, Daniel H. H., *et al*. Trans. The *Dhvanyāloka of Ānandavardhana: With The Locana of Abhinavagupta*. Cambridge: Harvard University Press, 1990.

Kehler, Dorothea. Susan Baker. *In Another Country: Feminist Perspectives on Renaissance Drama*. London: Scarecrow, 1991.

Kinsley, David. *Hindu Goddesses: Visions of the Divine Feminine in In the Hindu Religious Tradition*. London: University of California Press, 1986.

Lacan, Jacques. *Ecrits: A Selection*. Trans. Alan Sheridan. New York: Norton, 1977.

Lukács, Georg. *History and Class Consciousness: Studies in Marxist Dialectics*. Trans. Rodney Livingstone. Cambridge: The MIT Press, 1983.

Maclean, Ian. *The Renaissance Notion of Women*. Cambridge: Cambridge University Press, 1980.

Mahābhārata. Ed and trans. J. van Buitenen. Chicago: University of Chicago Press, 1975.

Mirashi, V. V. *Bhavabhūti*. Delhi: Motilal Banarasidāss, 1973.

Narayan, R. K. The *Rāmāyaṇa*. New York: Viking, 1972.

Newman, Karen. *Fashioning Femininity and English Renaissance Drama*. London: University of Chicago Press, 1991.

O'Flaherty, Wendy Doniger. *Asceticism and Eroticism in the Mythology of Śiva*. London: Oxford University Press, 1973.

———*Women, Androgynes, and Other Mythical Beasts* London: Univ of Chicago Press, 1980.

Pandit, Baljinnāth. *Vaiśanavadevi Rahasya*. Kulgām, Kashmir: Triyambaka Press, 1983.

Pinkham, Mildred Worth. *Women in the Sacred Scriptures of Hinduism*. New York: Columbia Univ Press, 1941.

Power, Eileen. *Medieval Women*. Ed. M. M. Postan. New York: Cambridge University Press, 1975.

Puhvel, Jean. *Comparative Mythology*. Baltimore: Johns Hopkins University Press, 1989.

Shakespeare, William. *The Winter's Tale*. In *The Riverside Shakespeare*. Ed. G. Blackmore Evans. Boston. Houghton and Mifflin, 1974.

Venkateśananda, Swami. *The Concise Rāmāyaṇa Of Valmiki*. Albany: State University of New York Press, 1988.

Woodbridge, Linda. *Women and the English Renaissance: Literature and the Nature of Womankind, 1540–1680*. Chicago: University of Illinois Press, 1984.

Zuntz, Gunther. *Persephone: Three Essays on Religion and Thought in Magna Graecia*. Oxford: Calrendon Press, 1971.

Vālmīki *Śrīmad Vālmīki Rāmāyaṇam*. Bombay: Popular Prakashan, 1976.

6

Ray's *Devi*

Norman N. Holland

To me, Satjayjit Ray's *Devi* (1960)* is a puzzling and (in the technical sense) mysterious film. I find at its core a paradox that flips back and forth like an optical illusion, an ambiguity like the one Freud called "the navel of the dream," a strangeness like the religiosity that bedevils India. Perhaps the best way to begin to unfold that ambiguity is to recall the film simply at its story level.

In Bengal of 1860, a husband, Uma (played by Soumitra Chatterjee), leaves his girl/wife, Doya (Sharmila Tagore), and his high-caste Brahmin home to study English at the university in Calcutta. He speaks in favor of the Brahmo Samaj, a movement founded by Ram Mohan Roy in 1828 (some aspects of which are discussed in Lalita Pandit's essay and references in this volume). According to this movement, one should learn the English language and ways and give up Indian cult religions for Christian-influenced monotheism. One should replace traditional medicine with modern medicine and support the younger generation against the total power traditionally accorded the Hindu father.

*Director, Ray; screenplay by Ray, after a novella by Phrabat Kumar Mukherjee; camera, Subrata Mitra; editor, Dullal Duta; b/w; 95 min. *Devi* was not approved for showing outside India until Nehru himself had passed on it.

While Uma is gone, life proceeds in the village in its sleepy way. Doya plays with her little nephew, Khoka (son of Uma's elder brother). She provides food and water offerings for the shrine of Kali, to whom Uma's father (Chabi Biswas) is particularly devoted. Kali is the mother goddess, addressed as "Ma," who is, like Persephone, both creator and destroyer. When associated with death, disease, drought, and destruction, her image is black, she wears a necklace of skulls and snakes, and she steps on the head of her husband Siva. Thus she shows her power, that she is as strong as Śiva, but she does not crush his head, thus showing she is not stronger than he. When she is the dispeller of disease, her name would be "Doyamoyee" (as Ray might transliterate the Bengali), her image is white, and she wears garlands of flowers. As a triple goddess, Doya plays with the child, and she tends her husband's father, who treats her as a mother just as much as Khoka does.

The old man has a dream in which he identifies the eyes of Kali with Doya's eyes. On waking, he bows down before her as the incarnate goddess, and the elder brother and the holy men of the village follow suit. A beggar brings his dying child to her, and the child recovers. The "miracle" convinces the rest of the community, and, when her distressed husband returns and tries to get her to run away with him, she demurs, wondering if she really is the goddess. Long lines of worshipers now seek the favors of the "living goddess." When her nephew Khoka falls ill, however, and the family puts aside medical care for "the power of the goddess," she fails to cure him. He dies, and when Uma returns, he finds father, elder brother, and sister-in-law all grief-stricken and resentful. His wife had gone mad. She runs out into the radiant fields, and her image dissolves into the smiling stone face of the ancient goddess.

The film begins, then, decisively enough, with an almost trite contrast between traditional Indian and modern English ways. The opening shot cuts dramatically from the animal sacrifice (of a castrated goat) at a festival for Kali to fireworks with a brass band playing "Col. Bogey's March" in the background. The "older generation" (the father and the elder brother) worship Kali. The "younger generation," Doya, Uma, and Khoka, enjoy the fireworks.

We see more of this contrast later, in Calcutta. There the young men who follow Roy's example wear socks and garters and English shoes. They ride carriages and smoke cigarettes (instead of hookahs). They lapse occasionally into English. They watch a play about laughing at your ancestors (it could even be a Bengali version of Aristophanes' *The Clouds*—after all, the issue is the same).

One young man talks about marrying a widow against his father's wishes. Uma asks advice, not of a holy man, but a professor (who has a picture of Shakespeare on the wall, instead of some guru—or is Shakespeare a guru?).

The cultural contrast, however, reflects others, between the generations and the sexes. All the men in the film are trying to possess a mother figure. Khoka wants Doya as a mother (and associates her with a story about a witch who eats the bones of little children). His grandfather uses Doya as a "little mother." Uma's elder brother worships her as a goddess. Her husband, of course, wants her as a wife, but, for all his modernism, he wants the submissive, childlike traditional Indian bride who will care for him. Uma's friend wants to marry a widow. The beggar loses the goddess, then gets her. The old holy men worship her.

We see males in the three essential roles of man to woman (as in Robert Graves's writings or Freud's "Theme of the Three Caskets"): child, lover, and dotard (about to be taken by the earth- or death-goddess). Indeed, the father, when he talks about walking with a cane, could be making an explicit reference to the Oedipal riddle. Anyway, we do see the three ages of man, as in the riddle of the sphinx: Khoka, just past the four-legged stage; Uma, two-legged; and the father, the three-legged old man with a stick.

The men are rivals for Doya, as wife, mother, and goddess. Moreover, the struggle takes place across generational lines in the classical manner of the Oedipus complex. Uma is the husband in the middle. The child Khoka charms his wife away as a mother. His father orders her away as his body servant.

Further, the cultural struggle mirrors the generations. The father and older brother (who also carries a cane and who does whatever his father tells him) represent the old culture. Uma, his friend, his professor, and the Calcutta scene represent the new generation. The relation between man and woman gets caught up in the generational conflict, as Doya mothers both the little boy and the old man—and stops being a wife to her age-mate.

There is a specifically Indian theme about the sexes here, too: Shiva and Shakti. Divine mates, they are respectively the male and female gods of creation and destruction. The worship of Shiva addresses what the father in this film recites from the sacred texts: "the male spirit, vast, all-powerful, unchanging." In worshiping Shakti, the female principle, however, the worshiper is to become like a child, abject, helpless, dependent, and that is what those who worship Kali become in this film: the beggar, the father, and the brother (drunk on holy wine). The beggar's two songs to the goddess, the first petulant, the second adoring, are like a child's moods with its mother.

Doya, the goddess, "*devi*," is both the astonishing image that opens the film, the appalling religious power, and the familiar, everyday nurturing Indian mother, the "Ma" repeated throughout the film. Thus, the relation between the sexes—is Doya Uma's wife or a living goddess?—becomes tangled up in the relation between the divine and the mundane. Ray develops this double level of the film through a variety of incidental images.

Repeatedly, birds fly in and out of the shrine. Because they go between heaven and earth, birds often symbolize (as in *Macbeth*) connections between the two. Here, they are sacred to Kali (as to Persephone), as one such connection between heaven and earth. In the house, however, there is a pet parrot, always speaking to humans—and adored by Doya in her secular aspect. This bird is earthbound, limited to a human, not a heavenly, dimension.

Developing the same theme, Ray repeatedly shows us feet. Doya washes her father-in-law's feet. When he decides she is divine, he bows down to her feet. She, however, curls them back, embarrassed and resisting the role he is forcing on her. When Uma returns and stares at his wife being worshiped, feet appear in the upper right of the frame. Perhaps Ray wanted to show feet because Kali steps on the heads of her foes and her husband, perhaps as another reference to the Oedipal riddle. Perhaps he referred to feet simply because feet are the way we rest on the firm ground of earthly reality.

I see as related Ray's many shots of people walking along the road home or in the house toward the mother-Doya. The film seems to me to ask: Who can walk how? With a cane? Down the hall to the goddess? Down the hall to the father? Along the dusty road? All are ways of reaching out toward—something.

Water. Kali protects against drought—that is why her images were thrown in the water after the opening shots of the festival. Doya gives water and candy to Khoka, places fruit and water in the household shrine, and administers medicine and water to the father. The beggar's sick child has not swallowed water in eight days. He is cured by having the milk (of Kali) poured between his lips. The husband wants to escape over the water, but Doya pulls back at the water's edge; she has seen the fragments of an image of Kali. It is at this point that she asks, "What if I *am* the goddess?"

In the end, of course, she is. She is both the dispeller of disease and the destroyer who has caused the death of her beloved Khoka. "*Devi*" means divine (Lat. *deus*, Gr. *Zeos*, etc.) It also means "to shine," and Doya dissolves into the light at the end. They are all gone into the fields of light.

Ray cuts from her disappearance to a stone image at the end that could be archaic Greek, southeast Asian, even Central American. The mother goddess is universal, and Doya in her madness has disappeared into that plane. Earlier, the grateful beggar had said, "Your face is not stone." Now her face is stone. On the wedding night, her husband said, "You are a china doll. You have the face of a goddess." Now she is and does in a different dimension.

The old man who believed her into being a goddess now asks, "How have I sinned?" A recurring question by all believers who don't get what they pray for, a justification for the goddess's failure. Rather than believe she isn't a goddess, the man of faith would rather say he himself sinned. And he did. He did not go on the begging pilgrimage ordained for all pious Brahmins (as, for example, the beggar does): "I couldn't walk without a stick." Having failed his obligations, having chosen instead to live in great comfort (Ray details the luxury of his life in the first third of the film), he is now terribly punished. The old man's delusion that Doya is Kali comes from his failure to observe the right pieties and leads to Kali's cruelty killing his beloved grandchild. That would be a religious reading. Whom the gods would destroy, they first make mad.

Ray cuts dramatically across the conflicts he has set up: from one sex to the other, one generation to another, one culture to another. But then he lingers in long close-ups on the individual face. I feel I am watching the characters' mental processes, the little boy savoring his candy, for example. But, of course, the camera can only photograph surfaces. It can never really show me a mental process. Thus, Ray's camera work builds on what seems to me the central ambiguity of the film.

The film exquisitely entwines the psychological with the supernatural. It leaves me no way to split off some religious being-beyond from our everyday being-in-the-world. The boy asks for a story about a witch—prosaic enough, as a story—but then she *becomes* that witch.

The film gives a perfectly rational, natural psychological explanation for a half-supernatural punishment. The old man believes in Kali too much—perhaps because he is a little enamored of his charming daughter-in-law. He justifies his adoration of her by believing she is the goddess. The beggar's child gets well. Then others believe in her, too. Instead of getting a doctor for Khoka, the old man and the brother insist on relying on a faith cure from

Kali. And they lose the child. All perfectly explicable. Yet at the end she has *become* the goddess. She *is* the creator and destroyer. Faith creates the object that creates faith (as in Shaw's ironic definition of a miracle: "an event which creates faith").

This is for me a film about belief and the way belief, trust, or faith itself, can become a creator and destroyer like Kali, because faith creates one reality and destroys another. We can no more live without faiths than we could survive without a mother—even if she be destroyer as well as creator. Our every act, our every perception, builds on hypotheses about the world, a basic trust in its constancy—in short, faiths. We could not see this film or any other without a system of faiths. Only by believing can we find the truth—which turns out to rest once more on belief. This is, then, a film about faith, about the terrifying duality of faith. Faith is not only our only way of connecting with reality, but also it allows us to disconnect. We can throw truth and reality, as much as we can know of them, to the winds and let ourselves fly on the magic and the hysteria of belief. No wonder she goes mad at the end. No wonder India herself, that most religious of lands, hovers between a pious search for peace and maddened genocide. But then, that is as true of the West as of India and the East, isn't it?—a reminder that Ray dramatizes in *Devi* a psychological truth we must all suffer.

7

The Poetics of Exile and the Politics of Home*

Una Chaudhuri

In the 1988 British film *Sammy and Rosie Get Laid*, a father pleads with his troubled son, an Asian immigrant in England, to return "home" with him. The son points out, not without irony, that he is home, that "This is the bosom." Exasperated, the father spells it out: "I mean home to your country, where you will be valued, where you will be rich and powerful."[1] The brief exchange articulates one of the most important disruptions of post-colonial immigrant experience, that of the link between the figure of home and the notion of belonging. The disruption is not a simple reversal. It is not quite the case that the immigrant's home is where he or she does *not* belong. Rather, the immigrant experience of today interrogates both concepts, home and belonging, and points to a renovation of the general discourse of home. That is to say, the problematic and asymmetrical relation between the immigrant and the traditional figure of home may allow for a revisioning of a concept that, as we shall see, has long been in crisis.

That there is a politics to simply being at home is no longer an unfamiliar idea; in terms of recent cultural practice, we saw one

*A slightly different version of this essay was presented at the Performance Studies International Conference, Tisch School of the Arts, New York University, October 4–7, 1990.

aspect of that politics in the transformation of the word "housewife" into the word "home-maker," a substitution that played out a whole reconceptualization of the power relations between women and domesticity. In the area that concerns me directly here, that of representation, a similar political thematics of home has prevailed. For example, in terms of theater history, the ideology we recognize as modern humanism was inaugurated by a decision not to remain in a home as artificial and stifling as a doll house. However, as both these examples show, there is a certain literalism in the concept of home as commonly used, which, if left undeconstructed, will inevitably produce only a limited and reactionary politics or identity. One of the cleverest schemas of this deficient and self-defeating mode of self-production is to be found in Poe's "The Fall of the House of Usher," where literalism forces an unwanted equivalence on several distinct entities—two individuals, a family, a family history, and a *house*. Poe's account of destruction by sheer reductiveness, by the denial of difference, is also a deconstruction of the grotesque, late-Romantic politics of singular identity, which feels itself too securely "housed" in a place where it can no longer be at home.

A new politics of home begins it seems to me, with an act of imagination, a plunging of the literalistic house into the tarn of metaphor. The metaphoric life of home is particularly in need of liberation, because this concept suffers more severely than most metaphors from a fact noted by Lakoff and Johnson in their book *Metaphors We Live By*, that "we typically conceptualize the nonphysical *in terms of* the physical."[2] Our dominant present-day concept of home is grounded in not one, but two, kinds of physicality, house and homeland, both of which work to curtail the political potentiality of the concept, and to recuperate it for an ideological thematic of fixity and essentialism.

The current ideological meaning of the home-as-house construct is ironically exposed, for example, by Spalding Gray in his piece entitled *Terrors of Pleasure*, the narrative of a disastrous adventure in real estate: "I was thinking that we should buy a house because renting wasn't enough for me; I wanted to have the sense of *ownership*. I thought it'd be kind of like growing up, like having a child, if you *owned* your own house."[3] This fantasy, according to which home is synonymous not only with family and self-respect, but also with *house*, that is, with private property, is deeply valorized by the social system. Any counter-proposals, any efforts to reclaim home from the logic of house ownership—for example, by putting up a city of tents in Tompkins Square Park—are swiftly rejected by the state and the community.

The theatrical version of the literalized home is to be found, of course, in realism, which from its inception has staged both the deterministic power as well as the crisis of this concept. One sign of the crisis is the violent ambiguity, in realism, of spatial signs. Ibsen's famous interactive architectural symbols—his climbable towers, slammable doors, and burnable buildings—help to construct domestic space as a problematic: both the *condition for* and the *obstacle to* psychological coherence. Again and again in Ibsen, the crisis of the concept of home appears as the collision therein of two incommensurable desires: the desire for a stable container for identity and the desire to deterritorialize the self.

The theatrical conventions of the realist drama made their own contribution to the practice of deriving identity from environment. The fully iconic, single-set, middle-class living room of realism produced so closed and so *complete* a stage world that it supported the new and powerful fantasy of the stage not as a place to pretend in or perform on, but a place to *be*. We tend to associate this fantasy primarily with acting theory, and specifically with Stanislavski, but its effects can also be seen in the new structural emphasis, in realist drama, on arrivals and departures. So literally global is the signification of the stage/home of realism that simply to enter or leave it becomes a decisive—perhaps *the* decisive—dramatic act.

This is precisely what Chekhov ironizes in his drama. In Chekhov's plays, as in Ibsen's, arrivals and departures are used as macrostructural devices, but Chekhov's arrivals and departures, unlike Ibsen's, are marked by a certain comic/pathetic arbitrariness. Shorn of its decisiveness, the act of displacement ceases to be a strategy for the formulation of a stable identity and becomes instead a symptom of its loss. In the legendary dispute between Chekhov and Stanislavski what was being contested, in part, was the whole politics of deriving individual identifies from environments, of grounding in a stage-home characters who were essentially homeless. By contrast, the more stylized, less realistic stagings of Chekhov's plays in many contemporary productions (notably Andre Serban's) recover the problematic of identity, which naturalism tends to bracket out. To the degree that the stage-home is deliteralized, it reveals itself as a complex and contradictory thematic, precisely an *idea* of home—not a place so much as a discursive field, laid out in such a way as to guarantee its inhabitants a certain psychological homelessness.

The realist discourse of home relies on a long-standing conceptual structure in which two figures are balanced—and constructed—as opposites: the figures of belonging and exile. The home as house (and, behind it, the home as homeland) is the site of a claim to affiliation whose incontestability has been established by a thick web of economic, juridical, and scientific discourses—which also construct the meaning of exile. It is a usefully ambivalent meaning: On the one hand, exile is branded by the negatives of loss and separation; on the other, it is distinguished by distance, detachment, perspective. For the individual (and exile is a decidedly individualistic figure), the poetics of exile offers a mechanism whereby suffering is exchanged for a certain moral authority, personal rupture for aesthetic rapture, as heard, for example, in Nabokov's reflection that "the break in my destiny affords me in retrospect a syncopal kick that I would not have missed for worlds."[4]

In Chekhov's drama, the discourse of home is deconstructed to produce the image of a static exilic consciousness, experienced by the characters as a feeling of being homesick while at home. Here the sentimental image of home—as an actual place correlated with a powerful emotional experience (the sense of "belonging")—unravels, as the logic linking belonging with exile is revealed to be not a logic of opposition, but rather one of supplementarity: The emotional structure that is most familiar, most habitual and home-like to these characters is the feeling of being displaced from somewhere else. They are not exiled *from* where they belong, but exiled *to* where they belong.

However, the literalistic and domestic space of naturalism contained Chekhov's deconstruction and stopped it short of any ideological reformulation of the politics of identity. Exilic consciousness, read either as upper-class malaise or as universal tragic alienation, was ultimately something the spectator could be at home with. That is to say, once situated in terms of an already well-coded "milieu and moment," the contradiction embodied by these characters is easily absorbed into a modernist account of psychological fragmentation and alienation, the same account, indeed, that has made exile itself a privileged poetic figure.

In the remainder of this essay, I want to look at two very different kinds of critique of the belonging-exile opposition, which structures the sentimental image of home. Both go further than Chekhov into ideological territory, one ideology ancient and religious (my example will be *Oedipus Rex*), the other contemporary and political (my example will be *Sammy and Rosie Get Laid*). Both these works extend the metaphoricity of home in ways that subvert the discourse of home I have associated with realism, the discourse of home that seeks to house singular identity. But while the first rejects all versions of that discourse, the second (*Sammy and Rosie*), as I read it, offers a rewriting of exile of a sort that might redefine belonging as well, and perhaps even home.

Oedipus Rex removes the figure of identity from its ground in home, in any spatiality whatsoever, and links it instead to a teleological temporality. The time scheme of *Oedipus Rex* derives its coherence from outside the play, indeed, from outside the human realm altogether; its operation is felt only in the effect that what has appeared to be a "play-before-the-play," the originary narrative of a self-creating protagonist, turns out to be meaningful only as a "play-beyond-the-play," authored by the gods. The source of identity, it suggests, is extrahuman and barely knowable. By contrast, the identity derived from belonging to a place is profoundly illusory.

The suggestion that home is a place not to *live in* but to *leave from* is suggested, I think, at the end of *Oedipus*, in one of the play's many enigmatic illogicalities. Most people remember the play's conclusion as inaugurating the exile of Oedipus, and exile is certainly one of the main themes of his last speeches, just as belonging has been the main theme of his earlier ones. For example, his very first words in the play—"My children"—invoke the most powerful and most literal mode of belonging there is: belonging through filiation. His next words confuse filiation with what will turn out to be, in this play, its opposite: affiliation. Speaking of being "nursed" at the "ancient hearth" of Thebes, Oedipus manages to suggest that one can be the son—and heir—of a *place*, a condition that, were it true, would benefit no one more than Oedipus himself.

In what follows his opening address, Oedipus repeatedly refers to his position in Thebes, frequently rehearses the logic of his belonging there, and often overstates his relationship to its people. As the play goes on, Oedipus is increasingly embedded within a conceptual system based on the opposition "belonging versus exile," a system that occludes the truth of his life, which is that he is utterly and incurably homeless. Even at the end of the play, his apparently heroic moral pleas for his own exile—"Send me from Thebes," he begs—are an attempt to preserve this system, to replace Thebes by Not-Thebes, which is to continue to position himself literalistically and geographically.

To remember the end of Sophocles' play as an image of exile is to fall under the influence of Oedipus's seductive system of spatialized self-definition. For the dramatic facts are somewhat different, and much more contradictory: When Oedipus finally leaves the stage, it is not for the open road, but for the palace, ushered in there by cautious Creon, who wants more guidance from the gods before granting Oedipus's exilic wish. Thus our final image of Oedipus captures all the paradoxicality of his stage existence. His exit is, perversely, an entrance. The ruthless logic—or pedagogic—of repetition is returning him to the place to which he should not have returned in the first place.

At one level, what is being staged here is a certain psychological meaning of home that was as crucial to Freud's reading of the Oedipus myth as to Sophocles', namely, regression. As the psychologist James Hillman puts it, "going home is always going *back* home." For Hillman, home is the place sought out by "the regressive needs of the soul . . . . [because] the bar, the bed, the boardroom and the buddies do not meet the full gamut of needs, which always limp along behind the myth of independent individuality."[5] But what Oedipus's final "regression" also suggests—since his homecoming begins his exile—is the even more terrifying idea that the mythical Self is limping straight into an illusion. There is no shelter, no comfort "back there." In Sophocles' play, set as it is not in the domestic home-space of realism, but in the public discourse-space of Greek theater, where all is contested and nothing can take up permanent abode, home turns out to be the rough mountain behind a facade of shelter and civilization.

It is a great leap from Oedipus to *Sammy and Rosie Get laid* (though both do end with a parent's suicide by hanging and both begin with the image of a devastated city). I choose this film because it links its deconstruction of home to a deconstruction of homeland, a connection that is essential to a nonreligious, ideological formulation of that lesson—that "home-truth"—which Oedipus (presumably) learned backstage.

Sammy is a young second-generation Asian immigrant whose father has gone back to Pakistan, leaving Sammy behind in England. This move significantly reverses not only the situation of Oedipus, but also the usual practice of Third-World economic immigrants, who often leave their families behind when they come to the West, like living signs of where one "really belongs." Thus Sammy is quite removed from the old discourse of home and identity, but he is not thereby automatically the representative of a new and alternative one. He is a paradoxically marginal protagonist whose claims to identity may depend on his ability (unproved by film's end) to exchange the individualistic poetics of exile for a collective politics of refugeehood.

The film begins with the return of the father, Rafi, to England, for avowed reasons that are shamelessly sentimental (not to mention politically retrograde): "before I die I must know my beautiful London again: for me it is the center of civilization—tolerant, intelligent. . . ." (9). Of course the film decisively decenters this image of London. As the sentimental London of Rafi's fantasy is replaced by an apocalyptic London of race riots and police brutality, Rafi's responses reiterate the various modernist myths of social alienation and individual fragmentation. "The natural bonds are severed," laments Rafi, "And love is sought everywhere but at home. What is wrong with the home?" To which his lover Alice answers (as Ibsen had), "Generally the people who live there" (41). In the violent social context evoked by the film, this explanation has a hollow ring. The film's own answer to Rafi's question is located at the level of the discourse itself, recharacterizing home as a system of homogenizing signifiers that is unraveling under pressure of new and insistent differences.

Meanwhile, Rafi's own self-decentering vis-à-vis the seat of empire is revealed to be less than innocent, to be, in fact, a fully self-serving and successful mimicry of power. We learn that Rafi has acquired great political power after returning to Pakistan and done so by means of terrible brutality and repression. He is accompanied by a ghost whom he alone can see, the battered and blinded representative of his many victims, to whom Rafi justifies his use of state terror, saying, "The country needed a sense of direction, of identity. People like you, organizing into unions, discouraged and disrupted all progress" (53).

Besides undermining Rafi's self-construction as patriotic nationalist, the ghost's presence also materializes the mode of displacement that has characterized exile from mid-century on. The new displacement is enforced mass-exile, large-scale refugeehood. Our huge and rapid movements of populations, transnational as well as regional, suggest a whole new demography, exchanging motion for place and difference for continuity. The people in *Sammy and Rosie*—the main characters, their friends, and the ubiquitous, extravagantly mobile group of street people who populate the gaps in the film's psychological space—confront and mediate for us the fact that, as Arjun Appadurai puts is, "exile is no longer the psychic privilege of an elite avant-garde."[6]

At one point, Rafi asks Sammy to leave the "cesspit" London has become: "You'd better come home, Samir." Sammy answers, not entirely ironically, "I am home, Pop. This is the bosom." To which Rafi makes his definitional response, showing no trace of recognition of his son's radically ambiguous situation: "What a sullen young man you are. I mean home to your country, where you will be valued, where you will be rich and powerful" (32).

Rafi stands on one side of the equation "home" = "country" = "where you are rich and powerful"; the ghost stands squarely on the other side. Floating somewhere in between are Sammy and his white wife Rosie, who take whatever place they can in society, but without any sense of natural entitlement, deriving an ironic identity from the complex, multi-layered urban scene. "We love our city and we belong to it," says Sammy. "Neither of us are English. We're Londoners you see" (33).

But the film finally subverts even this thoroughly ironic and attenuated fantasy of belonging. "Being Londoners" does not allow one to simply escape the mystifications of home and homeland; it intensifies the contradictions in them. For another reality of being Londoners, as refugees, is embodied in the multiethnic caravan community of homeless people, which, at the end of the film, is violently removed from the vacant lot it has occupied. As the property developer's bulldozers move in, the film script reads "The convoy is leaving the waste ground and heading for the road. The [homeless] kids remain defiant, cheerful and rebellious, like the PLO leaving Beirut" (56).

Here, momentarily, the reality of refugeehood displaces the poetics of exile and redefines the urban West not as a high ground of self-consciousness, but as another site for locating—and opposing—the sheer groundlessness of victimage and suffering. The image of the refugee convoy carries the possibility of redefining the discursive links between home, homeland, and identity, not only for the homeless and the displaced, but for everyone. Perhaps the sharp need underlying refugee identity can pierce that self-destructive modernist alienation of home and exile to which August Strindberg once gave such wonderfully exasperated voice: "No one can stop me from setting my writings in Sweden. I know that country and its language best and hate it most."[7]

Notes

1. Hanif Kureshi, *Sammy and Rosie Get Laid* (New York: Penguin Books, 1988), p. 32. All further references to this text will appear in parentheses after the quotations.

2. George Lakoff and Mark Johnson, *Metaphors We Live By* (Chicago: University of Chicago Press, 1980), p. 59.
3. Spalding Gray, *Terrors of Pleasure: The House*, in *Sex and Death to the Age 14* (New York: Vintage, 1986), p. 202.
4. Vladimir Nabokov, *Speak, Memory: An Autobiography Revisited* (New York: Putnam, 1966), p. 250.
5. James Hillman, *A Blue Fire: Selected Writings* (New York: Harper and Row, 1989), p. 200.
6. Arjun Appadurai, editorial. *Public Culture* 1, 2 (Spring 1989): p. 3.
7. Strinberg to Albert Bonnier, 22 Nov. 1885. Quoted in Michael Meyer, *File on Strindberg* (London: Methuen, 1986), p. 51.

Part IV

Hybridity and Universals: An Interlude

8

A Sense of Detail and a Sense of Order: Anita Desai Interviewed by Lalita Pandit

LP: I would like to start with something about your background, anything you feel like speaking about.

AD: I was brought up in old Delhi. It was a quiet, lonely place at that time. During the early part of my childhood, it was still the capital of colonial India, and probably the most traumatic event of my childhood was the 15th of August of 1947, when the British and Muslim populations disappeared overnight, bringing about the transformation of the old city I knew into the new city of the postpartition era. I went to school and college there. I suppose our house was a little different from the others in the neighborhood because my mother was German. It brought in a certain European element. In other ways, we were a part of this neighborhood in Delhi.

LP: It is interesting, your growing up in a house in old Delhi, because the house in *Clear Light of Day* is also an old, decaying house in Delhi.

AD: It was the most autobiographical of all my novels based on my memories of the childhood home and the neighborhood. Many of the characters in the novel are based on my memories of the neighbors, of course as they appeared in my imagination. It was the one in which I used the most of my childhood memories.

LP: The descriptions of the house in *Clear Light of Day* do have a certain evocative quality. Obviously, that is due in part to these associations.

AD: That is the house I grew up in. I have lived in dozens of other houses in different parts of the world, but that is the one I remember the most vividly. I think children experience their homes in a way adults do not. Adults may think of the rooms and the furniture, but children actually experience them. To them the house has a personality.

LP: That is true. I grew up in a house in Kashmir that I remember most vividly and have recurrent dreams about. This also brings to mind Raka's experiencing of Kasauli in *Fire on the Mountain.* It seems to me Nanda Kaul merely lives in Kasauli, she does not connect with the landscape or the place as Raka does. Raka rediscovers the place with a child's sense of wonder.

AD: Kasauli is a place where I spent a summer once as a small child and experienced the place as Raka does, who went on her own, in solitude to explore the place. But that is an experience one can lose as an adult. When you write about the experience as an adult, it ceases to have that mystery as well as the immediacy. It took me years and years to recover that. I did when I took my children there, and seeing them play on the hillside, wander around the pine woods, somehow brought back my own experience to me very vividly.

LP: One of the things I admire about your technique is your sense of detail, your sense of places and people. For example, in *Where Shall We Go This Summer,* the wife tells the husband that the only time she was happy (in Bombay) was when she saw a burka-clad woman outstretched on a sandy beach. Her companion—husband, lover, or father—touched the woman's pale face with great tenderness, as two girls at a distance played in the sand. This is a very evocative moment in the novel, and I feel you must have yourself observed such a scene, or something similar to it. Am I right? How many such moments of evocative detail in your novels/stories are based on real experiences? I have somewhere heard you say that you actually read about the Ila Dutt incident, the incident you write about in the *Fire on the Mountain.*

AD: You are right. That is a scene I had seen. I saw the couple in a park in Bombay and was struck by the wonderful tenderness of that scene, and I carried it in my memory as one carries what is valuable and significant. It expressed for me perfection of a relationship, and it does so for the protagonist in the book. Her own life is so imperfect, and she finds it so difficult to come to terms with that imperfection, her inability to compromise, so that she fantasizes about this ideal moment that suggests what a perfect relationship might be. There are other such moments in that book, the stranger she sees stranded and doesn't stop for or get to know. And of course, a book is really a coming together of such moments, all those moments that one accumulates as one makes one's way through life. There are certain moments we do not forget, that do not escape, to which the mind turns again and again, so that we *give* them a great deal of significance as we think about them, brood over them, and they finally enter our private mythology. Baumgartner's character is based on a glimpse I had of an old man in Bombay. He lived with his cats, begged around for food for them. There is another such moment *In Custody*, when Deven is absolutely at his wit's end and doesn't know where to turn next. He sits on a bench and looks at the dome and the minarets of Jama Masjid against the sunset. The picture he sees is a work of art, it is a vision of perfection, of perfect harmony. It gives him, if not hope, at least reason to continue. It provides him with a vision of art as philosophy, as a religion, and strengthens his faith in poetry, poetry as a revelation and as means to redemption.

LP: You told me before something about the postcards you had seen, postcards that had arrived from Germany with that specific number on them that Baumgartner sees on the last postcard sent by his mother. You said you combined your sense of your mother's background with the incident of the postcards in *Baumgartner's Bombay*.

AD: Well, I can't say Baumgartner is simply based on the figure I saw in the streets of Bombay, because many elements came together to form the character. It comes from years and years of trying to find a way to use the German part of my childhood, the German language that I heard as a child, and knowing how to put this into my Indian background. It was this man who gave me a key and provided me with the solution. I knew someone who knew him, who used to go to the races with him. He told me the man was not as poor as he looked, in fact, was quite rich and owned a racehorse. This stuck in my imagination. He happened to be an Austrian Jew. When he died—a natural death, not the violent death of my book—my friend was asked to go through his belongings and dispose of them. He brought me a packet of letters to read; they were written in German, and he wanted to know if they were important. They were not; they said very little, simply contained everyday questions and were filled with endearments. They were so empty that they were rather mysterious. These letters were all stamped with the same number. Later I read that Jews in concentration camps during the holocaust were allowed to write a certain number of letters, during the early years at least. These letters were stamped with the numbers they bore in the camps. Only then did I realize what that number had meant. I did not know this man's history or anything about his past. He was dead and could not tell me. I needed to invent one. I then realized I could use my mother's memories of prewar Germany in order to fill in the unknown past and provided him with a family and a background that actually belonged to my mother.

LP: There is a moment in *Baumgartner's Bombay*, when Hugo is still a kid growing up in Germany, somebody mentions Rabindranath Tagore and his *Geetanjali*. Would your mother, when she was in Germany, have heard of Tagore, or would she have read *Geetanjali*?

AD: I couldn't resist bringing that in. One of the memories of my childhood is a photograph of Tagore in a robe, attending a reception in Berlin given by the Indian residents there, of whom my father was one. He was a student in Berlin and met my mother there. When she married him, she knew nothing about India. She knew absolutely nothing. She was totally unprepared.

LP: A little like Baumgartner's mother.

AD: Yes! All she knew was a little of the poetry of Tagore and Sarojini Naidu. So she had the most romantic expectations. She spent the rest of her life trying to match them, and failing. The India of her experience was not romantic; it was very hard, and it demanded of her great courage and sacrifice. But it did save her from the Germany of the '30s and '40s.

LP: I want to backtrack a little to return to something you told me earlier about the genesis of Nanda Kaul in *Fire on the Mountain*. You said that you used to watch a solitary, melancholy woman when you were in Kasauli and that image somehow gave you Nanda Kaul.

AD: When I started the book, that was just a hazy and indistinct vision. Again, it was the emptiness, the barrenness of those hills that stayed in my imagination. The hills had character in themselves. When I started to write, I began with that empty landscape.

One of the people I used to see when I was in Kasauli later was a woman who used to go for walks alone. She wore an expression of such sadness, such melancholy. Her melancholy blended with the landscape which had been part of my childhood. The child Raka was there, too, from the start, as part of myself when a child in Kasauli. The third person who entered the book was an acquaintance of my mother's. She was a woman who used to visit us in Delhi when I was a child; she had the most awful voice—very much like Ila Dutt in the book. This woman entered the book quite against my will. I hadn't planned it; she broke into it. And then I remembered that she did go and live in Kasauli and was murdered there, in exactly the way I described in the book. She seemed to enter the book like a ghost, as if she, too, belonged in it.

LP: She does enter the book like a ghost, a very significant ghost. My next question is about the metaphor of the forest fire in the *Fire on the Mountain*. I cannot resist associating the phrase "forest fire" with the Indian word "*dāvanala*"—found in Sanskrit, Hindi, and various other Indian languages—which literally means "forest fire." As you must know. It is used as a recurrent metaphor in Indian literature and myth. I see you use the metaphor in different ways. You reconstruct it in a different context. Would you care to comment on your use of this metaphor in *Fire on the Mountain*?

AD: When I was writing *Fire on the Mountain*, I was not thinking of the traditional metaphor. I was thinking of the natural phenomenon of the forest fire, which happens to be a real presence in those hills. But, of course my imagination, my creative imagination and my consciousness, is a part of the larger Indian imagination, a fragment of it. It is natural that we should coincide, we should share the same symbols, give them the same significance.

LP: You give it a different significance, as I see it. For example, writers like Śaratcandra and other Hindi and Bengali writers often associate the figure "*dāvanala*" with feminine sexuality and use it to suggest the socially/morally disruptive consequences of sexual transgression of women, and so forth. There is always an implicit judgment (of women's sexuality) in their use of the metaphor. That is why I say you have been able to reconstruct the metaphor. As if to retrieve it out of the accumulated conventional associations, you transform its meaning. You may have been thinking of it only as an occurrence in the physical world that is so central to the book. Yet, in the novel, Raka, your child protagonist starts the fire and euphorically declares: "Nani! I have set the mountain on fire." This utterance and the act are then associatively linked with Ila Dutt's rape and murder at the end of the novel.

AD: The difference lies in that I wasn't using the forest fire as a literary metaphor. I was using it as an actuality, a physical actuality, and giving it a significance which would charge it with meaning. At the end of the book, it does acquire a symbolic dimension—it is the fire with which Raka devastates all the lies and fantasies of Nanda Kaul.

LP: Since your background does combine the East and the West, which Western authors have inspired you the most over the years? Who are the authors whose works have been of special interest and of imaginative use to you?

AD: One goes through periods of absorption in one writer or another. To begin with, I was swept off my feet by the Brontës, and they really opened my eyes to the power of literature. Then I read D. H. Lawrence, Joyce, Virginia Woolf, and other English writers of that period with great joy. Eventually I discovered the Russians, Dostoevsky and Chekhov, then roamed amidst the European writers—Proust and Rilke. More and more, it is poetry that excites me and to which I turn for the intense pleasure. At one stage, it was Japanese and Chinese poetry from which I learned to use tiny details of landscape and to employ subtle rather than broad brushstrokes in my prose. Now I read the modern Russian poets—Mandelstam, Pasternak, Akhmatova—with the most profound admiration. I have learned what I could use from all these writers. They are my teachers, my "gurus."

LP: You started writing at the age of seven. What sorts of things did you read at that age?

AD: I read the books on my parent's bookshelves—the Brontë sisters, for instance, and was greatly stirred by them, and then moved on to the classics—Jane Austen, Dickens, Hardy, Joyce. All these masterpieces of prose fiction that taught me whatever I know about writing and have provided me with the most intense pleasures of my life. We were a family of great readers and always had our noses in our books.

LP: What did you write when you were seven?

AD: I find it a bit difficult to tell you. I was filling notebook after notebook with my scribbles. I was always working on a novel. Another habit I had was to write down all my experiences, because that was one way of ordering one's world. Life and experiences seemed to me chaotic and haphazard till I placed them in a certain order, or pattern, upon the written page. It became a childhood habit to me, ordering thoughts and experiences into sentences, pages of composition.

LP: It is interesting that at that young age you were writing lengthy pieces. Rabindranath Tagore started writing at a very young age and wrote some very outstanding short pieces. In contrast, you wanted to write longer works. Could one say that the novel has been the perfect medium for you? You have written short stories, but the longer pieces seem to be what your imagination needs. Am I right?

AD: I enjoy writing the novel. It gives me time. It gives me space. I like to uncover layer after layer of the story till one arrives at its heart, its meaning. You can do that at a slow, meditative pace in a novel, while in a poem or a short story you would be required to provide it immediately, or very quickly. I like the scope the novel gives you to ripen your ideas slowly and naturally, not force them.

LP: Who among Indian writers and writers from other Eastern countries (China, Japan, Egypt) have you been influenced by? Apart from the context of your own writing, which of these authors have been of special interest to you? For example, what do you think of Naguib Mahfooz.

AD: I believe he has written a vast amount about life in Cairo; his work has documentary quality, but it is not the kind of literature that interests me. It is the poetry from that part of the world that interests me—particularly the Sufis, like Rumi. Amongst modern writers, there is an interesting, and poetic, Palestinian novelist called Anton Shammas. I do not know modern Chinese writers but love the work of the Japanese Nobel Laureate, Kawabata. Amongst Indian writers, I have recently rediscovered Tagore, as I told you, and I read R. K. Narayan with pleasure. The work of younger writers like Rushdie and Amitav Ghosh has been very exciting, too. But we all work in very different ways, so I won't say we "influence" each other.

LP: We spoke earlier about your introduction to Tagore's *Home and the World*. You said you have written another introduction to his works. What is this an introduction to?

AD: It is an introduction to a collection of his short stories.

LP: Have you translated any of his work into English? Did you read him when you were growing up? Were you at any time greatly influenced by him?

AD: Right from my childhood, I had the usual Indian child's response to Tagore, that he was something one had to read in school and not for any great interest or pleasure. I've only discovered him quite recently, in my adulthood. By reading biographies of his, studies of his paintings, and seeing the paintings and then getting back to his poetry and fiction, I realized how much more there was to Tagore than I had ever imagined, how much more complex, troubled and thought provoking. It is like making a new discovery.

LP: Growing up in remote Kashmir, I started reading Tagore when I was very young, and his works have had tremendous intellectual and emotional impact on me. Obviously, I read him with great pleasure and was never assigned to read him in school. A few minutes ago, you mentioned you were writing an introduction to a collection of his short stories. Is this something you are working on now?

AD: I was working on it this summer. I just sent it in.

LP: Is it an introduction to a newly translated collected?

AD: It is a new translation. A good deal of his work is going to be reprinted in new translations.

LP: Who did these translations?

AD: These translations have been done by Krishna Dutta and Mary Lago. He has another translator, also an English poet, William Radice, who had done a lot of his poetry and is working now on his short fiction.

LP: I see a lot of continuity between Tagore's representations of the isolation and entrapment of Indian women and your very incisive explorations of the same kind. Since you say you discovered Tagore pretty late, what I would like to know is how late? Did you read him in English or in his original Bengali?

AD: Really I have started reading Tagore only in the last four or five years. In a way, it was being asked to do the introduction to his *Home and the World* that started me, and I read him only in English.

LP: When I asked you about your influences, you didn't mention Shakespeare. Your Indian critics have made connections between

Voices in the City and *Hamlet*. I have not heard or read anybody identify another Shakespearean echo in *Where Shall We Go This Summer*. There are obvious similarities between this novel and *The Tempest*: the powerful politician of a father, the totally innocent daughter, and most interestingly, the mysteriously absent mother.

AD: I wouldn't have thought of claiming Shakespeare as an influence. That is such a tremendous arrogance. I wouldn't put myself in the same field, not even the margins of it. I think Shakespeare is something one imbibes. One does not consciously think of him as a model, or an influence. His work is of the kind that once having read it, it becomes a part of one's consciousness. I think one can trace echoes of Shakespeare's work in almost any author. I was not consciously making any connections. On the other hand, there are academics all over the world who have offered such theories. There is an academic in New Zealand who made a big deal of the fact that I had gone to a college in Delhi which is called the "Miranda House." He saw this as a link to *The Tempest*.

LP: I am not making a wildly associative connection here. Since Shakespeare is an icon in the West and has been widely read and held in awe in the East, his influence on postcolonial writers and women writers all over the world is not a nonissue. I remember reading something about it recently, and the annual conferences of the Shakespeare Association of America sometimes have sessions on what Shakespeare means to writers from previously colonized nations. References to him and his work in Indian and African writing is a valid subject of discussion. Besides, his *The Tempest* has been of special interest to postcolonial theorists and writers. For example, Aimé Césaire rewrote the play from a postcolonial point of view. The connection I made here between *Where Shall We Go This Summer* and *The Tempest* is not totally off the wall, but I am not assuming you actually made these connections.

AD: It is one of those coincidences, because, of course, it was based on a real island off the shore of the coast of Bombay. I am interested in its physicality and remember feeling the isolation from the city. The book does have literary antecedents, too, which come from a common source, a common ocean of themes that we all share and use.

LP: This leads me nicely to my next question, which is about your audience awareness, or readership awareness. I am thinking of an interview which was done in the early '80s, sometime between 1979 and '84. In this interview, you said something very interesting, and you said it in your characteristic imagistic manner. You expressed sadness at the fact that you were writing in a language that does not have a tradition in India. You described English language as "a refugee in the land" and added, "an astonishingly tenacious refugee." In this context, do you see yourself writing not only for Indians, but for larger audiences in lands where English is an indigenous language and not a "refugee"?

AD: One is always asked what audience do you have in mind when you write. I can tell you with absolute honesty that I as a writer—and I do not think any writer—can possibly write with an audience in mind. If it struck me likely that I was writing for a specific audience, I would put my pencil down immediately to forget the feeling that somebody is looking over my shoulder. But of course, there are readers. One is aware that one is going to be read. The fact that I write in English does put me in a rather strange position in India, at least it did when I started out. As I told you earlier, I had a feeling that we were not a community of writers. We were just some very isolated people who, for the reasons of their background, obviously, wrote in English. I was one of them, but we didn't share our experiences. I do not think we approached the English language in the same way either. Each of us was experimenting. I think, in the recent years, the situation has changed tremendously. In the last 10 years, everything has changed. We thought we were a dying race, the ones who used English, that we were probably the last generation who would do their creative work in English. We were made to feel that we had no real position in the Indian world of writers. And it is very, very curious. I don't think anyone has adequately explained it. What has happened in the last 10 years is exactly the opposite. Suddenly everybody is writing, writing in English, writing with tremendous confidence, a new confidence that I don't think we older writers had. We were much more hesitant, tentative, experimental in our use of the language. Where the writers today use it as if they do not think about it. They are simply writing in a language that they are used to speaking to each other in, and hearing, and writing.

LP: There was an article recently in *The New York Times*. I think the article is written by Barbara Crossette and she quotes Kushwant Singh singing the praises of young writers. In this article, you have been classified as one of the young writers. There is a picture of you next to Amitav Ghosh, and Kushwant Singh is heard vociferously praising the "new" writers for being realistic and socially conscious. The article does not deal with the language issue. Though like you, Kushwant Singh makes a distinction between the old writers and the new writers. Have you read any of Amitav Ghosh's fiction?

AD: I try to read as much as I can. I really put the date of change down to 1980, the year Salman Rushdie wrote his *Midnight's Children*. It was a very ambitious and bold book. And, partly because of the success of the book, it led to a whole generation of young writers and gave them the confidence they might not have had otherwise. He can be said to have set free the tongues of the younger writers—a tremendous influence upon their work.

LP: I was also thinking the Indian writers writing in English have a larger Indian reading public. If they were writing in their regional languages, they would not be read by Indian readers from all parts of the country. What do you think?

AD: It is not a large audience. If you look at the statistics, it is not a large audience. It is just a more varied audience. They have readers in more of the different states in India than they would if they were writing in Indian languages. But you would be astonished to look at the sales figures for the books written by regional authors. Some of them are best sellers.

LP: That is true. By large, I meant a multiregional readership. You and Salman Rushdie have a multiregional readership in India, while a Gujarati author doesn't have that advantage.

AD: That is to do with how soon and how well the author gets translated. There certainly is a lack of translation. Hardly any books are translated from one regional language to another, not more than a handful.

LP: The question of readership brings me somewhat prematurely to *Baumgartner's Bombay*. You already made some comments about how the book builds upon your German background and your early link with the German language. I notice that you do not translate all the German, especially the songs, into English. At the same time, you do render all the Hindi, Bengali, Gujarati expressions into English. When Chimenlal says, "Hugo *bhai*," you promptly insert "Brother Hugo." Perhaps you do this in order to preserve the character's perspective. In Hugo's linguistic awareness, German will always be German. It will not be translated into anything else, while Hindi, Bengali, and Gujarati might first be translated into English. Still, it seems to me this novel brings forth a new and different dimension in your awareness of readership.

AD: You have given me the answer to the question really, because it was an attempt to experience India through a foreigner, through Baumgartner, to see how what was familiar to me would appear to him. It is true that by writing *Baumgartner* I do seem to have taken a step outside my own area of experience. It is the first time I ever wrote about a character who was not Indian. By doing so, I seem to have stepped out of the languages I lived amongst—English, Hindi, and Urdu—and to have shifted not only my focus, but my perspective. Using German provided me with a German perspective. The translations would have detracted from what I was trying to do. The German language is essential to the conception of character in the book. The German language is Baumgartner's link to his German past. The German language is a legacy I received from my mother, and, in my childhood, it created a very intimate feeling, something I shared with my family and no one else. It was much later, when I started reading German authors, that I even realized it belonged to another part of the world, much larger and very far from my home. It made me see how a language can contain not only an individual experience, but a whole culture.

LP: You must have listened to the songs at some time.

AD: Those are nursery rhymes, lullabies.

LP: That is what I thought. Perhaps your mother taught you when you were young.

AD: Certainly if you knew German you would be able to read more into them, and there is a missing element if you don't, because like a lot of English nursery rhymes, German nursery rhymes do have a very sinister quality.

LP: That I assumed, judging from the German folk and fairy tales I have read. It is obvious that the very conception of *Baumgartner's Bombay* had something to do with the German part of your background. You also briefly mentioned that you were wondering whether what happens to Baumgartner is something India does to him, as if living in India thwarts his personality?

AD: Well, when my mother lived in India, there were very few Europeans there, just a handful. They tended to hang together, even though they were far apart in their nationalities and languages. In my childhood, I knew these women who even then struck me as very, very eccentric. I used to wonder what made them so eccentric—had they been oddities even in Europe or had they become oddities in India? And, while I imagined Baumgartner, I discovered it was neither one nor the other; it was history that had made them so. They themselves were passive agents that were formed by their strange histories, which was what happened to Baumgartner. What it is really about is how history affects totally passive characters, who don't have any defense against it, and no way of controlling or manipulating it. Some became heroes, others victims, but most just survived. That is why they concentrated on staying afloat, going with the current, surviving. None escaped from history either, and when Baumgartner is murdered at the end, it is his history that he seemed to have escaped from that hunts him down and overcomes him. The ending of Baumgartner is something that troubled me a great deal. I didn't have the ending when I started. I knew that Baumgartner will die and will be killed, but had no idea by whom. At one time, I had two alternative endings, and I played with them. The other ending was that he could have been killed by the poor man who lived on the pavement. After all, in that man's eyes, Baumgartner was wealthy. He could easily have wanted to rob Baumgartner, even murder him. But when I came to the end, it seemed to me that the only logical possibility was to have a German hippie kill him. There is a certain kind of historical logic in this which I could not deny or disguise.

LP: That answers the question I had about the ending. I had trouble with the ending. Aesthetically, it is the most fitting ending, but it comes across to me as such an outrage. I have a purely subjective response to it. As an Indian, I feel whatever happened to Baumgartner in Bombay or Calcutta should have been something that could have happened to any Indian. Whatever it did to him, India should have provided Hugo Baumgartner protection from Nazi violence. Early on, Baumgartner had saved a woman from being beaten by her husband. He could have done something like that again and been attacked and killed for intervening when everybody around him is just watching the spectacle of a poor man beating his wife.

AD: That would have been random street violence. That would have been almost like an accident, with no meaning.

LP: It is obvious that you have an unerring sense of an ending. Your endings are not simply tragic, they are catastrophic. For example, Ila Dutt in *Fire on the Mountain* is not simply murdered and thus eliminated; she is raped. She is violated and thoroughly destroyed. Even though you consider yourself a novelist who has chosen to concern herself only with the inner lives, the isolated psyches of your characters, the endings betray a strong concern with the terrible havoc that historical, social, and ideological forces play with the lives of people. Could you elaborate on this seeming contradiction a little bit?

AD: I'll try to explain this; I am not sure I can do it. To write about the private, enclosed world is something that comes easily to me, the stream of consciousness is probably the easiest kind of writing. It is also the most self-indulgent; I could indulge in it myself. At the same time, one has to be aware that there is a certain point at which the private world has to confront and meet the outer world. Just as in everyday, ordinary experiences the outer world and inner world confront each other forcing upon one clichés, compromises, and, sometimes, conflict. It is the confrontation of the inner and the outer that interests me as a novelist. The outer world is dominated by certain forces, the individual's force is enigmatic, variable, an imponderable. The clash between the two is capable of shattering the inner world, unless the individual finds the strength and the courage and imagination to protect it. Only very rarely can it overcome it.

LP: But those "outer worlds" are specifically historical.

AD: As you see, it could be society. It could be tradition. In the Indian society, tradition takes precedence over the individual. It could be history, culture. It is the force the individual cannot control.

LP: The question of endings brings me back to Tagore. I see a great difference between his endings and your endings. Many of his endings are compromise endings. For example, often his female protagonists go against custom and tradition, and he allows them a certain degree of freedom. But then, at the end, these women return to the place they had deviated from. It does not happen all the time, but often in his novels he muffles the dialectic that he starts out with. I see you do quite the opposite thing. Your endings are so stark and uncompromising. You show the outer world of tradition, history, culture ruthlessly mutilate the private lives of individuals.

AD: Probably it has to do with the fact that he was writing at the turn of the century. He was a Victorian writer in a Victorian society. It would be unrealistic of him to show societies changing, to show individualism change society. Whereas, in our lives, I have seen things change. Of course, I can't say Tagore did not experience violence. He did. Perhaps he had a greater belief in tradition than I do. I have never belonged to any tradition. I have always been outside the orthodoxy, the conventional. So it hasn't the same meaning for me.

LP: Most of your female protagonists are wives and mothers, except Bimla in *Clear Light of Day*, though she is also a mother of some sort. To see women as being trapped in the wife/mother role is certainly common across cultures. However, don't you think that Indian tradition and culture seems to have a greater and a more distinct commitment to the patrilocal nature of marriage? For example, Indian folk and classical cultures glorify the moment of the young girl's departure to her marital home. Somehow, this departure in the Indian tradition is set up to be more final and absolute. Certainly, in modern Indian society, the circumstances are different. They are not the same they were in Tagore's time, Tagore's child-brides, mothers, wives, or mothers-to-be were physically, as well as psychologically isolated. Your female protagonists live and move (for example, in *Voices in the City*) in a freer and larger world. But they are also victimized as a result of the culture's symbolic commitment to the patrilocal marriage. They are psychologically displaced because of that. The character in your *Where Shall We Go This Summer* makes a failed attempt to return to her natal home, where she has not been completely happy. Do you think this particular aspect of Indian culture is at least in part responsible for the distinct kind of displacement and dislocation many Indian women (as wives, mothers) feel.

AD: Surely. To write about an Indian woman as a career woman is very different from the way we can write about an American woman or a European woman. Even for educated professional women in India, there still is a much stronger commitment to family. Glorification of the moment of the young girl's departure to husband's family is part of the Indian culture. It is in the music and in the literature. However, that is not quite the way I see my female protagonists. That is not the moment I have focused on. I have written about them in that gray area between the moment of leaving and before the moment of arriving—the moment of doubt, hesitation, yearning, and great possibility.

LP: Do you think, because of the nature of Indian society, culture, Indian feminism is different from European, American, even

African feminisms? Do you think there *is* a vital feminist movement going on in India?

AD: There is a feminist movement in India, but it is very different from the Western movement. In the West, there is movement towards abandoning the old order, to bring in a new order. The Indian woman is always working towards an adjustment, a compromise. Few Indian feminists really contemplate total change. Working towards an adjustment through the traditional role is much less drastic, much more Indian. I think Indian feminism is more practical than theoretical. It is expedient rather than ideological.

LP: Sometimes, in the West, people say the Indian feminist movement is historically at an earlier stage. Do you think so?

AD: I don't think so. The Indian feminist movement probably predates the American one. But the nature of it is very different.

LP: Which Indian writers do you like most and identify with?

AD: I like some of Attia Hosain's work. I admire Ruth Prawar Jhabvala's novels. Recently I have read and enjoyed Bapsi Sidhwa's fiction.

LP: What do you think of Amrita Pritam?

AD: I like her poetry. I think she has written some fine poetry. I can't say the same thing about her fiction.

LP: You said earlier that Ruth Prawar Jhabvala is one of the Indian writers who has inspired you?

AD: Since my work is very different from hers, I wouldn't use the word "inspired." But certainly, I admire her very much. I think she has written about ordinary, middle-class, urban society with an accuracy, precision, and irony like no other Indian writer.

LP: In some of her fiction at least, she so often presents a very exclusive and negative view of Indian women. I find her representations of Indian women unfair. I feel as if there is an inordinate degree of negative stereotyping of Indian women in some of her fiction.

AD: That is what Indian readers always say about her. I do not agree at all. I think she has covered a much wider spectrum in representations of Indian women. She writes about women with different backgrounds, women with different aspirations. I do not agree at all with your view of her. She has a comic manner, a humorous manner, that people are misled into thinking is superficial, not serious. They miss the irony.

LP: No. I think it is serious. There are moments in her fiction when I completely agree with her criticisms. I also think she is a powerful writer, and I like her irony and humor. There is a certain kind of an Indian woman, of a certain class, with whom I would have the same interaction that the narrator in Jhabvala's fiction often has. However, there is another kind of an Indian woman she does not represent at all. There are readers in India and in the West who do think of her as somebody who writes a lot of stories about Indian women, covers a broad spectrum, as you just said. To these readers—I am certainly one of them—Jhabvala's depiction of Indian women seems one-sided, the sort that reinforces negative stereotyping of Indian women in the West.

AD: Is a writer obliged to write fiction that is representative of all kinds of people in a society? Every writer chooses the sort of characters that interest him or her, that he/she knows well and can write about with authenticity and feeling.

LP: Has you living and teaching in the United States given you a greater exposure to Afro-American and Chicano writing?

AD: No. There is so much reading and work to do that I am unable to read outside of my area. Here I teach a course on modern Indian literature, and I teach some writing courses.

LP: Do you include your own writing either in the creative writing or the literature course syllabi?

AD: No. It would be an awkward situation for my students, and myself, too.

LP: Which authors do you teach?

AD: I teach twentieth-century literature, starting with Tagore, in translation, then going on to Raja Rao and R.K. Narayan, in the original, and continuing through Attia Hosain and Ruth Jhabvala to Bharati Mukherjee and Salman Rushdie. I have also taught Bibhuti Bhushan Bannerji's *Pather Panchali* and some modern Bengali short-story writers. And the poetry of Kamla Das and Amrita Pritam; also of Nissim Ezekiel and Arun Kolatkar. The syllabus changes slightly all the time.

LP: Which Salman Rushdie novels do you teach most frequently, and how do your students respond, for example, to *Shame*?

AD: I generally teach *Shame* because it is so compact, and that makes it more accessible than the vast, sprawling *Midnight's Children* or *Satanic Verses*. Besides, it is a marvellous novel that displays all his faculties and his particular gifts. My students are always enthralled by it.

LP: Are you interested in contemporary critical theory, feminist theory, or any other?

AD: No. I keep miles away from critical theory, almost as if I fear it might have a negative effect on me. It seems to be so much the opposite of the creative impulse. I think the critical and creative impulse are very, very different. It is like looking at a view from two different ends of a telescope.

LP: Since the treatment of nature, space, and the world of objects is essential to your art of narration, the New England landscape must feed your imagination. Are you going to transport these impressions to the Indian soil, or will you write a New England novel?

AD: I wish I could find a way to accommodate them both, not keep them separate, but merge them as they are merged in my own experience.

LP: I want to return to an earlier question. You said you learned about concentration camps while you were writing *Baumgartner's Bombay*. I was wondering if you could tell us something specific about the concentration camps in India, if you did any research about these?

AD: Well, I did. You see, I was really looking for some material on the detention camps in India, and I could find nothing. Nothing exists. I got in touch with a few people. I did know quite a few, some German people, who had been in these detention camps, some friends of my mother's. I was only able to meet one of them who is still alive. He told me if you had come two years ago I would have been happy to talk to you. But now I am writing my own autobiography and I can't give that away to you. So it was no use. All I had to go on was the material about the detention camps in the West, camps that they would call internment camps. There was material about internment camps in Canada and England, and I read all of those. I had a friend in Sussex who found me books. So I had some idea of what these camps were like, how people were identified to be sent there and how they lived, what was the routine. Then I heard of two people who had been in the detention camps in India. So I sent them the chapters to check. They did make some suggestions which I incorporated. One was a Jewish professor in Haifa, Israel. He had, interestingly, come to India to teach at Shantiniketan before the war. He knew Tagore. Tagore was still alive. The Jewish professor was taken out of Shantiniketan to an internment camp. He was able to get out with the help of British friends. But others were trapped there for the duration of the war.

LP: I find the ignorance of Indian people, of the Indian government, and also of the British soldiers who were running those camps, appalling. To them Jew and Nazis were simply Germans, speaking the German language. That was all that mattered.

AD: Yes. There were many Jews put in those internment camps along with Nazis. There were some Jewish societies that came to the rescue of some of the Jews. But there were others like Baumgartner who stayed there, because they knew no one influential, and because they were too confused and muddled to help themselves.

PH: When you were talking about critical theory, you mentioned that creativity and the critical impulse were completely opposed. I was wondering if you thought that was contingently true or necessarily true, true of critical theory as it is today and/or true of any critical theory, whatsoever.

AD: I think it is a basic truth for one thing, because I am really aware that when I am writing the first draft of a book, I can only allow my creative impulse to work. I have to subdue my critical impulse. I have a critical impulse, of course. At that stage, I have to subdue it, to make quite sure that I don't use it. If I used it at that stage, it would destroy the writing, which is very tentative at that stage. I would just tear it up. After I have written that first draft, I deliberately arouse that critical impulse, to see the writing objectively and subject it to severe criticism. And in the end, it is a combination of the two. Critical theory, which is what you were talking about, is something that *follows* a work of art. It cannot come before it. When it follows a work of art, it makes a great deal of sense. Theorists can make all kinds of discoveries and arrive at an understanding of a text which you would not have otherwise. I think it is a matter of precedence, really.

PH: One reason I am asking is personal: I am a critical theorist. The other reason I am asking is that some of the things you said earlier struck me as very Greek, which is not to say they are un-

Indian; I do not want to oppose things in that way. Specifically, what you said reminded me of Aristotelian literary principles. For example, you were saying that the alternative ending of *Baumgartner's Bombay* of having the poor man on the pavement kill Baumgartner would have been random, whereas having the German kill him gave his death meaning. This seems to me to fit nicely with what Aristotle said about the structure of a plot having necessity and design. Design covers a broad range of things, it includes what we call poetic justice, but one could interpret design as "meaning" in your sense. Then, on the other hand, you were talking about society or history as a force overwhelming the individual. People who have studied Greek drama would no doubt think of this as the conflict between individual and fate. I am not saying you would have thought of these things or used them because of Aristotle. Presumably, Aristotle is a good theorist, and he isolated some of the things that artists do. You would be writing in a certain way because you are an artist, not because you have read Aristotle, but there would still be some sort of a kinship.

AD: Exactly. What is an artist doing but taking the raw material of life, which is fragmentary and random, but in composing it on a canvas, or a piece of paper, you need to find some kind of an order: what fits together, what doesn't, what belongs, what must be discarded. You find yourself using these little pieces, almost like working out a puzzle, fitting the pieces together in a way that would form the whole picture. This does sound arbitrary. But the word "design" has an arbitrary ring to it, as something imposed from outside.

PH: I didn't mean that as a criticism.

AD: It is a problem a lot of readers have had with *Baumgartner's Bombay*. It does seem too designed, too controlled.

PH: I actually am in full agreement with Aristotle about how valuable design is.

AD: I was fulfilling the purpose of art, not of reality. The purpose of art is to bring about some kind of order, even if you are giving reason to unreason, to madness.

South Hadley, Massachusetts
October 26, 1990

Part V

Interpreting Literary Contact: Translation, Influence, and Writing Back

9

Translating Indian Literary Texts into English

P. K. Saha

Theoretically, one may translate from any given source language to any receiving language. In practice, however, the translation of literary texts is limited to translations from earlier languages to later languages or from one contemporary language to another. For example, it is unlikely that anyone has ever translated *Hamlet* into Classical Greek or *For Whom the Bell Tolls* into Sanskrit. The very notion of undertaking such translations seems funny, and the well-known Latin translation of *Winnie the Pooh* simply highlights the humorous intent behind the translation. Thinking about the matter, though, does force one to confront issues that lie at the heart of translation theory. Translations of literary texts are meant for specific audiences, and consequently all translations of literature become obsolete sooner or later.

There is no way of predicting exactly what specific problems a translator will face in going from a given source language to a particular receiving language. Consciously or unconsciously, each translator sets up certain goals in relation to the receiving language at hand. In trying to translate Indian literary texts into English, one faces problems in four overlapping areas: cultural, aesthetic, linguistic, and stylistic.

Cultural

In Sanskrit literature, for example, gods and goddesses often play prominent roles. How exactly is the English-speaking reader to be informed what a name like Saraswatī (the goddess of learning or literature) or Lakśmī (the goddess of wealth) means for an Indian reader? By providing a glossary or footnotes or some other device?

On a more abstract level, will translating a term such as Bengali or Hindi "*jīvandevatā*" literally as "lifegod" or "the god of life" do justice to the original? For an Indian reader, the concept of a god of life presiding over human affairs may invoke exalted feelings, but, for a Western reader, such a concept may appear tinged with religiosity or sentimentality or both. Removal of culture-specific terms is likely to produce a denatured brew, and consequently the translator may have to take calculated risks with footnotes based on a careful evaluation of the audience in the receiving language.

Successful anthologies such as *The Norton Anthology of English Literature* routinely use such footnotes in a helpful manner and make earlier English literature accessible to today's English-speaking audiences. There is no reason why translators should not use similar devices that provide not only the bare meanings of unusual names or terms but also help to guide readers toward the spirit of the original text. Thus it might be helpful to inform an English reader that, when the word "*jīvandevatā*" appears in a Bengali poem by Rabindranath Tagore, it does not necessarily mean that Tagore believed in the existence of an actual god with specific powers over human life, but rather that he was concerned with a level of abstraction on which human events could be viewed as being governed by principles that transcend human knowledge and power.

Such attempts to serve contemporary readers should be carefully distinguished, however, from attempts to obscure significant cultural assumptions underlying the original text that might appear offensive to today's audiences. For example, Bharata, the most influential rule-giver of Sanskrit drama, laid down various rigid rules in his *Nāṭyaśāstra* (*The Principles of Drama*). One of these rules involved the type of language spoken by different characters in Sanskrit plays. Only exalted beings such as gods or upper-class males such as kings or noblemen could be depicted as speaking Sanskrit verse (the word "*sanskrit*" literally means "refined" or "cultured"). Lower-class males and females (except for goddesses or queens) had to speak Prākrit prose (the counterpart, to a certain extent, of vulgate forms in medieval Europe).

Consequently, in *Śakuntalā* by Kālidāsa (the fifth-century Sanskrit playwright who is sometimes referred to as "The Shakespeare of India"), characters such as the fisherman or the women in general do not ever use the type of language used by kings and holy men, and translators not only need to recreate the flavors of the original, but also to inform English readers (perhaps in an introduction) that Kālidāsa wrote under certain linguistic and cultural constraints. If today's assumptions about equal rights for men and women or for all citizens induce translators to gloss over such issues in some kind of a misguided effort to present a favorable picture of Indian culture, then literature and history will both become casualties.

Aesthetic

Aesthetic tastes can differ in ways that pose serious problems for translators. Puns, for example, are for the most part used humorously in English. In Indic languages, puns can be used with a solemnity that might seem strange to English readers. The pun is likely to be untranslatable, but, even if its presence can somehow be indicated, the desired aesthetic effect on English readers may be difficult to achieve. Consider the following lines of Bhartrihari, a Sanskrit poet of the fifth century:

mukhena candrakāntena mahānīlaiḥ śiroruhaiḥ
pāṇibhyāṃ padmarāgābhyāṃ reje ratnamayīva sā.[1]

With a face beautiful as the moon, jet-black hair,
and lotus-colored hands, she seemed made of jewels.

"*Candrakānta*" means "beautiful as the moon," and it also happens to be the name of a precious stone; "*mahānīla*" simultaneously means "jet-black" and dark "sapphire," and "*padmarāga*" means both "lotus-colored" and "ruby." In the original, the puns represent an important aspect of the description of the woman's beauty. Clearly the English translation loses this aspect, and the English reader needs an explanation of the puns in order to appreciate the spirit of the original.

The theoretical issue here involves the related concepts of

vagueness, ambiguity, punning, and polysemy. When language is vague, it is not possible to pinpoint all the semantic possibilities. If someone says that a given task will be completed at some time, then the possibilities concerning the time of completion are virtually limitless. Ambiguity also involves more than one meaning, but the possible meanings can be pinpointed.

Ambiguity can be of four types: lexical, constructional, derivational, and metaphorical. The following sentences illustrate the four types:

1. I will meet you near the bank.

1a. *Shay eshechilo.* (Bengali)
he/she came

2. Old men and women will be evacuated first.

3. Flying planes can be dangerous.

4. The man is an ox.

In 1, the ambiguity is caused by two different lexical items (one referring to a financial institution, and the other to the edge of a river) that happen to have the same spelling and pronunciation. In 1a, the ambiguity is caused by a single lexical item. In Bengali, the third-person, singular pronoun is not marked for gender the way English "he" and "she" are marked for gender, and consequently the ambiguity of "*shay*" cannot be retained in English translations.

In 2, the scope of modification of "old" in the construction "old men and women" is uncertain, because it might or might not be modifying "women." In 3, there is more than one possible derivational source for the phrase "flying planes," because "flying" could be either a gerund acting as the subject of the sentence or it could be a participial adjectival modifying "planes." In 4, "ox" is being used metaphorically, and in English, at least, "ox" has connotations of unusual strength or stupidity, and either one or both of these connotations may be operative in this sentence. Even though a specific context might resolve the ambiguity in some cases, the theory of ambiguity needs to accommodate the overall possibilities.

Sentence 1 also illustrates the overlap between ambiguity and punning. Since "bank" can be two different words with the same pronunciation, 1 involves a pun. The word "plane" in 3 could also involve punning. A pun generally involves lexical ambiguity, but not all cases of ambiguity involve puns.

Polysemy involves *a* word with more than one meaning. In a pun, two (or more) different words accidentally happen to have the same or similar pronunciation, while in polysemy, *a* word has more than one meaning and often one of these meanings is shared with another word. Thus "shallow" and "superficial" can both be used to describe "person," and the meaning will be more or less the same, but normally only "shallow" is used to modify "river." So "shallow" is polysemous because it has more than one meaning.

Ambiguity, punning, and polysemy can all converge in a single construction. Yeats's "Among School Children"[2] contains these lines:

> O self-born mockers of man's enterprise;
> Labour is blossoming or dancing where
> The body is not bruised to pleasure soul

The adjectival "self-born" strengthens the case for interpreting "labour" in the next line to mean both "childbirth" and "work." Historically, these two meanings of "labour" make the word polysemous, but many speakers of present-day English may differentiate the two meanings sharply enough to have two different words that cause "labour" to be a pun in Yeats's line. In the same line, "blossoming" involves derivational ambiguity, because the word may be either a gerund or a progressive form of the verb "to blossom."

What complicates a translator's task is not only the presence of puns like the ones in Bhartrihari's or Yeats's poetry, but also the interaction in the original text between polysemy and punning. "*Padmarāga*," the Sanskrit term for "ruby," (which was used in the Sanskrit lines quoted earlier) is a compound structure consisting of "*padma*" ("lotus") and "*rāga*" ("color"). The Indian musical term "*rāga*" is derived from this literal meaning ("color"). The traditional melody patterns were synesthetically viewed as different "colors" in the domain of music. In Greek, "*rhegma*" means "colored material," and "*rhegma*" and "*rāga*" are clearly cognates. The word "*padma*" is also heavily loaded, because the lotus has as many implications in Indian literature as the rose does in European literature. So if a lotus is a lotus is a lotus . . . then how can "ruby" ever by viewed as a satisfactory equivalent of "*padmarāga*" without some indication of the complexity of the Sanskrit word?

Additionally, the translator of Indian texts must not forget that, in contemporary English, puns are not as highly valued as polysemy, perhaps because puns seem to be linguistic cheap shots based on accidental similarity of pronunciation rather than on profundity of thought. In Indian literature, especially in Sanskrit literature, polysemy accompanies punning more frequently and pervasively than in English, and, consequently, aesthetic preferences may have evolved somewhat differently in the Indian subcontinent than in English-speaking countries.

In the Bible, too, puns have a more elevated status than they do in English today. For example, in the Old Testament (Exodus 3), God commands Moses to inform his people that he has been sent by God, and Moses asks what name for God he should use when he reports to his people. God's answer (in English versions) to Moses is "I am who I am." This English translation does not convey the original pun involving YHWH or Yaweh (God's name, which is introduced here for the first time in the Bible) and the verb HAYAH, "to be." In short, Moses is being informed that he should tell his people that he has been sent by the being who is the essence of all existence, the ultimate illustration of the verb of existence. Clearly, this pun is not to be taken lightly. It is solemn in the way puns often are in Indian literature.

Linguistic

Certain morphological, phonetic, and syntactic patterns may create difficulties. There are words in Indian languages that have no equivalents in English. Translating a Hindi word like "*tapasyā*" into English as "meditation" may not be adequate because "*tapasyā*" involves ritual austerities that are not included in the meaning of "meditation."

Compound nominals are common in languages like Sanskrit and Bengali, and translating these literally may be problematic. Bengali "*rupsagar*" simply does not sound right as "sea of beauty," and a line like Tagore's "*nilo anjanaghana punjochayay sambrita ambar*" ("dense blue eyeshadow-covered sky") is difficult to translate because the sound-pattern is as important in the original as the compound words.

Issues such as grammatical gender, illustrated earlier by sentence 1a, or syntactic factors can create problems. Since English has lost so many inflections over the centuries, word order in Modern English has been forced to play a stronger role. Thus in English

5. The cat ate the rat

obviously does not mean the same as

5a. The rat ate the cat

but in Bengali

5b. *beralta khelo indurtake*
cat-the ate rat-the-object marker

means the same as

5c. *indurtake khelo beralta.*

Clearly, the greater syntactic freedom of Indic languages makes topicalization or highlighting (by preposing of phrases) easier in these languages, and identical syntactic effects may not always be possible in English translations.

Stylistic

Style may be viewed as the way language is used in a given text or as the way in which the language of the text appears against the larger background of the language as a whole as used by native speakers.[3] In pedagogical situations, style is often looked upon as a matter of linguistic choice. The general hope in such situations is that awareness of such choices will lead to the realization of Swift's notion of style as proper words in proper places. This Swiftian notion does not conflict in any serious sense with the descriptive notion of viewing style as a composite of the significant linguistic patterns in any given text.

Consequently, any linguistic item in a text may be stylistically significant, depending upon how the item is viewed in the overall literary interpretation of the text. If this theory of style is valid, then features such as sentence structure, meter, rhyme, consonance, metaphor, and other details of the way language is used in the original are all crucial aspects of style.

In order to discuss how the translator of Indian literary texts deals with these four types of interrelated problems, it may be helpful to make an inventory of the different types of translation that are theoretically possible or available. There are six terms for different types of translation that we need to consider: (a) linguistic translation, (b) literal translation, (c) faithful translation, (d) idiomatic translation, (e) imitative translation, and (f) transcreation. The first four may be illustrated by translating into English an ordinary Bengali sentence containing a conjunctive participle:

	chan	*korey*	*bajarey*	*jabo*
6. *linguistic:*	*bath*	*do CONJ PART*	*market-to*	*go-will*
7. *literal:*	*bath*	*after-doing*	*to market*	*will go*
8. *faithful:*	*After bathing, I will go to the market.*			
9. *idiomatic:*	*After I shower, I'll go shopping.*			

Translation 6 conveys more information about the syntax and suffixes in the original than does any of the others, but obviously it cannot be used for literary purposes. Both 6 and 7 indicate word order, but the latter leaves out fine grammatical details.

The differences between 8 and 9 may be significant in certain contexts. If one wants a whiff of foreignness in the translation, the slightly slower pace of 8 with its uncontracted auxiliary may create the flavor of a foreign text. The idiomatic version in 9 has the kind of tone one would expect from a native speaker. Without a specific context, it is impossible to tell which translation is more desirable. The difference between faithful and idiomatic translations can be highlighted more dramatically by the following example:

10a. *ami eta televisioney dekhechilam.*

10b. *ami eta radiotey shunechilam.*

11a. I saw it on T.V.

11b. I heard it on radio.

11c. I heard it on the radio.

Sentence 11a is both a faithful and an idiomatic translation of its Bengali counterpart (10a, while the parallel 11b is a seemingly faithful but wholly unacceptable translation of 10b. Since English has semifrozen syntactic patterns that involve obligatory use or avoidance of the article "the," it is 11c that is the faithful and idiomatic translation of 10b. The differences among literal, faithful, and idiomatic translations may be significant or trivial; depending on the context at hand.

Imitative translations try to attain idiomaticity and simultaneously attempt to maintain the important aesthetic patterns of the original. For example, if one could successfully translate *Beowulf* into Modern English without losing the typical alliterative patterns of Old English verse, we would have an imitative translation.[4]

As for the sixth type of translation, many years ago in *The Illustrated Weekly of India* (April 15, 1956), I coined the term "transcreation" to refer to translations in which liberty is taken to change the original in creative ways for the purpose of producing the most desirable aesthetic effects in the receiving language. In this publication, I criticized a translator of Tagore's *Balāka*, a firm believer in faithful translations, for not living up to his own principles. I also pointed out that Tagore's reputation abroad had been hurt by some of Tagore's own translations.

Transcreations are risky ventures, motivated by the inadequacy of translations. A well-known saying of nineteenth-century France (coined undoubtedly by a male chauvinist) claimed that "translations are like women. If they're beautiful they are not faithful, and if they're faithful they are not beautiful."[5] Chauvinist though the remark may be, it does represent a universal feeling about the inadequacy of the translations of literary texts, especially of poetry.

True, as George Steiner points out, in some rare instances translations have actually surpassed the original in grandeur, resulting in what he calls "upward betrayal."[6] Nagging questions persist, though, even in such eminently successful cases. What exactly did the original say? How does it differ from the translation? Was the translator using the translation to promote some literary theory or political goal, or was he or she trying to be as faithful to the original as possible?

Let me indicate the kind of experience that tends to shake my own faith in the value of transcreations. Like everyone else in the English-speaking world I have been familiar for years with Edward Fitzgerald's famous translation of the quatrain from Omar Khayyam:

A Book of Verses underneath the Bough,
A Jug of Wine, a Loaf of Bread—and Thou
Beside me singing in the Wilderness—
Oh, Wilderness were Paradise enow![7]

In the countless illustrations I have seen of this quatrain, the "Thou" is always depicted as a beautiful young woman. Imagine my astonishment when I learned that in Omar Khayyam's original, the counterpart of "And Thou beside me . . ." is "And a comely youth beside me . . ." Obviously Fitzgerald did not want to offend his Victorian readers, but I felt betrayed upon discovering that Fitzgerald's transcreation had blocked my access to vital information available to anyone who had read the original even in a cursory manner.

This example suggests that in some situations the translator should provide a faithful translation (or at least some explanatory comments) along with a transcreation because it is generally impossible for most readers to know exactly where the original differs from the transcreation. Times change, and an alteration made in good faith by a translator in one age may appear to be an atrocious mistake in another age.

Here are two examples, one very brief and the other somewhat long, of how faithful translations and transcreations of Indian literary texts may enhance each other. The brief example is from Jibanananda Das, after Tagore the greatest poet of Modern Bengal. In his famous poem "Banalata Sen,"[8] there is a romantic-apocalyptic stanza that starts as follows:

> At the end of all days, evening falls like the sound of dew;
> The hawk wipes the smell of sunlight from its wings . . .

Dissatisfied with the verb "wipes" in the original, several translators[9] have transcreated the line by using instead the word "shakes." Presumably these translators feel that "shakes" creates a compelling visual image that is more effective for English-speaking readers. Perhaps they also feel that "shakes" creates a more plausible image because it may not be clear exactly how a hawk does "wipe" anything at all. With its beak? Or feet? Or by some other means? But even if Das did err in using "*muche phele*" (the literal-idiomatic counterpart of "wipes") the important question here is whether a translator should take the liberty of trying to "improve" the original text without indicating where the text has been altered. If "shakes" is used by the translator, an explanatory footnote may be needed to inform the reader about the verb Das actually used.

The second example is from Tagore's "Basundharā,"[10] a poem of some eleven pages. Considerations of length clearly make it difficult to reproduce the poem in its entirety, and so I will use only an excerpt here:

A.

Earth

You have been my earth
for many years. Mixing me
with your clay, you have traversed
on restless feet endless skies
and the whole universe
age after age
through countless nights and days.
So today
sitting alone, absentmindedly,
on the bank of the Padma, staring
in front of me with entranced eyes,
I feel with all my body and mind
how the tiny blades of grass shudder
as they rise through your soil.
A hundred years from today
won't my being quiver
amid the layers of leaves
of this beautiful forest?
In home after home, how many hundreds
of men and women will forever start
the game of life: in their love
won't I exist at all?

B.

Earth

You have been mine for so long.
Through the ages
you have gathered me in your dust
and carried me restlessly
through the universe. So today
here I sit, staring at the river bank
with entranced eyes,
feeling with every fibre of my being
the shudder of tiny blades of grass
pushing their way through your soil.

So ages hence, when the wind
blows through yet unplanted trees
with timeless couples in the shade,
won't I still be there, unseen,
amid whispering leaves and lovers?

A is a more or less faithful translation of the excerpt, while B is a transcreation. An interested non-Bengali reader can probably benefit from both versions, but, to those who object to B, I would suggest that, if Tagore himself had chosen English as the vehicle for his original version, he would have *thought* somewhat differently. One's thoughts are inevitably molded to a certain extent by the matrix of the language in which one thinks.

Neither A nor B comes near the glory of Tagore's Bengali original, but the important point is that non-Bengali readers have no direct access to the original. They simply have to manage with A and B or some other equivalent versions. Chances are that the rhythm of B will bring them closer to the spirit of the original than will A.

The syntax of B flows more in keeping with the natural rhythms of English, and B also has phrases with multiple meanings and consonance of the type that one frequently encounters in Tagore's originals. In the last but third line of B, the phrase "timeless couples" can mean that the couples are outside of time in the sense that they represent ongoing generations of couples, and they can also be "timeless" in the sense that lovers pay no attention to time. In the last line, the word "whispering" is made to do double duty through simultaneous modification of "leaves" and "lovers," while the /l/, /v/, and /z/ sounds in "leaves and lovers" create a delicate consonance of the type that is so common in Tagore's poetry.

Clearly there is no simple solution to the problem of translating literary texts, but, in the spectrum described here, ranging from linguistic translation to transcreation, there are possibilities that enable translators to reduce the gap between readers and original text. All such tasks of translation have, in the final analysis, the most venerable antecedents. As Peter Salm puts it, "The first comprehensible verbal transaction between separate peoples whose speech had previously been gibberish to one another must rival in importance the invention of language itself."[11]

Notes

1. Quoted in John Brough, *Poems from the Sanskrit* (London: Penguin Books, 1968), p. 34.

2. W. B. Yeats, *The Collected Poems of W. B. Yeats* (New York: The Macmillan Company, 1956), pp. 212–214.
3. For fuller discussions of this notion of style, see P. K. Saha, "A Linguistic Approach to Style," *Style*, Vol. 2, Winter 1968, No. 1, pp. 7–13; and "Style, Stylistic Transformations, and Incorporators," *Style*, Vol. 12, Winter 1978, No. 1, pp. 1–22.
4. Professor Ruth Lehmann's new translation of *Beowulf* (forthcoming, University of Texas Press) is specifically said to be an "imitative translation."
5. Quoted in Peter Salm, "Undoing Babel," *Gamut*, Winter 1986, p. 61.
6. George Steiner, "On an Exact Art (Again)," *The Kenyon Review*, Vol. IV, No. 2, Spring 1982, p. 12.
7. In John Bouryer and J. L. Brooks, eds., *The Victorian Age: Prose, Poetry, and Drama* (NY: Appleton-Century-Crofts, 1954), p. 470.
8. Jibanananda Das, *Banalata Sen* (Calcutta: Signet Press, 1969), p. 9.
9. Jibanananda Das, *Banalata Sen* [*and other*] *Poems* (Calcutta: Writers Workshop, 1962), pp. 1–4.
10. Rabindranath Tagore, *Sanchayita* (Calcutta: Bishwabharati. 1966), pp. 194–197 passim. The translation and transcreation, along with some of the other ideas in this paper, were presented by me earlier in a paper read at the Twentieth Bengal Studies Conference, University of Chicago, 1985.
11. Salm, p. 62.

10

Nauṭankī and the Struggle for Independence, National Integration, and Social Change: A Brechtian Analysis

Darius L. Swann

Westerners seeking to gain an appreciation of that theater genre called *Nauṭankī* or *Svāṅg,* will find that Bertolt Brecht provides the most accessible way, for Brecht's theories of dramaturgy, acting, and actor-audience relationship find an intriguing coincidence in *Nauṭankī.* First, there are strong similarities between Brecht's epic theater and the narrative structure of *Nauṭankī.* Second, Brecht's desire for an "alienation effect" in the actor's art is realized in the acting conventions of *Nauṭankī.* Third, the relation of song and dance to spoken dialogue, which Brecht uses to achieve the "A effect" is similarly used in *Nauṭankī.* Finally, the object of theater as moral instruction is common both to Brecht and *Nauṭankī.* In this essay, I shall explore these similarities and note some differences. While the similarities between two forms coming out of such disparate backgrounds may be intriguing, they should not be surprising, for the model that inspired a good deal of Brecht's theory was an Asian form, the Chinese traditional theater, or Chinese opera. It appears from his essay, "Alienation Effects in Chinese Acting," that Brecht drew his inspiration from witnessing a performance of Chinese opera by Mei Lan-fang's troupe in Moscow in 1935. He was particularly impressed that the incomparable Chinese actor, Mei

Lan-fang, was able and willing to demonstrate his art to a group of specialists, apparently at a social gathering in totally untheatrical circumstances.[1]

I say that the similarities between Brecht's theater and *Nauṭankī* are not surprising, given his inspiration, for Oriental theater genres generally display certain commonalities. Most important is the integral unity of song, dance, and dialogue in most of these forms. The manner of their use is rooted in the aesthetic sense of the people of those Asian societies. And this makes for a certain irony in Brecht's choosing Chinese theater techniques to illustrate a theater designed to instruct and to stimulate social change. For although the past three centuries, which saw Chinese opera achieve its finished form in Peking (Beijing), were not unmarked by revolutionary upheaval, the theater itself contributed little to the revolutionary ferment. Henry Wells is correct when he says that "the Chinese theater is for the most part one of the most profoundly and consistently traditional in the world."[2] When Wells wrote

> Chinese drama calls for a narrative line draw with a freedom close to that of fiction, blends naturalism with fantasy, insists on conventional morality, combines sung lyrics with chanted prose and speech, prefers pathos to tragedy and is in general clear in meaning and equable in spirit . . .[3]

with minor exceptions, he might have been writing of *Nauṭankī* as well.

The *Nauṭankī* theater is narrative in dramatic structure and operatic in style. It always tells a story, and its charm lies in its music, the lusty singing and strong instrumental accompaniment. Spoken dialogue holds a relatively minor place, for the interplay of characters is primarily through the singing. This powerful singing style grows out of a tradition of open-air performance, before crowds numbering in the thousands, in the days before electronic amplification was known. According to the testimony of old *Nauṭankī* performers, crowds of up to twenty thousand were not uncommon. The singer needed strength and endurance for a performance that lasted five or six hours. In fact they still do.

A *Nauṭankī* performance is announced by the *nakkāras,* a set of two kettle drums, one large and the other small, which are struck with sticks. These drums, played for an extended period before the performances are an effective public announcement, for the distinctive pattern of drumming can be heard for miles around.[4]

After the preliminary music by the orchestra, which also includes a harmonium or two and a *dholak* (a drum with two heads of equal size), the performance begins with the opening prayer or *Maṅgalācaraṇ*. When the opening prayer is finished, the stage manager (*Raṅgā*) immediately begins the story of the play, except when there is a preliminary variety show consisting of song, dance, and comic sketches.

After each verse of the song, the sound of the *nakkara* fills the interval and signals the singers to begin anew. Women performers and male impersonators often insert bits of dance during the drumming interval.

Three or four comic interludes, which are generally not written into the script, are standard features of any performance. Slapstick, double entendres, misapprehension, boasting, cowardice, stupidity, and gluttony are the standard ingredients of the comic routines.

Such is the nature of a *Nauṭankī* performance. When we look at the structure and form of this theater, certainly it departs from any Western notion of the well-made play; indeed, it is far from the theater of realism, which was the prevailing context in which Brecht entered the theater and against which he protested. Of course, Brecht, in his admiration of Chinese acting technique, says nothing about the form of Chinese theater. In spite of his silence in this regard, some of his plays show a striking similarity to the structure of the Chinese theater. The measure of this similarity can be seen by comparing two of his more popular plays, *The Good Woman of Setzuan* and *The Caucasian Chalk Circle,* with Chinese plays.[5] Both of Brecht's plays and Chinese traditional plays follow a common pattern: (1) The character appears and introduces himself/herself and (2) supplies a framework of time and circumstance. This is done simply and directly rather than through expositional dialogue as one would expect in a representational play. (3) The introductory speech also expresses the circumstances from which the plot will grow. (4) Immediately the character(s) who is (are) being waited for and who will set the plot in motion appear(s). The action that follows is rather loose and episodic, not tightly woven, as in an Ibsen play, for instance.

Indian *Nauṭankī*, like Chinese opera, is also susceptible to a Brechtian analysis in regard to its form. The plays are narrative and story-centered and do not press implacably to their climax; sometimes the story meanders and the audience is allowed to savor the pleasures that a detour may afford. That is to say, Aristotle's unity of action is not their main concern. They more nearly correspond to Brecht's concept of epic theater, a term he used to make clear his departure from Aristotle's dictum that the drama and the epic are different orders of literary creations. Aristotle defined tragedy (and by implication all drama) as the imitation of an action. By making action the definitive aspect of drama, he gave prime weight to the plot, the structuring of action to lead to a climactic moment of revelation.

Brecht's objection to this kind of play was that, when successful, it drew the spectators into such an empathetic relationship with what was happening on stage that they became prey to their emotions. He wanted his audience to maintain enough emotional distance to be able to think (and ultimately act) on what the play revealed to them.

> The spectator was no longer in any way allowed to submit to an experience uncritically (and without practical consequences) by means of simple empathy with the characters in a play. The production took the subject matter and the incidents shown and put them through a process of alienation: the alienation that is necessary to all understanding. When something seems "the most obvious thing in the world" it means that any attempt to understand the world has been given up.[6]

While *Nauṭankī* plays resemble Brecht's prescription in structure, they depart from it in dealing with emotion. In Indian traditional theater, the emphasis is always on impact and not on action. The imparting of flavor (*rasa*) is the aim of these plays; so a play frequently forgoes action in order to wring from a moment its full flavor or essence, its *rasa*. The aim of the play is not simply to evoke the emotional state, but to allow it to be savored. In *Arjuna's Vow*, the dominant *rasa* is the pathetic one. The action is slight; the news of the slaying of Arjuna's son, Abhimanyu, in battle allows the audience to experience the pathos that this event unleashes. In turn, members of Abhimanyu's family, his uncle Yudhisthira, his wife Uttara, his mother Subhadra, his grandmother Kurti, and Draupadi, wife of the Pandava brothers, lament while the action remains suspended. This is not the stuff of Aristotelian action; it is also not Brechtian, since such an emotional outpouring is precisely what he would have avoided. In dealing with character, however, *Nauṭankī* plays share a great deal with Brecht's. The characters here, like Brecht's, are simple, uncomplicated, and two-dimensional (e.g., the wicked king; the grasping whore; the virtuous, ever-faithful wife; the pure young man). The play is not a vehicle for the gradual revelation of character, for self-knowledge and decisive change as in an Ibsenian play. *In A Doll's House,* we see Nora transformed from a doll/child at the opening of the action to a woman (person) at its conclusion, and that decisive change is forced on her by the revelation of the true character of her husband and what she has allowed herself to become. In the play, we see the process of her becoming aware of the flawed nature of their relationship. Brecht's characters, as we have noted, tend to be simple and two-dimensional. Without interior exposition, they exist without the shadows and nuances that define a character in the naturalistic mode. Brecht's concept of the gest, while intended mainly to affect acting, has some relation to his conception of character. This difficult concept, which Brecht explains as the social attitudes that characters adopt toward one another,[7] reflects a fixed, agreed-upon point of view. "The social gest is the gest relevant to society, the gest that allows conclusions to be drawn about social circumstances."[8] As Brecht describes it, we are reminded of the neoclassical idea of abstraction, generality, the normative characteristic of a class or group. The application of such a concept results in the stereotyping of characters who behave according to established notions of propriety or decorum, to use two neoclassical terms. Ironically, the concept also brings to mind the social attitudes expressed in the Confucian statement of the fivefold relationship.[9]

In *Nauṭankī,* the basic character of the hero/heroine is established at the outset and the action of the play is a justification of that characterization rather than a revelation of it. For example, in *Satyāvadi Harīścandra,* Harīścandra, ruler of Ayodhya, is described at the beginning of the play as an upright, just, and truthful man, always generous. He was respected by his subjects and blessed by God. The series of horrible events that follow, at the instigation of the god Indra, test Hariścandra to the limit, but he remains true to character to the end. Finally, ordered to slay his wife, he is about to do so when God intervenes. "Hariścandra, you have been tested and found a most just, honest and upright man. Your name will be written in the books of heaven and you will always be remembered in this world as a most righteous man."[10]

Likewise in *Pūran Mal,* the young hero never wavers in his probity when he becomes the object of desire of his father's young second wife. He rejects her approaches, and in revenge she accuses him to his father of improper conduct. His moral stance derives both from strength of inner character and respect for the dharma of his society. On the other side, Phulande, his stepmother, is not shown to us as a tragic Phaedra, tortured and destroyed by passion. The play does not take us inside these characters so that we feel their struggle and conflict. The point of the play is not exploration or revelation of character, but the reinforcement of moral teaching through the justification of the hero. The emphasis is not on action, but the end of the action.

Imparting morals is an important part of what the play is. Here again there are striking parallels with Brecht, whose plays are characterized by didactic moralizing.[11] In the epilogue of *The Good Woman of Setzuan*, a character speaks these words to the audience:

> It is for you to find a way, my friends,
> To help good men arrive at happy ends.
> *You* write a happy ending to the play!
> There must, there must, there's got to be a way.[12]

Brecht's moralizing, however, seeks *change* in accepted norms.

Nauṭankī plays are full of moral teachings that mostly serve to undergird the traditional values of Hindu society even while titillating their audiences by depicting immoral human actions and circumstances. For example, a number of plays reinforce traditional male and female roles in Hindu society by depicting the faithfulness of wives in spite of the errings of their husbands. Plays like *Bhikārin* (*Beggar Woman*) and *Bahu Begum* (*Wife*) are built around the circumstance in which the hero becomes romantically involved with a beautiful prostitute. The husband in each case endangers the well-being of his family and household in order to satisfy the demands of the prostitute. The wife in each instance goes to extremes (from a Western viewpoint) to save the husband's honor and the marriage. At the end of *Bhikārin*, the husband begs forgiveness, and the wife replies, "What I have done for you is only what is the first duty of every wife. Give thanks to God; we can go home happy."[13]

In these plays, there is also a moral warning against becoming involved with prostitutes.

> The beautiful prostitute is . . . the bank bill of exchange. Whoever brings notes form his strong box will eventually be beaten and chased away. The one who today presses him lovingly to her bosom, gives herself to whomever has gold. . . .

As soon as the gold is finished, the prostitute looks elsewhere. Then the poor man exclaims, "Now life is miserable." This is the business of prostitutes; do not fall into their trap.[14]

Another social theme dealt with in a number of *Nauṭankī* plays is the evil of child marriage. The practice, which was common in an earlier period, was under attack by reformers from the nineteenth century on. Young girls were often wed to men several times their age. Not only was the match unequal[15] but, in the event of the husband's death, the young girl suffered all the disabilities of a widow in Hindu society. The abuses of child marriage were somewhat mitigated by the Sarla Act (1929), which prohibited the marriage of girls below the age of 14, but the scripts of the period indicate that child marriage was still a problem.

Śrī Kṛṣṇa Pahalvan's *Ānkh Kā Jādu* (*Trick of the Eye*), written in 1920 and '21, deals with this problem. Apparently the subject was popular, for the play ran for 27 consecutive days in Bareilly District. Natharam's play *Saṅgīt Katle-Śauhar* (*The Play of the Husband's Murder*) begins in this uncompromising fashion:

> O my friends, very evil times have come,
> India's boat is sinking in the sea of sin,
> Those who covet wealth nowadays have no fear of sin.
> Old men are wedding young virgins.
> Some, already wealthy, are coveting wealth
> and are marrying off their young daughters in childhood.
> From this mismating what will be the future result?
> Many will suffer the sad fate of child widows.
> And some will become prostitutes to be sure.
> But living itself will be great misfortune.
> Whoever gives his daughter in such a match is her enemy.
> He never thinks of his honor nor reputation
> In this connection I will tell you a story.

Nauṭankī plays, then, are didactic to a degree. A moral lesson is frequently given and in very clear terms. Here they clearly exceed Brecht's didactics, for his "message" is sometimes so indirect that it may be missed. One cannot otherwise account for his popularity in the capitalist West. The message is so subtle that an anticommunist public finds no offense in him.[16]

Of course, the *Nauṭankī* plays can afford their directness, for, unlike Brecht, they tend to reinforce rather than attack traditional values and views.

Brecht clearly sees that the distance that exists between the contexts of various historical theater genres may make their usability problematical. For example, he readily acknowledges that the style and tendencies of his epic theater have forerunners in medieval mysteries, and Elizabethan, Spanish, and other theaters, but he sees these latter as separated from the former by their objectives.

> It is well known that the Chinese theatre uses a lot of symbols. Thus a general will carry little pennants on his shoulder, corresponding to the number of regiments under his command. Poverty is shown by patching the silken costumes with irregular shapes of different colours, likewise silken, to indicate that they have been mended. Characters are distinguished by particular masks, i.e., simply by painting. Certain gestures of the two hands signify the forcible opening of a door, etc. The stage itself remains the same, but the articles of furniture are carried in during the action. All this has long been known, and cannot very well be exported.[17]

Although Brecht writes off a great deal—convention and, by implication, form—he seizes upon the actor's technique as a very useful, transportable element for realizing the theater he desires. Given his conviction about the relationship of form and historical context, how can the acting technique of such a theater be useful? Brecht answers in the following way:

> It is not entirely easy to realize that the Chinese actor's A-effect is a transportable piece of technique: a conception that can be prised loose from the Chinese theatre. We see this theatre as uncommonly precious, its portrayal of human passions as schematized, its idea of society as rigid and wrongheaded; at first sight this superb art seems to offer nothing applicable to a realistic and revolutionary theatre.
>
> The Chinese artist's performance often strikes the Western actor as cold. That does not mean that the Chinese theatre rejects all representation. The performer portrays incidents of utmost passion, but without his delivery becoming heated. . . . The coldness comes from the actor's holding himself remote from the character portrayed. . . . He is careful not to make its sensations into those of the spectator.[18]

Looking at the *Nauṭankī* style of acting through Brecht's critical vision, we recognize some aspects of this coolness, this alienation ("making strange") effect in it also. The actor's art is usually displayed on a simple platform stage enclosed with canvas backdrop and sides. Or there may be only the bare platform, in which case, the audience sits on all sides of it. In either case, there is no mistaking that the stage is a stage.

This kind of stage calls for a different kind of acting. In earlier days, before the advent of microphones and amplifiers, the audience commonly sat on all four sides, and the actors were obliged to sing each line four times, once on each side of the stage. Even today, one occasionally encounters such a performance. In such situations, the actors keep moving in a circular fashion around the stage, and the intervals between the lines are filled with snatches of the dance, which has come to characterize *Nauṭankī*. Generally that dance, whether done by female performers or male impersonators, is erotically suggestive. The dance, therefore, may be quite foreign to the character of the individual being portrayed. This would probably have intrigued Brecht, for it achieves an alienation effect that is striking. As audience, we are constantly reminded that the actor is *showing* the character, but is not himself the character.

That the audience understands and accepts this convention is made clear by offerings of money made by spectators during performance following a song or dance that someone finds especially pleasing. The performer troupe leader accepts the money and then and there publicly acknowledges it. The leader or the performer will announce, "Mr. X of (place) has given X (amount) of rupees in appreciation of the fine singing of Y (name of actor). We thank him sincerely." Sometimes the words of thanks are improvised in song on the spot, and the song may be punctuated by a drum beat and grind and bump of the performer's hips! The performance then resumes where it was interrupted.

Nauṭankī performers are traditionally all male, and the female roles are played by males in female makeup. This gives an added dimension to the alienation ("making strange") effect, for though the female makeup is usually skillfully done, no attempt is made to disguise the male voice.[19]

Since the late 1930s, female performers have been introduced into *Nauṭankī*. With rare exceptions, these actresses have not mastered the traditional *Nauṭankī* music, and their repertory is restricted to film tunes. Indeed, their presence in *Nauṭankī* is mainly to compete with the glamor of the silver screen. In most cases, the female performers, considered by the public as prostitutes, provide prelude and interlude of dancing and singing; usually they lip-synch the words to popular film songs and dance in showy costumes.

The alienation effect is most evident in the singing of the songs that are characteristic of *Nauṭankī*. Brecht made abundant use of songs in his plays and directed the actors not to "drop into" a song but let it be clearly marked off from the rest of the text.[20] This intended to emphasize the episodic nature of Brecht's plays and at the same time provided a comment that served to stimulate the audience to think rather than experience emotion and/or empathy.

> For its part, the music must strongly resist the smooth incorporation which is generally expected of it and turns it into an unthinking slave. . . . It cannot simply "express itself" by discharging the emotion with which the incidents of the play have filled it![21]

Another feature that serves to inhibit the climactic and illusionistic effect in *Nauṭankī* is the comic interludes, three or four of which are inserted into each performance. The comic interludes are usually not written into the scripts and generally are not related to the action of the play being performed. They are generally improvised by actors for whom they are a specialty. In the hey day of *Nauṭankī*, each *akhara* or troupe had members who were skilled in creating clever comic interludes. This feature is still popular with audiences today.

Brecht's use of the allied arts—song, dance—are intended to disassemble the theater of identification, supported by Stanislavskian acting methods, by shifting "the focus from the character themselves to what happens between them."[22] Rouse observes that Brecht concentrated on the sociological behavioral aspects of characterization. This draws our attention to a basic assumption underlying the playwright's work:

> The Brechtian theatre's most fundamental principle is its commitment to *social change* [italics added]. The dramaturgical principle most basic to fulfilling this commitment is, in turn, that theatre must attempt to present society and human nature as changeable.[23]

It is in this basic commitment that Śrī Kṛṣṇa's *Nauṭankī* is most foreign to Brecht's dramaturgy. While Brecht's theater was politically revolutionary in having social change as its ultimate objective, Śrī Kṛṣṇa's *Nauṭankī* was not socially revolutionary, though it was in a sense political. His plays, far from attacking traditional values and views, tend to reinforce them. Śrī Kṛṣṇa, the leading shaper of the Kanpur style, did use *Nauṭankī* effectively in the political arena. It is in his career that we can see that *Nauṭankī* is capable of accomplishing what Brecht wished for but seemed not to have succeeded in actually doing: moving men and women to political action for change.

Brecht seems always to have been something of a political misfit throughout the most influential years of his adult life. During the years of his exile spent in the United States, 1941 to 1948, his Marxism made him suspect. In 1947, he was called before the dreaded House Un-American Activities Committee, where he denied forcefully that he was ever a member of the Communist Party. His plays, which were sly but strong indictments of the capitalist system, war, greed, and profiteering, were probably too subtle for his American audiences to grasp their ideological bent. This was made easier by the fact that, in some productions of his most popular plays, the prologues and epilogues, which spelled out the moral teaching more clearly, were not used.

In 1949, he returned to East Berlin to become artistic director of the Berliner Ensemble. Under a regime in which the revolution had supposedly already occurred, what was he to say? In spite of his efforts to hew a true Marxist line, his work was met with faint praise and sometimes sharp criticism within the communist world.[24]

Śrī Kṛṣṇa, by contrast, was able to use his *Nauṭankī* plays to engage in the struggle to free India from British tyranny. His first work was under the sponsorship of the Ārya Samāj, a conservative, militant Hindu reform group that glorifies traditional Hindu culture and seeks to strip away all Western and other foreign accretions.

His first play is entitled *Haḳīḳatrāi* and tells the story of a young Hindu boy who remains steadfastly true to his faith even though it results in his death.

After the boy, Haḳīḳatrāi, has mastered Sanskrit, his father, Bagmal, sends him to study Urdu with a Muslim *Maulvi*. One day when the teacher is absent, one of the Muslim boys falsely accuses Haḳīḳatrāi of having made insulting remarks about the Islamic religion. This is reported to the teacher who takes him before the magistrate (*Kāzī*). The sentence for this offense is determined to be death. The mother and father plead for the boy's life but to no avail. His case is referred to the governor. He offers Haḳīḳatrāi one way to save his life: accept the Islamic faith. The boy refuses. His parents come and also try to persuade him to accept this way out, but he adamantly refuses. He is tempted with material wealth but remains steadfast. Finally, the governor, unable to shake his resolve, orders his execution. Before he wields the sword, the executioner says

> Blessed are you, son of Bhārat,
> For you have upheld the Vedic religion.

The author closes with an exhortation to his listeners:

> Friends, behold Haḳīḳat's faithfulness;
> With his very life he guarded the Vedic religion.
> My message is this: do not give up your faith. Victory
> to Dayānand. The story is finished.[25]

The Rail Bazaar Ārya Samāj, Kānpur, printed thousands of copies of the play and distributed them without charge. The reception this play received inspired Śrī Kṛṣṇa and made him famous. In 1913, he formed his own performing company, and *Haḳīḳatrāi* was its first production. His success as a writer, producer, and publisher of *Nauṭankī* scripts placed him in the front ranks of this theater for three decades. To this early period also belongs his play *Chhatrapati Śivājī,* based on the life of the great Maratha Hindu opponent of the Moghuls.

The story of Śivājī ranks among the first in restoring Indian national pride and inspiring struggle against oppression. During the Muslim emperor Aurangzeb's rule, Śivājī carved out a Hindu kingdom in the southern Indian plateau and established the Marātha nation.[26] With a mixture of shrewdness, daring, and brilliance, he ignited a national revolt that was to inspire Indians for generations to come.

Chhatrapati Śivājī, written in a period of increasing Indian struggle against the British, gave the common people a national hero. The play, which deals with the assault upon Singhagarh Fort, illuminates the courage of the Marātha warriors and adds a note of pathos at the loss of Tannasingh, Śivājī's trusted lieutenant.

By 1927, Śrī Kṛṣṇa had imbibed the influence of the great nationalist leader, Bal Gangadhar Tilak who was given the title *"Lokmanya"* ("Respected by the people"). Tilak at that point represented the revolutionary, or radical, wing of the Indian Congress forces agitating for Indian freedom from British rule. This was not an ideological change of direction for Śrī Kṛṣṇa, for Tilak represented an extremely conservative, sometimes reactionary Hindu nationalism quite compatible with the Ārya Samājist views that influenced Śrī Kṛṣṇa earlier. For the next decade, he was deeply involved in the work of the Congress Party. He used his pen and his troupe to bring the message to the villagers of North India. During the Non-Cooperation movement of 1920–21, Śrī Kṛṣṇa wrote a play called *Non-Cooperation Pickles* (*Asahayogya Chatni*), which he sold for a pice or two per copy in villages and towns.[27] With his plays on patriotic and nationalist themes, he helped elect officials in the political campaigns of 1922 and 1926.

It was in this period that he wrote his famous *Khūn-e-Nāhak* (*The Senseless Massacre*), which was produced on the stage of the Baikunth Talkies in Mulganj, Kanpur. The play was based on an infamous and tragic incident that occurred in Amritsar on April 13, 1919. On that day, some 10,000 persons—men, women, and children—were gathered in a public garden, in contravention of General Dyer's order prohibiting mass meetings. The order had been issued on the day before to counter Indian agitation against the Rowlatt Acts, which gave "preventive detention" powers to the British rulers in India. General Dyer drove with 50 soldiers to the walled garden and deployed his men across the one entrance. At his command and without a word of warning, they opened fire on the crowd. After ten minutes, they had expended their ammunition—some 1,650 rounds—and 400 people lay dead and 1,200 more wounded.[28] It was a fusillade that united India and galvanized diverse elements to unity in the national cause.

The reenactment of the drama within a few years of its occurrence must have had a powerful impact upon its audiences. The spirit of the play is expressed in these lines, which refer to the repressions used to control Indian agitation:

> Such atrocities shake the foundations of justice.
> In the garden of India the harvest is ripe;
> Now we are the sacrifice offered for our country
> We shall face the bullets and sleep in the breast of
> our motherland.[29]

In contrast with his earlier period, Śrī Kṛṣṇa points to the unity between Hindus and Muslims in the common struggle. The characters depicted in the play include both Hindus and Muslims who enjoy the festive occasion as one.[30] They share a common hardship and a common rededication to India's liberation. A Hindu woman roving over the body-strewn park gives water to a dying Muslim man and counts him among the true sons of Hindustān.

The impact of the play was such that the British police placed Śrī Kṛṣṇa under strict surveillance. He paid no heed to this, but presented this play again in Najibabad (Bijnaur). Finally, by order of the collector, he was compelled to leave Bareilly District.[31]

The play *Baliyā Kā Śer* comes from a later period. It is based on the 1940 Satyāgraha movement, but the spirit of resistance is expressed in even stronger terms. The *Rangāćāra* (narrator) announces at the outset that his subject is freedom, and the play opens with a women's procession led by Śilādevi. As the crowd shouts—and doubtless the audience joined then—"Long live the Revolution" ("*Inkallābzindabād*"), Śilādevi admonishes her companions:

> What calamity must be undergone, we will accept.
> We will not be daunted even if they cut off our heads.
> We will not moderate our call for freedom even if we must
> die . . . If in this service we must give our lives,
> Our names will be written eternally with the martyrs.
> The pure white *Khaddar*
> Shall cover our wounded bodies
> And on our coffins with our own blood shall be written,
> "Bandemātaram!"[32]

The procession is soon halted by the police, and, upon their refusal to disperse, the women are arrested. The words of Śilādevi seem intended for the audience watching:

> Here is a lesson which if you remember
> Our motherland shall be free of bondage.
> If you irrigate the land with your blood,
> Then the lovely garden of India shall be free.
> The blows upon your head,
> Which show love like Farhād's for Shirīn,
> Will free our mother from her pain.
> If you form a courageous army,
> And remain undaunted, unafraid,
> This tyranny will be wiped from the face of the earth.[33]

Śilādevi's example inspires a boy Surajkumār to enter the struggle. Eventually he is jailed. Like a string of lighted firecrackers, the spark passes from one to another. One after another, the characters of the play opt for the lathi-charge and jail on behalf of the nation. Ćittū Pānde urges government workers to plant the Congress flag over the court buildings, police stations, and post offices and to perform other acts in defiance of British raj. The heroes of the play die for the advancement of their country with the cry *"Jai Hind!"* ("Long live India!") on their lips.

In conclusion, it is clear that Śrī Kṛṣṇa, through his writing and staging of *Nauṭankī* plays, contributed to the struggle for independence in India, and there is evidence that these plays had a measurable effect.

These plays of Śrī Kṛṣṇa, though they are cast in a form that bears a strong resemblance to Brecht's plays and they employ an acting technique of some similarity to Brecht's as well, differ in some important ways. They draw heavily upon emotion, which instead of being kept disciplined, is nourished and drawn out until its full *rasa* (flavor) is savored. Further, in the "political" plays of Śrī Kṛṣṇa, cool analysis is set aside, and a fervent emotional call to action is issued. It should be said that history was kinder to Śrī Kṛṣṇa than to Bertolt Brecht. The former found his moment in history and made his theater count toward the liberation of his country. Brecht, for reasons described above, never found that happy moment or place in which his work could speak to bring the change he desired.

Notes

1. John Willett, ed. and trans., *Brecht on Theatre* (New York: Hill and Wang, 1964), pp. 94, 99.
2. Henry W. Wells, *The Classical Drama of the Orient* (New York: Asia Publishing House, 1965) p.5.
3. Wells, p. 5.
4. The *nakkāra* has a traditional association with temple ceremonies, large ceremonial processions, and congregations and with group dancing.
5. Brecht makes no attempt to represent accurately the settings of these plays. Rather, he uses the historification technique to distance the situation from his audience in order to reduce empathy. *The Good Woman* is set in Setzuan, a Chinese province (not a city), and *Chalk Circle* is based on a Chinese story.
6. Willett, p. 71.

7. Willett, p. 198.
8. Willett, pp. 104–105.
9. The Confucian fivefold relationship may be stated as follows:

   The father is loving; the son is reverential.

   The older brother is gentle; the younger brother is respectful.

   The husband is good; the wife is listening.

   The elder friend is considerate; the younger friend is deferential.

   The ruler is benevolent; the subject is loyal.

10. Harīścandra may be considered a culture hero of Hindu, India. Śrī Kṛṣṇa, Sangīt Satyāradi Harīścandra (Kānpur: Śrī Kṛṣṇa Khatrī, n.d.).
11. In his later years, Brecht seems to have backed away from his earlier view of the theater as an instrument of instruction to assert that its first aim is to entertain. (See "A Short Organum for the Theatre," Willett, p. 180.) The fact that he does not forswear an objective of social change leaves one to wonder how significant his change of view was or whether it was a matter of political expedience. (See Willett, pp. 274–275).
12. Bertolt Brecht, *The Good Woman of Setzuan.* Revised English version by Eric Bentley in the anthology *Drama,* ed. by Otto Rienert (Boston, Toronto, 1966). pp. 477–548.
13. Śrī Kṛṣṇa, *Sangīt Bhikārin* (Kānpur: Śrī Kṛṣṇa Khatrī, 1965), p. 48.
14. Śrī Kṛṣṇa, *Bhikārin* (Kānpur: Śrī Kṛṣṇa Khatrī, 1965), p.2.
15. Cf. the situation in *Pūran Mal* where the father marries a young second wife.
16. His postwar productions in an area ruled by a communist regime also show some relinquishing of his earlier objective.
17. Willett, p. 91.
18. Willett, p. 95.
19. Willett, p. 197.
20. Willett, p. 203.
21. Willett, p. 203.
22. John Rouse, *Brecht and the West German Theatre* (Ann Arbor: V.M.I. Research Press, London, 1989), p. 30.
23. Rouse, p. 40.
24. Martin Esslin, *Brecht: The Man and His Work* (Garden City, New York: Anchor Books, 1961), pp. 149–198.
25. *Sangit Haḳīḳatrāi* (Kānpur: Śrī Kṛṣṇa Khatrī, 1957), p. 32. The reference is to Swāmi Dayānand Sarasvati, the founder of the Ārya Samāj.
26. Stanley Wolpert, *India* (Englewood Cliffs, N.J., 1965), p. 61.
27. Unfortunately, I could not find a copy of this play, but it is clear from

the title and what has been written about it that it supported the Non-Cooperation movement against British rule.

28. Wolpert, *India,* pp. 125–127.
29. Śrī Kṛṣṇa, *Khun-e-Nāhak* (Kānpur: Śrī Kṛṣṇa Khatrī, 1947), p. 4.
30. Śrī Kṛṣṇa, *Khun-e-Nāhak,* p. 6.
31. From biographical note on the program at the presentation of an award to Śrī Kṛṣṇa by the Sangeet Natak Akademi on February 22, 1968.
32. Śrī Kṛṣṇa, *Baliyā Kā Śer* (Kānpur: Śrī Kṛṣṇa Khatrī, 1948), pp. 2f.
33. Śrī Kṛṣṇa, *Baliyā Kā Śer,* p. 5

11

Caste, Race, and Nation: History and Dialectic in Rabindranath Tagore's *Gora*

Lalita Pandit

Tagore's *Gora*, named after its main character, is a novel about an Irish foundling raised by Bengali Brahmin parents in colonial India. Tagore's biographer, Krishna Kripalani, has speculated that the character of Gora is based in part on Sister Nivedita (Margaret Noble), an Irish woman who became a disciple of Swami Vivekananda. Nivedita had unwavering enthusiasm for Hinduism and used to preach Hindu orthodoxy to Tagore. Tagore was himself a dialectical product of Hindu orthodoxy and the liberalism of the early Brahmo Samaj. Nivedita's adopted Hindutava provides, as if an objective correlative for Tagore's nonimperialist, abstractly utopian idea of universalism. Since many anticolonial critiques of culture equate universalism with imperialism, it is important to remember that Tagore's universalism is different and it refers to a moral/intellectual/emotional discipline based on the principle of empathy. The imperialistic notion of universalism, in contrast, is nonempathic, fixed, and hegemonic. The imperialist universalist expects to see only its own reflection in the Other, tests the value and validity of the Other solely in terms of an already established normative self. In its most aggressive forms, it seeks to annihilate the Other. Tagore's universalist philosophy developed as an antidote to this annihilating, nonassimilative, separatist universalism.

In his own writings, his teaching and educational reform, he sought to synthesize Indian and Western modes of thought. The adoption of Western ways by Indians becomes problematic only because this transformation occurs within a framework of polarized hierarchies that serve the aims and goals of the colonizer. In their defiant adherence to Indianness or in their pursuit of Westernization, colonized Indians are constituted only as means that serve the ends of the raj. Thus the history of colonialism forecloses the possibility of free choice in either direction.

In *Gora,* Tagore explores various dimensions of the biocultural genesis of the universalist human self in a novel that Krishna Kripalani has rightly described as the epic "of India in transition" (207–209). The novel was first serialized in a Bengali language journal in 1907. By 1910, it was translated into English by the author himself. Tagore's Gora does not only incorporate the contradictions of caste and race; this hybrid figure makes the dividing lines between the nation and the world blurry. Tagore's constitution of Gora as the "universal man" has a certain intellectual beauty and humanistic value; at the same time, it is implicated in the politics of race, caste, religion, and class. In the following pages, I should like to place a discussion of Tagore's novel, which is about growing up in the late colonial period, in the contexts of history and dialectic that are necessary for understanding the subtext(s) of culture and politics that shape the aesthetic structure of this text.

In Bengal and in the rest of India, the novel has consistently enjoyed immense popularity. When they first appeared, the English versions of several of Tagore's novels, for example, *The Wreck, Gora,* and *The Home and the World,* were read in England and America as if they had originally been written in English. It was under this misconception that E. M. Forster wrote an unflattering review of *The Home and the World,* criticizing it for its language and style, evidently unaware of the fact that the novel was originally written in Bengali for a Bengali audience. Isolating several sentences from the novel, "Babu sentences" as he called them, Forster claimed to find a consistent imbalance of sophistication and vulgarity, which vitiated the novel (Lago *Tagore* 124). This review and similar responses by other critics were at least partly responsible for the subsequent lack of enthusiasm for Tagore's novels in the West. In India, however, all of his 10 novels, written between 1883 and 1934, are widely read. Amongst those who read Tagore in his linguistic and historical context, there is little or no talk of vulgar "Babu sentences," even among readers who read him in English.

Besides being critiqued for his language, Tagore was stereotyped in the West as the mystic of the East. The devotional song lyrics of his *Gitanjali* and his other poetic works solidified this reputation. A review of *The Gardener*, published in *The Baptist Times*, confuses the elements of Vaiśnav Bakhti in Tagore's writing with affirmations of Christian devotional sentiments. The reviewer enthusiastically remarks, "We have been waiting anxiously for some indication of the effect of Christian ideas on a truly representative Hindu Mind. Here, surely is the person we have been longing for—one sent from the chariot of the Lord to make his path straight" (Kripalani 231). The Vaiśanavaite piety and Buddhist humanism of Tagore's devotional poetry is equated with Christian piety. In any case, the excessive emphasis on the religious aspects of Tagore's poetry was problematic. It made the non-Indian readers less accepting of the polemical nature of his fictional writing, and it made the theology of Tagore's poetry appear as an "obscure" mass of Eastern mysticism purified of all pagan aspects by the refracting rays of Christianity.

The second factor that could have led to misreadings of Tagore's fiction was the inevitable associative connection of *Gora* with *Kim*. Such an association would have harmed the reception of the novel at a time when Kipling's versions of Indian society and the Indian personality were regarded by many Western critics/readers as authentic, unbiased representations. Whatever stray grains of authenticity and sincerity might be visible in between, representations of Indians in Kipling's early journalistic writings are straightforwardly racist and imperialist. Even in *Plain Tales*, he refers to the educated Indian as the "hybrid, university educated mule" and the illiterate native "as timid as a colt." Kipling consistently evoked sets of imperialist beliefs about the Indian Mind, the Eurasian Mind, and so forth. He describes the latter as "the borderline where the last drop of White Blood ends and the full tide of Black sets in. . . . The Black and White mix very quaintly in their ways. Sometimes the White shows in spurts of fierce childish pride—which is the Pride of Race run crooked—and sometimes the Black in still fiercer abasement and humility, half-heathenish customs and strange, unaccountable impulses to crime" (*Indian Tales* 73).

In his earlier news writing, Kipling continually offers analysis of "native" behavior, character, habits, and handwriting to construct ideologically informed explanations for newsworthy catastrophes and to provide daily bites of native lore for his leisured Anglo-Indian readers. He speaks of the "clinging dependence of the native on the Anglo Indian," of the native's "slackness," "incompetence," "stupidity," and "dishonesty." Often, in slandering the personality patterns of Indians, the young Kipling employs his brilliant powers of irony, wit, and his very "English" humor to invent a journalistic discourse that is singlemindedly dedicated to the task of documenting vices/defects/flaws that years of Anglo-Indian conversations at tea parties and *bura khanas* (formal dinners) had accumulated around the figure of the "native." In these discourses, the "native" is often seen as lacking, fragmentary, only partially human, and different in some absolute way. In "The City of Evil Countenances" (see Pinney 81), Kipling takes a deeper plunge; here he temporarily departs from recounting the defects of character and produces a more sinister representation of the people of Peshawar:

> Under the shop lights from the sweet-meat and *ghee* seller's booths, the press and din of words is thickest. Faces of dogs, swine, weazels and goats, all the more hideous for being set on human bodies, and lighted with human intelligence, gather in front of the ring of lamplight, where they may be studied for half an hour at a stretch. Pathans, Afreedees, Logas, Kohistanis, Turkomans, and a hundred other varieties of the turbulent Afgan race, are gathered in the vast human menagerie between the Gate and the Ghor Khutri. As an Englishman passes they will turn around to scowl upon him, and in many cases to spit fluently on the ground after he has passed. (Pinney 83)

At least the natives of "the city of evil countenances" show resentment toward Englishmen, not the "clinging" dependence Kipling speaks of elsewhere. This conjuration of the sinister aspect of the "native Other" relects the nightmarish dread that most of his Anglo-Indian readers would have shared with him: the dread that made them send their small children home to England to be raised by hired foster parents. Kipling's journalistic writings mirror the schizophrenic psyche of the colonizers, a psyche that at once constitutes the natives as clinging, childlike dependents and as the threatening, "demonic" others; these constructions reflect the paternalism and the paranoia of imperialist racism. Therefore, it is not surprising that Tagore felt uncomfortable with being called the Kipling of India. The "Bengali Babu," as Kipling might have characterized someone like Tagore, did not like the fact that his novel should be abstracted into its central motif: the "poor-white boy" raised by "native" parents, acculturated in "native" ways. Such a reductionist comparison with *Kim* would have seemed inappropriate to Tagore, especially in light of Kipling's essentialist conception of the White-Indian boy (Kim) who possesses a white soul/mind, the racial nature of which remains unaltered underneath thick layers of acquired Indianness.

As a writer, Tagore's project was very different. Tagore sought to fashion the Bengali language into a sophisticated literary medium at the end of a long period of the hegemony of state languages like Sanskrit, Persian, and then English. As a socially conscious writer, he offers an internal critique of Indian society, its indigenous forms of oppression, and its marginalization of women and of lower castes/classes. His short stories that have often been critiqued in the West for not having the "single effect," a quality that Edgar Allan Poe set up as an aesthetic norm for the short story, are very successfully and powerfully dialogic. In this context, the term "dialogic" does not refer specifically to Bakhtinian dialogism, but to the technique of multimodal framing used in India's ancient arts of story telling, amply evident in works such as *The Kathā Sarita Sāgar* (the *Ocean of Stories*) and many other popular and elite story sequences. Most of Tagore's stories are spoken not in the authorial voice, but in authenticated voices of the downtrodden, the doomed and the damned of Indian society: the tragically oppressed and the marginalized. The real life prototypes for most of these voices were derived from the people Tagore came to know during the years he ran his father's estate in rural East Bengal. Some of the most poignant among these are the voices of young widowed women passing their days in a living death, poor working girls, many of whom are only children. Others are servants, old people, childless women who facilitate their beloved husband's second marriages to acquire progeny, married women doomed to waste their talents (and desires) in the claustrophobic inner quarters of rich households, adolescent "bad" boys. Tagore speaks of the isolation of sensitive small children, of low-caste Hindus and poor muslims. In giving them their own speech patterns, he developed a fictional discourse, an idiom in the vernacular language in which such voices, doomed to the silence of an age-old solitude, could be articulated.

Aesthetically, many of Kipling's fictional writings on India are indicative of a similar aim and have a similar effect. He, too, wrote about individual Indian people who are lonely and lost in the muddle of life: Tota, Mohammad Din, Ameera, Puran Bhagat, and numerous others. Like Tagore, he, too, experimented with a new idiom, inserted direct vocabulary items from Urdu and Hindustani into his English prose, and preserved the nuances of spoken Urdu in English. However, Kipling's authorial empathy is invariably mixed with his often brilliant, but ideologically grounded, satire. In his fictional transformations of Indian life, Kipling does not altogether abandon the imperialist attitude and rhetoric. Still, many of his short stories show abiding traces of genuine warmth and human fellowship. After all, India was his country of birth. He spent the first six years of his life there and learned to speak in the "native idiom" from his Indian caretakers. During this period and even later, he thought in Hindustani and dreamed in it. Some of his stories contain traces of this childhood love, which Kipling's English upbringing must have attempted to erase.

In spite of their contrary politics, diametrically opposed ideological affiliations, and mutually resisting narcissistic investments, Tagore and Kipling were both perceived in England as voices from India, producing "new writing from the colony." Their being read in relation to each other became, thus, an unavoidable legacy. The association of *Gora* with *Kim* is particularly inevitable, because each novel centers around the birth and growth of a White orphan in India, the white boy who lacks the benefit of English patronage. For the most part, such an event in colonial India could only be imagined. Most Anglo-Indians shipped their progeny out of the "heathen" land into the homes of willing relatives or hired help in England. There was a great social pressure to ground these "Indian" English children in "good Christian values," to lace them with "proper" imperialist attitudes, and to reform their speech by facilitating an early acquisition of "proper English" to prevent the damage that the differing vocal habits of Indian languages might do. In this typically Anglo-Indian fashion, Kipling and his four-year-old sister were farmed out to a Southsea suburb in England, away from the "Mahim Woods," where Kipling "loved the voices of night-winds through palm or banana leaves, and the song of the tree-frogs," where his *āyah* sang "Indian nursery songs all unforgotten," where he spoke "English" haltingly translated out of the vernacular idiom that [he] thought and dreamed in" (*Something of Myself* 4). Since a majority of the English living in India did not allow their children to stay long on Indian soil, even under parental and missionary supervision, Tagore's and Kipling's fantasy of a White orphan raised entirely by Indian parents inserts mythic reality at a place where history functions as a deterrent. In Kipling's case, there was a heavy narcissistic investment in inventing such a myth. At age six, he felt abandoned by his parents, exiled from the home and the land he had come to love. In the "House of Desolation" in Southsea, he was "regularly beaten" (*Something of Myself* 6–7). The wild freedom of Kim's growing up in India contrasts with the rigidity and deprivation of Kipling's childhood house of desolation.

Even though a comparison between *Kim* and *Gora* is unavoidable, specific differences between the two outweigh generic similarities. Tagore's Gora is not a rootless street kid like little Kim. Gora has roots in India and his Indianness is not tentative; it is definite, and its consequences are irreversible. Forced by circumstances to play hide-and-seek with the ghostlike estate of his "Sahibness," Kim lives in stolen time; growing up in India is like a fantastical holiday for him, and he finally becomes an indisposable Anglo-Indian part of the administrative machinery of the raj. Nevertheless, the two novels tell two versions of a single myth, and at the center of each is the protagonist's quest for self-definition and self-identity. For both characters, the imperialist imperative separates the agencies of nurture from the agencies of culture.

Kim knows by hearsay that he is a sahib; even this vague knowledge functions to separate him from the multitudes of India among whom and with whom he grows up. This trace of his biological origin, like a talisman, functions as a protective shield. Kipling literalizes the figure by having the pieces of evidence that prove Kim's racial origin locked in an amulet case wrapped around the boy's neck. To provide his hero double protection against the nurturing and threatening native environment, Kipling endows him with a genetically determined "white consciousness." Kim's essentially "white soul" manifests in him an instinctual dread of snakes ("the white man's horror of serpents" or "the white man's love of animal flesh-meat." When his tattered figure struts "on the brickwork plinth under the great tree," Kim's "white blood sets him upon his feet" where "a native would have lain down" (41). In contrast, Tagore's protagonist lacks any conscious or unconscious intimations of his racial origin. The phantom of "Sahibhood" that Kim has a reluctant relation to does not at all affect Gora. The secret of his birth is simply a set of facts that Tagore saves to mark the final, epiphanic moment in the life of his protagonist, who, like any protagonist in a bildungsroman, progresses from relative ignorance to self-knowledge, narrow egotism to a more expansive, fuller selfhood.

For Gora, growing up in Calcutta is neither a fantastical holiday nor a punishment; it is a stable, fully comprehensible, plausible reality. He is bound by the ties of kinship, obligation, and duty to family, society, and the nation. He is not spared the rigors of formal education, nor is he spared the colonialist ironies of growing up in India. Gora's adoptive family represents a microcosmic view of the upper-class/caste Bengali elite. The voluntary caste observances of the eccentric members in this family are varied. Gora's mother is nonorthodox; she eats food cooked by a low-caste maid servant. She is different from her husband. The novel starts at a point when her husband has decided to make a postretirement transition to the most rigid forms of orthodoxy. Gora's older brother's family live in conformity with the codes and customs of their class, yet they are all members of the same extended household. Their diverse caste preferences, their assertion of varied brands of individual faith, effectively mirror the pluralism of the Hindu way of life. At the same time, these bear witness to their privileged class status. Their prosperity makes possible separate sets of maids and servants, cooking arrangements, food taboos, and separate order of fasts and feasts. Without being grounded in wealth and status, such complicated caste observances within one family would not be possible.

Kipling's Kim enjoys a different kind of freedom, that of the very poor. As "the poorest of the poor white," Kim grows up on the streets of Lahore, learns the ways of the world from the beggars and fakirs of Taxali Gate, and "is burned black as a native" (*Kim* 1). Yet he, too, has his Indian family. He is virtually adopted by Mahoob Ali and Keshoo Lama, the horse-trading secret agent and the Buddhist monk from Tibet. The Buddhist and the Mohammadan poles of Kim's wandering family remain segregated like a pair of unpleasantly divorced parents. The half-caste woman who raised him and claims to be his aunt is already a thing of the past when the novel starts. When Kim is claimed by the mavericks, his dead mother's white origin is promptly established, and the possibility of any kinship with the half-caste woman is eliminated. At this point, the fact of Kim's unadulterated Caucasian origin is firmly established. Even prior to the discovery of his mother's white identity, Kim's half-caste pseudo-aunt had broken her bond with him when she sent him out into the wide world with his entire inheritance wrapped around his neck in a leather amulet case. The inheritance is, of course, nothing but three pieces of paper, two of which are Kimball O'Hara's "clearance certificate" and Kim's birth certificate. His father, a gangforeman on the Ferozepore railway line dies of opium addiction. Kipling's comment on the Indianized Irishman's addiction is noteworthy; he refers to "opium that is meat, tobacco and medicine to the spent Asiatic" (*Kim* 206).

The fetishized fragment of a destiny (Kim's encounter with his father's regiment)—"the Red Bull on a green field, the Colonel riding on his horse, and nine hundred devils"—springs from the drug-induced ravings of Kimball O'Hara. It is handed down to Kim by the same half-caste woman (6–7). The dead father's prophecy is processed through many minds and mouths. This results in a queer mixture of facts and fantasy, creating a web of magic and superstition. In spite of the fact that Kim is inscribed into this exotic web as an orphan child of a poor drug addict, his native "whiteness" manifests itself in his ability to draw rational conclusions from empirical evidence, and such other genetically white traits. The colonialist author's dichotomous perception of the East and the West is evidenced here; Kim's Eastern upbringing represents magic and superstition (among other things), and his Western, biological origin represents intuitive intimations of science and rationality. His father has been corrupted by the Asiatics, and he has learned from them the grandiose art of mystification. The dying Kimball O'Hara's hope that his orphan son may some day be claimed by his regiment and be looked after is offered to the reader as an enigmatic prophecy, grounded in cultural practices that are alien to Kim and his father but to which both have adapted themselves. Since they are Irish, a group of whom Kipling did not think particularly well, their greater susceptibility to India's corrupting influences seems natural from the omniscient narrator's point of view.

At a basic plot level, the total concealment of the birth and racial origin of Gora and the partial concealment of Kim's origin protect both boys from being sent to some Masonic orphanage in India. Instead, both characters come to have an adoptive Indian family. At the pristine hour of his birth in Anandmoyi's basement, Gora finds his designated place in the waiting arms of a childless Bengali woman, a highly sentimentalized mother, as benign as Kim's Lama, only more capable, the mother who becomes for Gora an emblem of India: the familiar nation that is as naturally his as it is Tagore's. Just as Gora is saved from being sent to the orphanage by the intervention of the mother, Kipling's "poor white boy" is also saved from this fate by the intervention of his Teshoo Lama. The Buddhist Lama takes it upon himself to pay the required tuition and make sure his *chela* goes to Xavier's. In this manner, even though the fake *chelā* acquires an English education at Xavier's, the Lama assumes a parental debt and pays it in full, thereby binding Kim to India (or to Tibet).

Tagore's sense of the cultural indigenousness of Gora is well expressed by the fact that his Indian readers and critics have identified Brahmobandhab Upadhyay, a revolutionary who died tragically in a British prison, as another real-life prototype for Gora. Gora's life does not end tragically, but he shares with Brahmobandhab a staunch anticolonialist commitment and revolutionary idealism. In his brief reference to *Gora*, Ashis Nandy mentions that an earlier version of Tagore's novel, *Cār Adhyāy*, had a moving preface in which Tagore made reference to the "personal tragedy of a revolutionary friend who, to fight the suffering of his people, had to move away from his own ideas of *svabhāva* and *svadharma*" (*Intimate Enemy* 8). This revolutionary friend is no doubt Brahmobandhab, and, in *Gora*, Tagore deals with the alienation of the colonial as well as anticolonial Indians and the paradoxes of self-definition that Ashis Nandy explores in his discussion of the psychology of colonialism.

In addition, Nandy thinks that Gora's hypermasculinity, his robust physicality, is immediately reminiscent of Brahmobandhab. He sees the exaggerated emphasis on masculinity as one of the many modes of self-definition and self-production in colonial India. According to Nandy, the construction of masculinity as a necessary virtue is part of the patriarchal ideology carried over from imperialist modes of thought (*Intimate Enemy* 6–8). To patriotic Indians, masculinity also represents the strength that would free India from foreign rule and afterwards help in nation building. This may all be true, but the emphasis on masculinity has roots in Indian culture as well, and it has traditionally been associated with the virtue of masculine asceticism. The virtue of asceticism becomes sharply defined in ancient India as the hegemonic intentions and motives of patriarchal structures work themselves into the cultural discourses. In any case, the narrative logic of the Brahmobandhab connection in *Gora* goes far beyond the advocacy and critique of the masculinity obsession in its colonial and precolonial contexts. The Brahmobandhab allusion sets up a historical referent that adds metaphorical resonance to Gora's character, his speeches and writings. This resemblance ultimately renders the fact of his biological (racial) origin irrelevant. His character is taken over completely by the complex and paradoxical, the immense reality of growing up in British India as a Hindu Indian, not as a sahib, not even as a Bengali babu. Seeing Tagore's Indianized bildungsroman hero as a fictionalized Brahmobandhab helps to distance *Gora* from the imperialist context of Kipling's India and situates this literary figure in the anticolonialist contexts of Keshob Sen's, Tagore's, and Vivekananda's India. Since Brahmobandhab's life serves as an allegory for parts of all their lives, a brief summary of it would allow us to have a clearer understanding of the narrative logic and the political implications of Tagore's text.

Brahmobandhab's real name was Bhawani Charan Bannerji, and he was born in 1861. Coincidentally, Tagore was born in the same year. Brahmobandhab's mother and father died when the boy was still very young, he was brought up mainly by his uncle Kalisharan Bannerji, who was a famous Bengali Christian lawyer and nationalist. Brahmobandhab, like Tagore and Gora, went through a series of identity crises and personal transformations based on acquired notions of essentialist difference between the alien colonizers and the native colonized. Contrary to the commonly held view that imperialism is universalist, colonial rule in India was rigidly and invariably grounded in hierarchies of cultural difference. Furthermore, India is not an exception in this regard; imperialist domination is always grounded in essentialist notions of difference (Balibar and Wallerstein 24). Hence the fragmentary, transient assumption and abandonment of mutually resistant and differing identities was the only mode of self-authentication for colonized Indians. In Gora, Tagore imagines a utopian universalist self as a holistic substitute for the divided psyche that Brahmobandhab and others like him act out. During his early adolescence, right after his sacred thread ceremony, Brahmobandhab refused to attend the Duff's English School and chose instead to study Sanskrit language and literature at the Batpatra Academy. At the same time, he was fond of swimming and wrestling and considered body building a necessary requisite for nation building (Kopf 201–202).

Perhaps in an attempt to counterpoint the focus on ascetic masculinity, the revolutionary and nationalist discourses of these years strongly invoke an emotionalized, aggrandized notion of femininity that constructs Durga (or Kali) as the always desired and forever forbidden object of desire and worship. In a highly Sanskritized Bengali poem, a poem that is used in modern India as one of the two national anthems, Bankim Candra evokes an anthropomorphic image of the physical land of India as the Mother/Earth/Goddess emblematic of the resistance and cohesion of the agencies of nature, culture, religion, revolution, and politics. Individual women for these revolutionaries symbolize Śakti, and they are invited to join revolutionary activities, to infuse nationalism with destructive energy associated with the divine feminine. As an ascetic revolutionary, Brahmobandhab uses this brand of Śakta symbolism in his writings; so does Gora in Tagore's novel. Gora's relationship with his own mother, and later on with Sucharita, is grounded in this specifically Hindu construction of the women as an agent of change, of reform, and of revolution.

Another significant dimension of Brahmobandhab's identity that we find in Tagore's Gora is the latter's involvement with an disaffection from Brahmo Samaj. In his youth, Brahmobandhab was greatly influenced by Keshub Sen, the founder of India's Brahmo Samaj. In its purest forms, an instance of which would be the Adi Brahma Samaj of Tagore's father, it was a revival of Upanishadic Hinduism. Again, in its final development as universalist theology that searched for a faith that would transcend the hegemonic categories of caste and race, Brahmo Samaj is very appealing and suggests a revival of libertarian Hinduism. In its most offensively colonialist form, Brahmo Samaj incorporated and propagated the imperialism of the Christian Church in India. It gave rise to a new bourgeois sectarianism, dividing the Hindu masses from the educated elite. Tagore's Gora and all the other characters in the novel are caught up in the contradictions of a society and a culture in transition, contradictions that are best mirrored in the conflicts between Hindus and Brahmos.

Brahmobandhab and his fictionalized prototype in Tagore's novel, like many other figures of the Bengali Renaissance, enthusiastically embrace the Samaj at first. They are gradually disillusioned and feel betrayed by its layers of imperialism. Inevitably, they renounce the Samaj and return to orthodox Hinduism. When once again the hegemonic structures of orthodox Hindu practice become intolerable, they return to a universalist Brahmoism in a futile search for a nonimperialist, nondogmatic, nonhegemonic religion: a religion that would link the nation with the world. Brahmobandhab's search for such an interethnic system of religious faith met with dismissal, opposition, and censorship from the Christian Church and its missionaries who wished only to convert and were, therefore, antogonistic to the theological dialogue that Brahmobandhab sought. He realized too late that the apparent intercultural plurality of colonial India was grossly perverted by the power politics of imperialism and differentialist racism.

When Brahmobandhab's initial disillusionment with the Samaj led him to Christianity, he sought to reconcile the "pure" forms of Christianity with the "pure" forms of Hinduism. In 1891, he converted to Roman Catholicism and changed his name to Theophilius (Kopf 207–208). He tried to rewrite Vedanta theology in the form of a Hindu New Testament and founded an Indianized Catholic order called the Kasthalic Math. When the local missionaries tried to put an end to his Hindu-Christian experiment, he went all the way to Rome to appeal his case. Once there, Brahmobandhab was denied an audience with the pope. This denial, after he had traveled all the way from Calcutta to Rome, was Brahmobandhab's first official confrontation with religious imperialism.

After his return to India, he started a strongly pro-Hindu journal *Twentieth Century*—gave up wearing Western clothes, and took on a saffron robe. In 1895, he changed his name from Theophilius to Brahmobandhab Upadhyay and lectured frequently on Hinduism and neo-Hegalianism. Even though the last phase of his life was a militant, nationalist-Hindu phase, the name he used during this time retains an early kinship with Brahmo Samaj. By 1907, Brahmobandhab had completely abandoned the Samaj and had become a revolutionary like most ambitious young Indians of the time. Like many of his contemporaries, Brahmobandhab discovered that Indians (Hindus) must first respect themselves; only then would they become a nation. Tagore's Gora echoes these views. Brahmobandhab died in prison in 1907, the year Tagore started writing *Gora*. He had been arrested on charges of sedition, the British police closed down his revolutionary newspaper, *Sandhya*, the daily circulation of which was 15,000 copies. They also destroyed massive tomes of his unpublished manuscripts; included in these destroyed documents were records of his correspondence with Tagore (Kopf 212–213).

The parallels with Gora's life are obvious. Gora is supposed to have been enthusiastic about the Brahmo Samaj; this phase of his life is narratively recalled and remains outside of the text of Tagore's novel. Despite his English education—the degree-oriented format of which Gora and his friend Binoy have just completed—Gora's *svadhyāya* (self-study) in Sanskrit metaphysics and theology has fully acculturated him in the Brahministic tradition. Like Brahmobandhab, Gora favors celibacy, chastity, and asceticism and has decided to remain a bachelor and devote his life to the service of the motherland. He is not a radical revolutionary like Brahmobandhab; there are traces of Gandhi, Vivekananda, and Tagore in him. Yet his patriotic writings and speeches use the Śakta symbolism that both Brahmobandhab and Tagore's radical revolutionary in *The Home and the World* use. Śakta symbolism, as I have pointed out, presents an iconographic representation of various phenomenal forms of the divine feminine; the icon and patriotic rhetoric emerging from the symbolism invokes the feminine principle as the source of strength (Śakti) and justified aggression. Though Gora never really turns into a radical anti-imperialist like his real-life prototype, he fights oppression at many levels. He goes to prison for defending a group of Calcutta students who are arrested and beaten by police for using a "whites only" drinking-water facility. The students use this forbidden facility only because one of their teammates was injured and they needed clean drinking water to revive him and to wash his wound (154). In contrast with Brahmobandhab's, Gora's prison term is very brief and quite harmless.

In the first chapter of Tagore's novel, when the reader makes his/her first acquaintance with them, Gora and Binoy are said to be members of the Hindu Patriot's Society and the former is supposed to have just begun his orthodox Hindu phase. Tagore treats their opening conversion with light irony. Gora has just started observing caste taboos while Binoy does not follow them. His writings of this period, which Binoy and other characters in the novel frequently read and quote from, equate decolonization (of the mind) with a return to traditional Hinduism and a rejection of Brahmo Samaj. Bengali readers of Tagore's novel would have been conscious of allusions to Brahmobandhab's writings and speeches in words fictionally attributed to Gora. This resemblance, following in the wake of the revolutionary's questionable death in a British prison, would have made the resonances all the more meaningful to them. They would not have considered this talk "irrelevant," as an impatient British reviewer did. The issues that are brought up in this talk, issues of caste, race, history, and dialectic are relevant even in the current, postcolonial phase of India's decolonization.

At the level of human particularity, Brahmobandhab's interest in Christianity is no different from Margaret Noble's interest in Hinduism. What distorts his intellectuality and spirituality is the differentialist power politics of imperialism and the imperialist presence of the Christian Church in India. Brahmobandhab's name change to Theophilius and his conversion to Christianity is clearly indicative of the self-alienation, self-division of the colonial psyche that Fanon speaks of in *Black Skin, White Masks* (16). His return to Hinduism is no less schizophrenic, because of the reactionary nature of this second conversion. Tagore's imaginary reconstruction of history and dialectic constitutes a dream and a nightmare, a universalist utopia and a sectarian anti-utopia. Gora's narrow, Brahministic nationalism is as sectarian and limiting as the classist and imperialist sectarianism of Brahmo Samaj. However, the secret truth of Gora's biological racial origin and its final revelation allow Tagore to set up history, race, caste, class, and religion as determinants that are tentative, not absolute and final.

In the context of Western models of novelistic structure that

Tagore may have used in *Gora*, his work is most like a nineteenth-century bildungsroman. Kipling's *Kim* is a cross between the picaresque and the bildungsroman. Kim is an adolescent picaro, the white picaro adventuring in the East. However, Kim's adventures—which are meant to terminate when he meets with the mystified construct of his father's regiment, his imperial destiny—are fused with Teshoo Lama's search for the legendary river of enlightenment. The latter introduces the quest (for truth) motif into the adventure novel. Tagore's Gora is a political activist, thinker/writer, and nationalist. In the course of the novel, he pontificates, teaches and is taught, rejects others and is rejected by them; life changes him as the novel moves toward a teleological ending, which reveals the secret of a child's birth and the awakening of the adult to larger dimensions of human experience. Tagore links his telic ending with the Upanishadic telos of pure, illusion-free knowledge of the self. However, the metaphysical wisdom of the Upanishadic concepts is qualified by the dialectical politics of race, class, gender, and caste. As a white man, *Gora* discovers firsthand what it means to be an Indian in colonial India. His life is a political allegory, and Tagore's novel could not have engaged fully in the dialectic of race and caste without deferring the revelation of the fact of Gora's biological origin.

This contingency of birth is not essential within the tradition of liberal Hinduism, since Upanishadic metaphysics puts the highest emphasis on thought or knowledge (*jnāna*). It also gives priority to karma (action) over birth (*janma*). A human subject's caste and his/her theogenetic orientation is thus determined by lifestyle, or *svadharma*: one's authentically chosen vocation or work. I use the terms "*svabhāva*" and "*svadharma*" as Ashis Nandy uses them in the context of his explorations of psychosociological development of individuals in colonial India (*Intimate Enemy* 8). In this sense, the term is radically different from the term "dharma"; the latter refers to an ideological system that is necessarily a hegemonic system of beliefs that define codes of day-to-day conduct and behavior. On the contrary, *svadharma* and *svabhāva* refer to self-development, self-culture, and enlightenment. Upandishadic thinkers, like the existentialist philosophers of the West, define spirituality of the individual in terms that go beyond the limiting categories of dogma, doctrine, and convention. In colonial India, imperialist assumptions about native character preempt the possibilities of *svadharma* for individual Indians—Hindus, Christians, Muslims, Buddhists, and others. Being an orthodox Hindu or Muslim makes one an unassimilated, resistant, or even apathetic native; conversion to Christianity and adoption of Western ways means one has been "properly" acculturated. Either way, the individual Indian's actions and choices, his/her *svadharma*, serves only to situate him/her as a fictional construct within the larger frame of the colonialist order of the state, society, and culture.

In Tagore's India, the British rulers had invented a vast inventory of myths about what the natives were capable of doing and what they were unfit to do. More importantly, the exclusionist policies of colonialist economy determined how the native labor force could best be utilized to serve the ends of the empire. This imperialistic mindset and political economy dictated the choice of *svadharma*, *svakarma*, and even *svadhyāya* (vocation, work, and self-study) for a vast majority of urban Indians. Moreover, the policies of the raj that most directly affected the work structure were exclusionist in the same way in which the cultural practices of the caste system were exclusionist. In purely practical terms, what an Indian of this time period could choose as vocation was determined by what the system of English education prepared him for. The only authentic choice they could make was to become freedom fighters, reformists, and revolutionaries, these being the most honorable yet the most difficult and problematic forms of *svadharma* and *svadhyāya* for people of colonized nations anywhere in the world.

Tagore's novel starts with the two friends, Binoy and Gora, contemplating possibilities for work and vocation in the Colonial City. Since Binoy is not an ascetic like Gora, he is thinking of marriage and women as well. For their more complacent peers who might have chosen to remain insulated in ancient customs at home—and who would inevitably have become tiny instruments of the empire at the workplace—the transitional ethos poses no problem. Gora's elder brother, Mohim, represents this type. In contrast, Gora and Binoy represent the intellectual elite, and their lives are inextricably caught up in the immediate historical processes: the rise of Indian nationalism, the revival of Hindu orthodoxy in the service of nationalism, the relatively new sociocultural/religious/intellectual phenomenon identified as the Brahmo movement. When Tagore wrote this novel, his family had accumulated a history of enthusiastic alliance, disaffection, and a partial realliance with the Samaj. No doubt, *Gora* contains an insider's critique of the Brahmo rhetoric and ideology. However, Tagore's novel is not a period piece, though Tagore assumes prior knowledge of the history and politics of the Samaj.

The Brahmo Samaj was formally founded by Raja Ram Mohan Roy in 1860 as a form of protest against the decadent customs associated with orthodox Hinduism. Ram Mohan Roy sought to return to a purer Hinduism of a mythological golden age. At the same time, the Brahmo redefinition of Hinduism sought to move away from the pantheon of Hindu gods. Brahmo thinkers set up a metaphysical return to Brahma, the absolute, ultimate, formless deity, highest in the hierarchy of manifested deities, as their rhetorical point of reference. This clearly marked a return to monotheism and a departure from polytheism. More accurately, the popular Brahmo rhetoric marks a denial and censorship of polytheistic practices of worship, dismisses them as decadent, and claims that the Hinduism of an earlier period was exclusively monotheistic. The genuinely attractive feature of Brahmo Samaj, which had nothing at all to do with monotheistic worship, was its commitment to social reform. The Samaj made significant contributions toward removing taboos against widow remarriage, stopping child marriages, and the custom of sati. Most importantly, it worked successfully in its program to liberate women by ending their centuries of seclusion, their confinement to the women's quarters. It opened new opportunities of education and work for women.

The most unattractive feature of Brahmo Samaj was its acquired sense of a separation from the "idol worshiping," "caste-difference-ridden" (Hindu) masses whom it sought to reform. The rhetoric of separation and difference allowed the Brahmo Bengalis to establish for themselves a superior caste identity. In this manner, it served to produce and propagate a home-grown variety of imperialist ideology based on differentialist principles. The paradox of Brahmo Samaj was that its members set themselves up as a dissenting group who wished to stand up against the hegemony of traditional Hinduism, but in doing so they adopted a hegemonic point of view identical to that of the imperialist outsider and master. Thus, despite what it had to offer in terms of much-needed social reform, the Samaj served only to duplicate the imperialist ideology and to bring it closer to home. The opposition between the Brahmo and the Hindu views is nowhere more evident than in the dialectical verbal exchanges between Gora and Haran Babu, a Brahmo dogmatist. The long stretches of dialogue that take place between Gora and the other characters in the context of Haran's supremacy generates a powerful dialectic of ideas, attitudes, and perspectives. The plot complications and resolutions of the middle and the last sections of the novel emerge from this dialectic.

At the center of the dialectic of ideas are two family units: Gora's family and Paresh Babu's family. Binoy, Gora's lifelong friend and companion, lives alone but is a part of Gora's family unit because he has no close relatives of his own. The "other," "alien" family is the Brahmo family of Paresh Babu—His wife, Barodasundari, and their four daughters: Sucharita, Lolita, Labanyo, and Lila. These women are somewhat of a rarity because they are "free" women who are not committed to the seclusion of the inner quarters of the household. The oldest of the sisters, Sucharita, is an adopted daughter, the child of a long-dead, Brahmo friend of Paresh Babu. The opening chapters of the novel, through a series of ordinary, everyday events bring various young members of these two families together and introduce narrative sequences dealing with romantic love, passion, infatuation, male-female friendship: a network of cross-gender interactions that would have been forbidden within the traditional family structure of Indian society. For Binoy and Gora, an introduction to the Brahmo girls of Paresh Babu's household, a social opportunity to engage in intellectual discussions with them, is a new experience. Paresh Babu's home becomes a signifier for a changed world, an alternative zeitgeist, a place where women have stepped out of the women's quarters, where they serve tea in the living room, where they entertain the guests or engage in polemical arguments with them. Tagore's narration treats this section with light irony in the style of the comedy of manners; the battle of sexes is also treated in a comic/satiric mode.

Brahmo homes in a lot of Bengali literature of this time function as sociosexual spaces that provide free access to women; they constitute signifiers of forbidden desire, of forbidden contact and conversation with women. For example, Śarat Candra Chattopadhyay, a contemporary of Tagore, incisively explores the politics of desire that centers around Brahmo households and their relation to the orthodox Hindu surround. In his treatment of the Brahmo-Hindu dialectic Tagore chooses not to plunge into the politics of the profane and the sacred, the permitted and the forbidden, in the manner in which Śarat Candra and many other writers of this period do. In *Gora*, Tagore makes Binoy's first erotic fixation on Sucharita as innocent as possible. As she enters his room, Binoy sees Sucharita's reflection "in the mirror," and this mirrored image of a woman fascinates him. It opens to him "a new world of tender brightness" that the socialization patterns based on seclusion and segregation had kept in abeyance (2). In this scene, Binoy's confrontation with Sucharita is fortified not only by the mirror image; it is shielded by the amiable chatter of her younger brother. Seen from the eight-year-old's perspective, the sleepy city of Calcutta appears "motionless like a disconsolate dog curled up with its head resting on its tail" (5); it is not a moon-drenched romantic city or a drizzly city framed by low-lying rain clouds—dark as the body of Kṛṣṇa, the god of *jouissance*. The conventional chain of signifiers associated with erotic desire is deliberately substituted by the child's image of a disconsolate dog. Furthermore, the mirror scene promptly inserts forbidden desire into a scenario of marriage, because in a traditional Hindu ceremony the bridegroom first sees his bride's reflection in a mirror. Still, an invitation to have tea at Paresh Babu's house raises expectations of forbidden eros. An automatic refusal to enter a Brahmo household, a course of action that Gora orders for the terribly infatuated Binoy, functions in this case as a sociomoral imperative, and such an unmannerly adherence to rules of segregation would be considered a necessary masculine virtue. The hostilities between Hindus and Brahmos of this time period owe a great deal to this type of separatism and ambivalence.

As indicated earlier, the Brahmo dogmatism in *Gora* is represented by Haran Babu who is a scholar/teacher and a frequent visitor at Paresh Babu's house. He is also the designated husband-to-be for Sucharita. Barodasundari and Haran, as Brahmo enthusiasts, are very sanctimonious in their disdain for orthodox Hindus. At one point in the narrative, a long-lost aunt of Sucharita turns up at Paresh Babu's house when the mother and the daughters are vacationing at the district magistrate's mansion. The aunt is Hindu and observes appropriate food and other caste taboos; Paresh Babu puts her up in a small room in an isolable part of the attic. It is easy to sympathize with Barodasundari's dismay at this unforeseen intrusion into the established order of her household. However, when her Brahmo friends try to forcibly enter into the widow's room with shoes on—determined to desecrate the idol of Lord Kṛṣṇa that she has set up in a corner—the manifestations of sectarian bigotry take on an ugly aspect. This incident and many others initiated by Haran Babu make Lolita and Sucharita turn their backs on the Samaj, the very Samaj that has freed them and empowered them and allowed them to escape repressive gender roles, a contemporary institutional structure that has enabled them to demand respect as women.

Similarly, it is the colonialist context of Brahmo righteousness that alienates Gora and prompts his defection and his subsequent adoption of Hindu orthodoxy. When he first enters Barodasundari's drawing room, he invites the wrath of the girls and their mother by observing food taboos. He appears at their door with a prominent caste mark on his face that completes his "war apparel," as Sucharita describes it later. She thinks he has made it known to them, not in words, but in something more articulate than words: "From you I am different." This dramatic confrontation with the Other magnifies Sucharita's acquired sense of "difference" from the masses of India. At the time of their first encounter, Gora appears to Sucharita like an ancient Rishi from the banks of Ganges or the foothills of the Himalayas. This is no doubt an imitative disguise to invoke a context of the mythological past of India, just as the coats and ties of the Calcutta Bhadralok serve as imitative disguises of a different sort. Gora's costume has a serious ideological purpose, but in its exaggeration it is also meant to be ironic and parodic. However, the mythic past of India was a living tradition even in colonial India, potently linked with the deeper psyches of Indians. Hence, in his war apparel, Gora arouses in Sucharita a desire that she has not known before. He presents himself to her as Śiva in Kālidāsa's *Kumārsambhavam* presents himself to the ascetic (and desiring) Pārvati, as a paradoxical embodiment of *tapas* and *kāma* (monastic discipline and eros). In this case, the politics of colonialism necessitates that Gora enter Sucharita's world as an antagonist, the Other that they (the smug Brahmos) must contend with. His return to and insistence on this somewhat exaggerated orthodoxy is not free from the taint of egotism, but as Tagore's narrative of erotic desire and of political dialectic proceeds, Gora transcends some of his early sectarian prejudices.

In the first half of the novel, Paresh Babu's house becomes the battle ground for the politics of desire, of nationhood and caste. The Anglo-Indian congeniality of the afternoon teas, the presence of beautiful young women is not enough to dispel the ghosts of divisive ideologies. At one of these occasions, somebody casually mentions that two Bengali students recently passed the civil service examination with distinction. Haran Babu—who is by this time clearly established as Gora's antagonist in terms of their relationship to Sucharita and in the context of their opposing politics—promptly exhorts, "What does it matter how well Bengalis may do in their examinations, they will never be any good as administrators" (44). Haran does not realize that he is echoing a standardized cliché. He waxes eloquent on the "defects and weaknesses of Bengali character" and the "evil customs" of Bengali Hindus (44). The tone of moral righteousness that he adopts sets him up as someone who stands far above these "customs" and the "defects of character."

In the 1860s and 1870s, many Calcutta Bengalis were getting advanced technical and professional education but were denied positions to which their merit entitled them. British administrators uniformly agreed that it would be a mistake to advocate the claims of the natives to higher employment. In one official report (1875), Lord Northbrook expresses anxiety at the growing numbers of "a mass of people with a smattering of English education, just enough to make them conceited and ape the British habit of grumbling at and criticizing everything done by the government." "It would have the worst effect," he continues, "to flatter this class and make them suppose their merits are equal" (Ray 34). Haran reiterates this view without realizing that Lord Northbrook does not exclude him (Haran) from this mass of people "with a smattering of English education." Gora has just received his Master's Degree; he understands that he is included in this mass of people. He strives therefore to align himself with the other mass, the mass of "un-(English)educated" Indians. Tagore intends Gora's return to the dogmatism of popular Hinduism to serve as an antidote to the neo-imperialist ideology of the Brahmos.

One of the stereotypical gripes that oral and written discourses of Brahmo Samaj reiterate tiresomely concerns the native Hindu's "superstitious" nature. Like the imperialists, they dismiss an entire realm of mental phenomenon as "superstition," a phenomenon that provided human beings problem-solving (conceptual) tools for centuries, tools with the help of which they could make complex ecological and rational choices. To connect superstition with irrationality and to assume that Europeans are not "superstitious" is at best a cognitive error. "Superstitions" of various kinds have facilitated irrational use of power in the West and the East: witch burning and Nazi killings, sati and untouchability taboos. However, the Brahmo Indians' twisted world view determines that Indians (Hindus) are being "superstitious" when they refrain from eating beef and conserve their cows as milk-giving animals; on the other hand, Englishmen are being "rational" in their racist beliefs about people of dark skin. The paranoic and superstitious nature of racism escapes them entirely. It is simply to question such assumptions that in the middle of a heated debate at Paresh Babu's house, Gora declares, "what you call superstition is my faith." When Haran harps on "reform," Gora says, "Reform? That can wait a while yet. More important than reform are love and respect. Reform will come of itself from within. . . . Because forsooth our country is superstitious, you the non-superstitious must keep superior and aloof" (508). "First establish kinship with us," he adds, "then come to reform us." In his retort, Gora does not justify superstition nor does he dismiss the need for reform.

What he really objects to is the irrelevance of such standardized clichés in the lexicon of the native imperialist ideologue. Gora's use of the divisive terms "us" and "you" is necessitated by the differentialism of Haran's imperialist discourse. To Sucharita, Gora says, "Come Inside India, accept all her good and evil, if there be deformity then try to cure it from within, but see it with your own eyes" (102–103). The Brahmo native who stands outside India is an alienated colonial subject whom Gora wishes to reform, subverting the imperialist assumption of moral superiority and redefining it in nationalist terms.

Gora's and Binoy's entry into Paresh Babu's house does not only produce the dialectic of contending ideologies of orthodoxy and Brahmo Samaj, it also sets in motion the plot of romantic love. Binoy falls in love with Lolita, the darker girl who is less conventionally beautiful but the most outspoken and independent of the girls. Gora fights his growing interest in Sucharita, remains unwaveringly adamant in his asceticism, and surrounds his object of desire with signifiers of Śakta worship, a worship offered by the bachelor revolutionary to the Mother Goddess. But, to become a worthy object of worship, Sucharita must first reassume her Hindu identity fully. Held in Gora's gaze of sublimated eros, she becomes a "complete" woman and makes his nationalist ideas "intensely real" to him; he sees in her "a truth revealed" (101). He regards her as chaste and beautiful, different from a "woman who sets fire to the hearts of men" (6). "The altar at which woman may be truly worshipped," according to Gora, "is her place as Mother" (6). Fortunately, Gora grows out of his early mother cult as his attraction for the Brahmo girl becomes more sharply defined in terms of *śringāra*. Meanwhile, Paresh Babu permits the growing attractions, Barodasundari and Haran work as antagonists and blocking agents; the liberalism and sectarianism of caste and religion are clearly associated with the consummation and blocking of erotic desire. At this point, Tagore makes innovative use of stock imagery from Sanskrit love poetry. The Calcutta sky, the rain, and the sun, the streets and houses, gardens and flowers, codes of dress and hairdo, posture and gesture, facilitators and blocking (human) agents, the subtle semiosis of an Indian (Hindu) love constitutes *śringāra rasa* in Tagore's dialectical novel about colonial India.

Everywhere, the conventionally forbidden is sanctified. When Binoy awakens fully to his mature love for Lolita, he feels as though "his very soul was moved, as if he had heard the chanting of Vedic mantras in some ancient forest retreat" (70). This sanctification is only superficially indicative of Tagore's traditionalism;

its political significance emphasizes the dialectic of history. Tagore decolonizes Lolita and Binoy's Hindu-Brahmo romance and situates it amongst indigenous signifiers. The "ancient forest retreat" of Binoy's imagination clashes sharply with the suburban retreat where Barodasundari had taken her four daughters to sing silly English songs, to act in an English play—to entertain, to please, to flatter, to seek the approval of the British magistrate. When, in the wake of Gora's arrest and the police beating of college students, Lolita leaves with Binoy to dissociate herself from this colonialist mimicry and sycophancy, she cuts off all ties with her Brahmo family and joins the Hindu fold. Her return to Hindu society is facilitated by heterosexual eros as ancient and perpetual as the waters of Ganges, the shadows of pine trees in the remote Himalayan foothills, red and white flowers signifying discord and harmony between lovers. Hers is not an anglicized love; it is rooted in India's mythological past, and it gives her the courage to fight colonialist cowardice and the sectarianism of Hindu decadence.

When they finally marry, Binoy and Lolita are ostracized by their families and friends. The narration of romantic love and marriage—despite its associative connections with Vedic chants, the fragrant flames of ritual fires in ancient India, and the "cadences of festival music" (154)—is not immune to the marginalizing politics of caste, class, and race. Yet such marginalization at a time when Indian society is in transition sets Lolita and Binoy free as man and woman; it sets them free to aspire to gender equality in love and marriage. At the end, Gora is also freed from his Brahministic hubris when he discovers that he lacks the privilege (or bondage) of a Hindu birth. However, the theogenetic contingency of birth alone would not have freed Gora; at the end, he grows out of his early romanticization of the masses of India. He encounters the fact of his difference from them, not as an English man, but as one of the Calcutta elite.

During his wandering in the villages, Gora discovers that the *svadharma* of service (of the mother country) is much more problematic than he had at first imagined. In his revolutionary idealism, he had romanticized the oppressed masses, and he had expected to find in them a source of strength; he had expected to find in Bengal's villages the real India. In his scheme of things, the villages were to present an antithesis to the colonially alienated atmosphere of the city. Once he is there in Bengal's villages, he finds an alienation of a different kind. He finds out that the centuries of imperialist/capitalist exploitation has impoverished the villagers so much that their blind faith in tradition—similar to Haran's blind faith in modernity—has crippled them. He finds out that the father of a poor man has been ill for a very long time; nearly all of the man's money is spent on caring for the father. When the old man dies, the village community insists that the son do a penance, because the protracted, uncured illness of the departed dead surely indicates some unknown, unreckoned sin of a past life. The dead father's atman, according to them, must be freed from this sin and be restored to spiritual health and mobility. In other words, in the villages, he finds an ironic confirmation of the values and cultural practices of the Indian masses that the imperialists and neo-imperialists base their criticisms on.

From the perspective of a decolonizing ideology, one can see that the villagers demonstrate rigor and consistency in their belief systems, values, and normative standards of living. If the traditional Hindu faith is what they live by, what they use to order their lives destroyed by capitalist/imperialist economy, the least they can do is to be consistent and maintain an illusion of a spiritually ordered universe. At the other end of the rigidity of their beliefs is an arbitrary, bourgeois modification of the claims of duty in light of an ethos of convenience and comfort. The villagers' insistence on penance does not seem irrational, because they believe in the laws of karma, they believe the long illness bore witness to an unacknowledged sin. They believe a penance will free the spirit, mobilize it to flow unimpededly in eternal and/or temporal Time. It is only in the context of the son's poverty—itself a product of economic imperialism—that the irrationality of the penance becomes an issue. Even though he is there to establish kinship with them, Gora does not fully understand the villagers' point of view. He is quickly discouraged. His class background, his education, separates him from them.

At home around the same time, his father's illness precipitates the disclosure of the secret of Gora's birth. After the initial shock is over, his kinship with his mother remains unchanged. His self-imposed restraints regarding Sucharita become irrelevant. The revelation of his birth brings with it a sense of momentary loss of identity, and he says to Paresh Babu, "From one end to the other end the doors of every temple are today closed against me—today in the whole country there is no seat for me at any Hindu feast" (515). These words echo Kim's poignant confession: "Now I am alone—all all alone. . . . in all of India there is not one so alone as I" (167). Kim is, at this point, already initiated into the "Great Game" of British government's secret service. He is no longer the disciple of his eccentric Lama. Gora's fictional existence, as we have seen, is conceptualized differently. It is clear that in situating

Gora inside the symbolic order of Hinduism, Tagore makes a clear distinction between liberal and dogmatic Hinduism. Formerly, Gora had chosen a lifestyle consistent with dogmatic customs and beliefs to establish kinship with the masses of India so that he wouldn't "stand above" them. During his wandering, he comes face to face with his differences from popular, dogmatic Hinduism.

From the authorial perspective, which is shared by a majority of Tagore's Indian readers, the revelation of his biological racial origin does not exclude Gora from the universal order of liberal Hinduism. He is a Hindu (Brahmin) in his search for a vocation (*svadharma*) that would most meaningfully actualize his atman. The self-culture he has acquired through his readings of scriptures (*svadhyāya*) is an accumulation of indelible *saṃskāras* in his psyche. From Tagore's point of view, Gora's identity is not a hybrid identity. Like any upper-class Hindu, he has the privilege of an elitist Brahmanistic liberality of thought, contemplation, meditation, and pursuit of self-knowledge. It is a privilege that the Brahmin villagers—who spend their days in back-breaking labor and their nights worrying about the English collectors' visits, droughts and rains, floods and famines—do not have. Gora is different from them, but not in the way Haran envisions himself to be different.

In the light of an illusion-destroying, self-liberating knowledge, Gora is connected at the end with a fuller, larger truth; at this moment, he turns to Paresh Babu to note, "Today in a single moment that fortress of my creation has vanished like a dream, and I, having got absolute freedom, suddenly find myself standing in the midst of a vast truth" (520). The deliverance of the self from a narrow egotism into a larger truth, into a more authentic state of recognition of the universalist nature of one's atman, is consistent with the principles of Vedānta, Sānkhya, and Śaiva metaphysics. It is appropriate that Gora refuses to hear the name of his real father: "there is no need to hear his name," he says. Thus, the non-Hindu, absent father remains unnamed in Tagore's text. The world of Gora's Hindutava is not intruded upon by the dead father's first or last name. Gora's acquired Hindutava remains whole and intact.

Complications related to the theogenetic notion of caste are introduced into the text when Gora's hypochondriac father decides to reveal the secret of his son's birth only when faced by the terrifying prospect that Gora will take part in the postfuneral rituals. According to Krishendayal's narrower view, only a person who is Brahmin by birth can take part in this ritual. Doing otherwise would violate the order, which connects the living with the dead, the divine with the human, and carries within it the eternal assurance of *Mokṣa*, or of rebirth. Gora does not need such assurances, because he has chosen the path of *jnana* and karma (thought and action). Freed from limiting doctrines, from the present and the absent father, Gora "feels great relief." His life seems to him an "extraordinary dream," because he seems to have "no mother, no father, no nationality, no lineage, no God even" (528). All "false" ties are broken; in the light of the new truth, all previous kinship relations are reappropriated. Gora's character incorporates Tagore's memory of Brahmobandhab/Theophilius's larger Hindu-Catholic identity, Sister Nivedita and her Hinduism, combined with a utopian universalist ideal of the human self, a self that transcends the legalities and normativities of family, caste, nation, and religion. However, this authenticated individual does not break his ties with the mother, who represents the agency of nurture, though he is freed from the inhibiting influences of culture.

Formerly, when the certainty of her motherhood was not in doubt, in his enthusiastic adoption of orthodoxy, he had refused to eat the food prepared in her kitchen because she observed no caste taboos. On caste grounds, he had opposed Binoy's marriage to Lolita. After his short prison term where he was not able to observe caste taboos, he had decided to do a ceremonial penance. However, the ceremony is never completed. Gora's asceticism and personal sacrifices (of letting go of Sucharita) also becomes unnecessary. He can now freely claim kinship with her. The displaced individual caught in the imperialist and anti-imperialist politics of India assumes a normal human identity as a son and as a lover. Nevertheless, the politics of caste, class, race, and nation looms large, and the haunting memory of Brahmobandhab's life and death, his thwarted personal growth, the colonial subject's twisting and tossing of alternatives—these phantoms of the colonial past persist in postcolonial India. That is why in his preface to *Cār Adhyāy*, written 27 years later and only a few years before India's independence, Tagore returns to morbid broodings and resurrects the ghost of his revolutionary friend.

Bibliography

Balibar, Etienne. Immanuel Wallerstein. *Race, Nation, Class: Ambiguous Identities*. London: Verso, 1991.

Fanon, Frantz. *White Masks, Black Skin*. Trans. Charles Lam Markmann. New York: Grove Press, 1967.
Kipling, Rudyard. *Indian Tales*. New York: John Lovell Co., 1890.
Kipling, Rudyard. *Kim*. Intro. Morton Cohen. Bantam: New York, 1988.
Kipling, Rudyard. *Something of Myself*. Ed. Thomas Pinney. New York: Cambridge Univ. Press, 1990.
Kopf, David. *The Brahmo Samaj and the Shaping of the Modern Indian Mind*. New Jersey: Princeton Univ Press, 1979.
Kripalani, Krishna. *Rabindranath Tagore: A Biography*. New York; Grove Press, 1962.
Lago, Mary M. *Rabindranath Tagore*. Boston: Hall and Co, 1976.
Nandy, Ashis. *The Intimate Enemy: Loss and Recovery of Self Under Colonialism*. Calcutta: Oxford Univ Press, 1983.
Pinney, Thomas. Ed. *Kipling's India: Uncollected Sketches 1884–88*. New York: Schoken Books, 1986.
Ray, Rajat Kant. *Social Conflict and Political Unrest in Bengal: 1875–1927*. Delhi: Oxford Univ Press, 1984.
Tagore, Rabindranath. *Gora*. London: Macmillan, 1910.

Part VI

Theorizing Colonial Contact: Hybrid Identities and the Possibility of Postcolonial Culture

12

The Postcolonial Critic: Homi Bhabha Interviewed by David Bennett and Terry Collits

On 13 July 1992, Homi Bhabha of the University of Sussex presented a keynote address to the "Literature and Opposition" Conference at Monash University convened by ASPACLS (Australian and South Pacific Association for Comparative Literary Studies). Bhabha is well known as a theorist of "postcolonial criticism," and his paper at the conference was entitled "'Race,' Time and the Revision of Modernity." The following day, David Bennett and Terry Collits of the English Department of the University of Melbourne interviewed Homi Bhabha for *Arena*. What follows is an edited version of that interview.*

Bennett: The term "postcolonial criticism" is a comparatively recent addition to the Western academic lexicon. Given that its perspectives are said to emerge from the subversive, "subaltern" discourses of minorities and the anticolonialist testimonies of Third-World countries, could you comment on the institutional provenance of the term and the kinds of affiliations that it identifies, projects or —perhaps falsely—presumes?

*This interview was first published in the "Postcolonialism" issue of the Melbourne journal, *Arena*, 96 (Spring 1991), 47–63.

Bhabha: I think we should be very attentive to the fact that the Western liberal academy, by its nature, requires new topics, new disciplines, new connections between the disciplines; otherwise it's unable to represent the kind of liberal pedagogies that it is concerned with. But these new disciplines and new topics are not entirely generated at the institutional level. For instance, the emphasis on postcolonial work, "minority" discourse, and so on, has happened not because the professoriate have invented these areas of interest, but because the universities and colleges have in this particular historical period, postsixties, been in some ways infiltrated—"infiltrated" is a strong word—but entered by a lot of people from colonial historical provenances who are asking questions that come from their histories. The danger, of course, is that there is a kind of universalist cultural relativism which tires to appropriate new topics and put them into a perspective that then deprives them of their cultural innovation, their historical reinscription, and their political and social purposiveness. So I think we should guard against that kind of appropriation. But we should not be oversuspicious or overironic; the more general intellectual importance of these forms of work should not be minimized. For instance, I feel that the emergence of these, broadly speaking, postcolonial, subaltern minority discourses raises very fundamental questions about what the social contract is today, what the academic contract is and, indeed, in the inscription of disciplines in histories, what the narrative contract may be. And here I think you see a moment where what happens in the university as the assertion of new disciplines is also happening in various other social sites as the assertion of new ethnicities, problems of racism, problems of nationality, of law, of discrimination, problems of the assertion of particular communities. So the kinds of new social contracts that we are epistemologically negotiating around these specific questions of difference emerging from the postcolonial are actually part of wider debates: in councils about funding, about discrimination, about minority rights.

Bennett: It's a question of the affiliations that are named, however provisionally, by this term "postcolonial criticism". Does it carry the implication that there is a common history, or some common structure of experience, as it were, that can provide a meeting point for all sorts of apparently quite disparate histories and experiences—or is there a danger in homogenizing these experiences in postcolonialist terms?

Bhabha: Again, I think I would have to answer this in two ways, with my own love of doublenesses and ambivalences. There is clearly a danger in producing kinds of facile generalizations which say things like: "We're all migrants now, we're all refugees, we're all homeless, just as indeed the signifier is homeless, we're all slipping around, sliding around." I'm not only being funny here, because very often the one at the linguistic level is metaphorically taken to reflect another diasporic experience, in more sophisticated ways than I'm doing, and I very much resent that. All our histories are not magical realisms all of a sudden. But having said that, I think there is a project that does link questions of slavery, indenture, migration, diaspora refugees, the colonial past, the present of migration, and so on, and that is a project that has two immediate aspects that I can think of. One is the kind of argument I have been trying to make in my work and put forward yesterday again, which is a more general intervention within the field of modernity, of civility, both as an epistemological and as a political project. I think that there could be a nonhomogeneous construction of a kind of narrative that would link these different aspects of minority discourse, by suggesting that these histories of diaspora refugees, these postcolonial histories, actually provide us with an epistemological and, indeed, political and historical critique of Western modernity. I think that might be one way of looking at it. So, not that we are simply interested in authenticating our different histories as Caribbean indentured subjects, as postcolonial Indian-British subjects, or subjects of the great Puerto Rican migration to New York—not simply on that basis, but on the basis that the cultural experience of those forms of displacement and exploitation might show us the other face of modernity and might then enable us to construct cultural signs, symbols, and temporalities by which we might, for instance, begin to renegotiate what it is that we consider to be forms of communal living, what the ethics of the recognition of personhood are, or, indeed, what cultural interaction may be. And I've made some suggestions in this direction, for instance, by saying that if we do take this postcolonial reinscription of modernity, then maybe we have to think of culture, not merely as the production of great works of art or architecture, nor merely the great countercultural narratives of liberation, but that we should be conscious of the much more interstitial, contingent images, symbols, art, songs, writings, memories, dreams that people create when those two grand options—the grand opera on the one hand, or the grand overthrow of the state on the other—are not available. And here I think a very important aperçu is Fanon's statement, somewhere towards the end of *The Wretched of the Earth*, where he says that there are people whose lives and whose oppositions, political oppositions or cultural oppositions, are not grounded in great theories, great ethical positions, complete or totalized forms of knowledge; rather, they are actually struggling to make those meanings, and it's this kind of notion, what I might call culture as a strategy of survival, that I think would be very important. Now, can I just say this: I hope it doesn't sound as if I'm romanticizing despair, pessimism, loss; that's not what I want to suggest at all. I'm saying that much of the weave, much of the text and texture of culture is construed in the strategy of various kinds of survival—psychic, social, the survival of the family. After all, if you just think of the metaphors by which we now live, we talk in a way about the tenuous survival of clarified forms of sexuality, where we're negotiating all sorts of forms of sexual expression and sexual identification. If we talk about economics, even the great nations like the United States are *surviving* with their vast credit problems. The middle classes are also surviving. If you take the issue of AIDS, for instance, as a central issue of the national health, the politics of life today, it has brought to our attention the question of survival. Surviving, for me, is obviously a profound sort of marginal and boundary problem; it's where polarities, social polarities and binaries, are brought into question. If you take the women's issue: It was again about how you survive as a mother, as a professional, as a lover. I mean to use survival, then, in this very strong sense, not merely as the form of diminished existence, and I want to suggest that philosophically what we learn, for instance, through psychoanalysis and its use of the questions of ambivalence, is precisely about the survival of identity, or the struggle for identification. Intellectually, epistemologically, I want to retrieve the notion of survival as a way of actually making articulations and connections while recognizing the problems of incommensurability, difference, and resisting the great temptations of universalizing.

Bennett: It's more common to conceptualize culture as "resistance" or as "dominance" than as "survival." What are you suggesting survives and what is *being* survived? For example, if we're talking not about bodies, but about identity, and if identity is never unitary or stable, then in what sense can we talk about the survival of identity—and what is it surviving, or outlasting?

Bhabha: The models of resistance and dominance assume that the struggle goes on between preconstituted agents of cultural change. My point is that the thing we name as culture—our awareness of what a culture is, and of cultural difference—is always a naming in response to a crisis, a crisis of survival. What that naming does, with all its ambivalences and problems, is show discursively the absence of preconstituted cultural agents. Let me illustrate how my concept of culture as survival emerged as a form of postcolonial critique. In colonial cultures and in the ways in which advanced European forms of technology and techne became part of the lives of Third-World peoples—those whose labor was actually *producing* such technologies—people constituted their lives in a kind of agonistic struggle between indigenous practices and imposed forms, a negotiation that couldn't be reduced to the polarity between a preconstituted Western tradition and an authentic native tradition. People were weaving their cultural existence in a much more strategic, interstitial, in-between kind of space. Take the movie and television industry in India, where advanced Westernized technology and its accompanying secularism is used to produce—is the *enunciative condition* of—a heavily mythological, atavistic, Hindu nationalist message, which stresses indigenous cultural authenticity. At the level of the production of the image, there is a *collusion* between technological advances, which presuppose secular and democratic forms of social and economic organization, and a conservative, hierarchical, traditionalist, often religious content. There are therefore conflicts between the producers of technology and the social identities that are being produced in relation to it—between the subjects of *énonciation* and the subjects of the *énoncé*—and it is as a naming of these conflicts, this crisis, that the discourse of culture is evoked.

Collits: Can we return to the point in your first response where you talked about those newcomers to the academy from the margins (to use an older language) who entered the universities from the sixties onwards and in entering them were related to changes that they have been through? You talked about them as "infiltrators." It's a strongly political word. These infiltrators became in your discussion a new "we." "We," I presume, includes those who are politically motivated to effect radical change in the institution. However, there was a shift from your original infiltrators to a current group whom you talked about more in terms of "cultural interactions," something not necessarily so politically charged, so full of agency, as infiltrators. Can you tell us something about the political position of the group you include as a "we"—who are "we"?

Bhabha: I suppose I was talking about many different forms and therefore forces of the agency of change, or the agency of infiltration and reinscription, of innovation within the general description of the postcolonial or the minority, which is what I assume you're referring to as "we." Now, there's a very obvious answer to this question, which is that I first have to acknowledge most immediately that the "we" refers in this conversation itself, not only to myself, who has a very specific kind of postcolonial history, but to yourselves, too, as an Australian and a migrant Briton, who have another obvious kind of colonial history. But if you take my earlier point, where I said that for me the major project is the construction of a countermodernity on the basis of the intervention of the colonial moment at the very inception, in the very matrices of the construction of ethics, rationality, the myth of progress, the myth of the nation, I think then that "we" becomes a more general intellectual project of social discourse for those amongst us who are socialists, who want to transform the conditions of the academy and, indeed, society and culture more generally. We need to be able to articulate forms of different identities and constituencies, but also to be aware that, in order to do that, we will not have some easy, uninterrupted narrative, but will have to deal with many forms of incommensurabilities. So, to the extent to which I've tried to define a wider intellectual project which affects the very history of modernity, to that extent I think I would include in "we" those who want to understand this double or contramodernity, the postcolonial contramodernity. In that sense, welcome to the "we." Having said that, there are obviously very specific issues which have very specific institutional histories. The kind of discourse that is produced now in the name of postcolonial critique has its inclusions, its "we's" and those whom it seeks to represent at a more general political/ethical level. Here the problem is as fraught and as difficult as that of the theorists of class speaking in some ways for or about the working class, or of the feminist intellectuals speaking about those who are in a position of being unconsciously tethered to various forms of domestic labor without actually realizing their own position. Now, from the postcolonial perspective, I have made reference to questions of refugees, of migration and so on, and there are a number of things to say about this. One: It is in my notion of culture as survival that I want somehow to garner that experience, understand that experience, bear witness to that destiny, to see how it then changes the epistemological basis of the work I do. To that extent, I'm part of this mediatory, transformative process which is a very dangerous one; the whole process of translation is very precarious, ambivalent, problematic, but I think it has always been so, whether you are a Marxist literary critic talking about the working class or, indeed, whether you're a postcolonial critic talking about these forms of marginality or minority which have largely been appropriated ethnographically or else resolved through some notion of liberal multiculturalism. To that extent, one has to grab the thorn of translation if one wants to change the terms in which these issues will be seen both within the culture industries and in the academies, where certain important institutions like schools and universities and the media overlap; if we can effect certain redefinitions there, then that actually does press upon policy institutions. But there is another aspect of the "we," and I think that is a form of communality that is to some extent specific to what I understand to be the most exciting, but also some of the most ambiguous conditions—political conditions, discursive conditions, historical conditions—of postcolonial critique. This is the fact that, unlike, say, Marxism and its academic or theoretical manifestations or even its political applications, postcoloniality doesn't have a master text. Various critics have noted this: Gayatri Spivak speaks about the catachrestic gesture of postcolonial criticism, basically a more Derridean deconstructive gesture; Edward Said speaks of the contrapuntal nature of the postcolonial critique in relation to the West; in other texts, the interruptive, the interrogative—I'm just trying to suggest to you my wider sort of theoretical idea that the construction of the colony makes an epistemological intervention in, and displacement of, the construction of Western civility. To put it very simply, I think we are in a position which is much more amorphous than the project of just class-led liberation. To talk very practically for the moment, it's very interesting to see that in many post-independence movements in the Third World, the destinies of the new nations have been articulated in avant-garde film or innovative experimental poetry, where the old realist paradigms have actually receded and have been associated with a much more debased, bourgeois, patriarchal form of nationalism. It's interesting to see that in the emergent black consciousness of a new ethnicity in Great Britain, the art work, the films, the music often participate in a cultural theory. It's interesting to see how the language of black feminist critique in the United States is troubled by essentialism, even if it is relation to its sometimes emulatory or ambivalent, but it's a major issue, and critics, black critics in the United States, are very aware of the problems of signification and its areas of complexity. In Australia, even from what I've picked up in a few days and through acquaintance with a number of people here, there is a profound attempt to understand public political events in relation to the languages of affect, the languages of identification and discourse. Now, perhaps one could say that the colonial moment, when seen as part of the whole matrix of the production of modernity, introduces such a contradiction into our historical awareness of the event that the disciplines we are now using to describe that disjunctive moment are inadequate as long as they're seen in their more traditional forms. So that, if ethnography was one of the major ways of the early twentieth century and midcentury to talk about other cultures, when we now try to talk about an ethnography of the West in relation to migration, or to diasporic communities, the very body of anthropological knowledge leads on into psychoanalysis, literature, rhetorical studies. Again, whereas twenty years ago "Commonwealth Literature" was an area study—you studied the history of an area, the politics of an area, the literature of an area, you became a kind of native surrogate, and the whole idea was to keep your voice as authentic as possible to the texts you studied—today that whole notion of an area is breaking up into a much more fraught and tense attempt to understand how we may talk about a problematic inter- or intra- or transnational culture. Consequently, literary studies can no longer function at the level of sophisticated metaphoric, formalistic, narrative image analysis. We are actually now trying to understand the specific enunciative conditions of the text, and this immediately leads us into a number of areas; there are histories local to the texts that we study which jostle with theories of other provenances and other cultures. So I believe there is a kind of international moment which is actually followed by a kind of intertextual and indeed interdisciplinary study. I have elsewhere said something very similar when I said that my project of postcolonial countermodernity is as much transnational as it is translational.

Bennett: Talking of translation, your own education took you from the tertiary study of English literature in Bombay to the study of English literature at Oxford. In a sense, you were living a grand narrative which took you from a "periphery," where things may have seemed simulacral, to a "center," where you might have found the "original." I know you were deeply disappointed; you found an absence. Where did you find the theory that enabled you to rewrite that fall from innocence as a knowledge?

Bhabha: First of all, let me say that my position in India as a part of a Parsee minority (that is, of Persian origins) already places me in an interesting kind of border position. On the one hand, it's a generally prosperous community: bourgeois, Westernized more than simply Anglicized, professional; but on the other, despite the commercial and professional status, it is a community that has noticeably had very little political influence or power. Again, it's generally a highly educated community which has, until recently, not been noted for making an enormous intellectual or creative contribution in India. What I'm trying to say is that there's a number of such anomalies that one has to live through as a Parsee, quite apart from the fact that in a poor country one was often seen as more European than Indian. There was an almost Kierkegaardian sense of original guilt that one had as a Parsee—which the Parsees, of course, deflected in often rather racist ways—so that in my own life in India, even before I went to educational institutions and took this sort of bourgeois colonial trajectory of the move from Elphinstone College, Bombay, to Christ Church College, Oxford, which is of a grand-narrative kind, I had already encountered, albeit in a very privileged way, a number of anomalous social positions. There were moments of immense adolescent angst and anxiety associated with not being authentically Indian, not having a real Indian language—the Gujurati that we spoke at home intermingled with English was a debased form of Gujurati. We didn't have many great nationalist leaders to call our own or to identify with. All of that created a lot of problems. But I think it gave me a sneaking sort of humorous sense of what it was to be seen as the belated one, who comes too late. In some ways, I quite enjoyed that; so that, whereas the Hindi novel or the Marathi theater or the Bengali intellectual tradition could boast many great things, we could boast the setting up of the Central Bank of India or the large commercial house of the Tartars, that we were supposedly honorable accountants, and so on. But on our New Year's Day, instead of having the great Indian mythological performances that other Indian communities had, we had these Bombay-Parsee farces that were set up by a distant relative of mine who was a kind of Parsee national figure. That's what we did on our New Year's Day. We went and laughed at ourselves in very slickly done, but rather humdrum, Parsee *Nataks* (*Nataks* being plays of a very popular kind). It also has a link with the Marathi theater, which was of a burlesque tradition, and from very early on, I remember thinking this was a wonderful thing, that where other people could go on New Year's Day or on a High Day or a holiday and see some edifying thing, we went to these farces—whole families would go. We would have a celebratory meal and then go and sit and laugh at ourselves at these low-level productions, and everybody would be there, from the working-class Parsees to the rich ones—only, one group would sit in the front of the house and the others would sit in the stalls or in the gods. And I think my taste for taking seriously certain kind of border positions, marginal positions, hybrid situations emerges from that. And, yes, I was much later very angry with my closest friend and my wife on occasions, because they took a much more classically Marxist line on the Parsees, seeing them as an Anglicized, bourgeois community whose cultural problems were of a trivial nature, given that, while they were a small minority in India, it was a privileged minority. But it was also an alienated minority, and I somehow felt, at that point, that there was something about cultural hybridity and its lower registers which ought not to be neglected and, indeed, many Mandarin Marxists could actually not see the complexities of that kind of cultural anxiety, ambivalence, and intermixture that is, in a way, the Parsee condition. If you can imagine it, it's like a Jewish ironic tradition functioning at a level of a certain kind of verbal and intellectual facility, but it doesn't have the great Jewish intellectual tradition behind it to point to.

Bennett: So what you are saying is that you had the theory long before you could formulate it, let alone. . . .

Bhabha: No, no, I don't know whether I had the theory; I had the experience. Everybody shoots me down for having had no experiences: I have no anecdotes, people say, I only have theories. They say, "We only remember you for the theory of so-and-so, we don't know anything about your history." But I'd like to make a plug here and say, *"I had these experiences."* But then there is the other part of your question, about my "grand-narrative" trajectory from studying English literature at Elphinstone in Bombay to Oxford. It was rather like the V.S. Naipaul moment in *The Mimic Men*, where he says that he always thought that the golden stones that were used to build the great edifices, the great façades of London, were invested with a particular gravity and weight and that actually when he went to London he found that stones were stones; it was that kind of feeling.

Bennett: What kinds of affiliations did you have to form in order to get the theory which turned disappointment and absence into a critical practice?

Bhabha: Well, I think this was a very specific problem in my case. I remember struggling over trying to write a dissertation on V.S. Naipaul, which I did at Oxford as a graduate student, working specifically on *A House for Mr. Biswas*. I found that I couldn't fit the political, the cultural, the existential, the chronological experience of that text into the tradition of liberal novel criticism of the Anglo-American school, where there has been, as you know, a proliferation of images of the home or the house as a way of talking about the novel's accommodation of life: Henry James' house of fiction; Iris Murdoch's idea that a novel should be like a free house where many people can live, indeed, even in a kind of a tortured, anguished hope; Rushdie's latest recent pamphlet, "In Good Faith," where he says at the end of it, fiction is like a house—in good faith, I think, but with a kind of paradoxical, ironic, tragic turn to that image. I'm saying the image of the house has always been used to talk about the accommodative, accommodatingly true nature of the novel, and here you had a novel where the realism, if you like, was unable to contain the anguish of displacement and movement as poor Mr. Biswas went looking for his house. So part of it was to do with the breakdown of that particular ethical, aesthetic tradition of novel criticism. I couldn't work it that way. This was also the period in the mid-late 1970s where the Machereyan reading of texts, the symptomatic reading of texts I should say, was current and the presence of Terry Eagleton and his seminar at Oxford was certainly very vivifying for me. I did, however, find at that time that none of that theory based itself for its sociopolitical conditions of possibility or invention on the colonial experience; it neither set itself in relation to the colonial historical situation, nor did it actually address the specific problem of "interpellation" that was very apparent for me in a number of colonial texts, amongst them Naipaul's preeminently—that the, if you like, the illusory nature of ideological interpellation, which was always supposed to be the thing that was disallowed to the subject, was precisely that which constituted the colonial subject. The colonial subject was actually very aware of his or her inauthenticity; indeed, the whole thing was about that, and about that in a very public sphere, so it was not like the more Sartrean or Camusian problem of the inauthenticity of the existential self; this was a form of inauthenticity which was clearly seen to be culturally, politically, and socially constructed and which then turns into a kind of inward experience, through which most of political and social life is negotiated. This is not only part of the colonial condition, it then becomes part of the nationalist bourgeois ideologies, at which point, in some senses, it can then turn. This is where I got very interested in the way in which mimicry could then stop being just a form of passive imitation and become a way in which the inappropriateness of the master or the model comes to be visible. That can be a way of both freeing oneself and then framing the colonizer's culture through experience of its colonial dissemination; it actually leads you to a very interesting place, because then you become aware of the contextual culture (the indigenous culture or native culture) and of the interaction between that and the imposed colonial culture. You're aware of the way in which that hybrid displacing space deprives the imposed imperialist culture not only of the authority that it has for so long imposed politically, often through violence, but even of its own claims to authenticity. In its attempt to be imposed or to be imitated, colonial culture actually raises the question about its own origins and its own authenticity and, I believe, produces a transitional mode, a subversive act. It is also, in a way, a freeing act, but it does not free you to a kind of liberal utopia, nor does it send you scurrying to look for your own authentic roots. What it opens up are dangerous, problematic areas of self-recognition, but ones I think that are very important because they put under erasure, make problematic, the binary division between native and imperialist cultures or between your roots and what is imposed on them. It raises this nonpolarized, nonbinary area which is genuinely problematic for the imposition of authority of an imperialist culture. The breaking down of the binaries is also genuinely problematic for the nationalist, bourgeois interest which is trying now, in order to assert its own power, to assert its own authenticity. At the same time, the breaking down of these oppositions actually opens up some of the most difficult cultural and political questions about democratic societies. It is in this sense that I have also tried to look at Naipaul's very avowedly antinationalist sense of a national culture.

Collits: I'd like to come back to the problem of the speaking position of the postcolonial critic. Contemporary ethnography is beset by anxiety over this problem, the problem of the ethnographer who reports from the margins back to the metropolis and tells the metropolis about strange things that have been visited. That has now become a problem. In many ways, I suppose arising out of the autobiographical experiences you have just given us and fitting these with many of the concepts you employ, you seem to bypass this problem or simply slip out from under it. I wonder, though, if I can ask you to specify your own speaking position as postcolonial critic in a space to which you have now invited an Englishman and an Australian as well. Do you speak, for example, as some kind of Tiresias figure? What I've got in mind is the Tiresias who was given the privilege of becoming a woman and then returned to being a man, so that having experienced both, the difference between "same" and "other" disappears. Tiresias could answer the unanswerable questions for the rest of humanity, and knowingly compare male and female experiences from his own "lived" experience. Does that ring any bell with you, either autobiographically or in terms of the problem of postcolonial speaking positions?

Bhabha: I'll just mention two starting propositions which relate to this problem. One, I hope that if you accept some of what I say about the need to redefine, from the postcolonial perspective, a contramodernity, not a postmodernity, then I think you will indulge me in thinking that the metropolis is in a way peripheralized and is a much more disseminatory reality than in any sense an organic national entity. In my own experience of living in London, I like to think how, for instance, Brixton is not a exclusively ghetto area at all, but is marked by a certain ethnicity and a certain sense of identification amongst Afro-Caribbeans. Isaac Julian's new film *Young So Rebels*, which is set in the Jubilee Year, takes Dalston in the East End of London as a kind of space where there isn't ethnic exclusivity, but a profound new ethnic identification with the place. Southall, equally, with Asians. And so I think, in a not unproblematic, but very productive way, the metropolis is not what it was, and, in a rather unfortunate way, the point was made in *The New York Times* a couple of years ago when a series of articles about the squalor of New York were entitled "New York: the New Calcutta." Now I think this is a profound historical mistake: The decline of New York cannot be compared to the problems of urban Calcutta, and it is just indulgence and inaccuracy to imagine that. A much more practical illustration of what I am talking about is the construction through histories of displacement, diaspora, postcoloniality, of the environment of my theoretical concept of a countermodernity. So, in this context, I would suggest that the Tiresian experience is very much an experience of doubling or splitting, terms which you know I explore from the cultural histories that I work. And, in that sense, it is not that "same" and "other" disappear, but that, if you are interested in the moment of disjunction, in the complex moment of the articulation of different temporalities such as I've been speaking about here in Melbourne and Canberra, then the polarities that are encountered in a number of political, historical, textual moments can be seen not as a starting point, but as effects. By studying the moment of enunciation, the moment of articulation, you see how certain forms of antagonism come to be constituted, and you begin to see polarities like "self" and "other" differently. It's not that one or other of them disappears, nor do you start from the one or the other; instead, if you like, you start from in between the two, and you see that each term is itself conflictual and itself constituted in a differential way. I mean the self may be Western and white, and there is the question of gender, the question of class, the question of age; there is the question of generationalism, of province, of the rural, the nation, the north and the south, and so on. My point would be that each of those polarities are in themselves, as they constitute themselves, much more complex and that it doesn't allow the self/other polarity.

Collits: I understand what you are saying, but I still have reservations. Let's just bring it back to things that you articulated in a usefully compressed way a short while ago, terms that you have made famous: "hybridization," "mimicry," and other such terms. Now, I feel that it would not have been possible for me, as a white, to coin such terms, because of their intense colonialist and racist overtones. You seem simply to be able to use these in a quasi-technical way that is voided entirely of such history. Yet I take it you are not using these terms with such a lack of awareness. Can you gloss these terms in a way that brings them into relationship with what you've just been saying?

Bhabha: Let us remind ourselves that what I've done with these terms has a history. The wrenching of the term "black" and turning it into "black power" is a kind of catachrestic reversal, a revaluation, a snubbing out of the primary, racist reference. Skip Gates, in *The Signifying Monkey*, does it with the simian stereotype, and indeed the notion of signification. Likewise, Huston Baker talks about the black vernacularism, takes vernacular with its pejorative force, and turns it back. Hortense Spillers takes the notion of the mulatto, that in-between position, to actually articulate another theory of race and representation. Now, because I feel each subject position, to use your term, even when it is in an apparently binaristic or polar opposition, is itself profoundly differential (which is what finally makes that polarity problematic), I feel that the question of what I've actually said about mimicry, for instance, is part of a more general theory of authority—authorization/de-authorization—that is actually visible in a number of situations of oppression and discrimination. Still, I take your point that there's a long colonial governmental history where Indians or Africans were only seen to be capable of imitating their masters and therefore the moment of freedom was delayed. Indeed, the question of a hybrid culture was always seen to be a way of actually propagating imperial rule: the idea that if we mixed up their culture enough, then we could discontinue the administering. Yes, there is this kind of catachrestic or ironic reversal, in keeping with a short history of the other terms that I've given, which I've also tried to effect. And I've tried to show that authority or authenticity are most capable of being subverted at the point at which they think that they are most originary, most authoritative. So my interest in "mimicry", to use one of those terms, arose precisely because I'm assuming that all modes of imposition, the very demand to be like the colonial master, is inhabited with its own failure. In that sense, mimicry is not so much about that demand as about its deplorable effects. The term "mimicry" is therefore about the way in which authorization, because it assumes that it is itself authentic and is producing the effects of mimicry, is in a way blinded, tragically blinded. We can do the same with "hybridization". For me, hybridization is again about a site—a site of political negotiation, a site of the construction of the symbolic, the construction of meaning—that, besides displacing the terms of negotiation, opens up an interaction or a dialogism of the powerful/the powerless, and it is this site—again for me a temporal problem—which enables another distribution of meaning, a change in the ratio of powers, because neither of the two (or more) settled moments prior to this hybrid site are imported into it in their previous form. The hybrid site is the moment that opens up through something that has been disavowed, a reinscription of that disavowal; but it is also a moment of the displacement of the previous antagonism, and, indeed, it opens up because that antagonism cannot be contained within it. In my essay "The Commitment to Theory," I've talked about this, where I say the important thing about the hybrid site is to see that the contenders in any antagonistic interaction are never unitary, in themselves they are themselves disseminated, and their interaction therefore has the possibility always of setting up other sites. I just want to say two brief things in relation to this. First, the moment of indeterminism, of contingency, is necessary because, without it, we would not be able to disarticulate authority. Authority functions because of the accident of something in relation to which it has, through its appropriated powers, to impose its own authority; in a way, authority has to lose itself to gain itself, otherwise it is to be part of the game, unable to show up its authority. But that moment of contingency is never entirely contained. The interesting thing is that, in order to be authoritative, the contingent or the indeterminate has to emerge. Sometimes, of course, that indeterminacy is normalized, rolled back into the discursive authority, and that is also the moment at which the authority can be disarticulated. Now, the second point I want to make relates more directly to certain issues about the politics of theory, the politics of some of the temporal concepts that I deal with, the notion of indeterminacy and so on; and that is that usually we assume that the problem with poststructuralism, as it contributes to social and political thinking, is always a problem of closure—it never tells us about closure, which is what we want, as if somehow our politics depend upon forms of closure and fixity. Supposing I suggest to you that the real anxiety posed by poststructuralism is that its temporality is such that it always makes you pose the question of where you are beginning. It's not the problem of ends; it always re-poses, as it were, from the end the question of where is one starting from, where is one demanding one's authority from. It makes the moment of beginning contingent, so that then one can never rest in a kind of primordial, culturally supremacist, historically ascendent position. If one is aware of the problem of beginning, as I put it, then one is always having to see other disjunct minority histories, other moments of beginning, in relation to one's own. So in a sense it's not—as, say, Terry Eagleton sometimes says—the open-endedness which is the real problem. I think what it problematizes, very properly and very usefully, although as always dangerously, is where it is that I am putting my mark in order to initiate or establish. It makes that point of beginning properly belated, so that nobody can claim that kind of priority. It always strikes me as being very strange, to put it in very simple terms, that people who attack the starting point of conservatism—the conservatists' belief in their own organic origin, or constitution—will then want to propose an alternative theory, whose content may be progressive or revolutionary, but whose form demands that an equally profound priority of origin is also imposed. That's when we get caught in this notion that we must have polarities in order properly to perform or execute political antagonisms.

Bennett: You suggested yesterday that the Rushdie affair has been misleadingly framed as a conflict between modernity and archaism, or between Western secularism and Muslim pietism or religiosity; in what ways can the binary terms of this debate be displaced—by, say, a third term?

Bhabha: So much of the problem of the Rushdie affair has actually been the problem of names and naming: fundamentalism, liberalism, the renaming of the Prophets' wives, taking the name of the Prophet in a profligate fiction—so I don't want to add another, third term or to name simply a thirdness. What I do want to say, as I said yesterday, is that accepting the problem in the very polarized way in which it was set up, not only did a disservice to a whole oppressed community, on the one hand, and to a man hiding for his life, on the other, but it didn't allow us to perform, quite simply, the process of negotiation. What do I mean by negotiation? I'm not talking about some kind of wheeling and dealing—which later actually happened to no good effect in the Rushdie affair when mediators set themselves up, no doubt good-heartedly, and suggested that some kind of middle ground should be established. For me, the hybrid site that is set up or that gets produced is not such a middle ground where the meeting of men's—and I repeat, men's—minds usually solve a problem. It would be something like the simple recognition that, however foreign to the Muslim experience Rushdie's text was, it was also in another sense (read or unread) internal to it, which is precisely why it created the enormous affective cathected crisis that it did. Equally, however external the ideologies of the Bradford Mosque might have been to Rushdie's way of writing, still, as he said himself, the very presence of that site of cultural difference was profoundly intimate to his own text. Now, for me—to use your term and a term I've used, too—the third space or the hybrid site of this debate emerged very much in the way in which it was taken up by feminists who acted in ways not to be trapped between the liberal writers and the fundamentalist mullahs, but to raise wider questions about the administration of cultural difference, the problems of gender within it, the problems of a wider metaphor of marginalization, the problems of education and schooling, the problems of communities controlled by certain kinds of patriarchal power centers, and the problems of interpretation—of their own lives as well as of certain texts. The way in which the affair became a feminist issue, a black feminist issue in the British context, is for me a very clear illustration of how elements of the antagonism are then reinscribed into another site, which does not necessarily either speak to the preconstituted polarity between liberals and mullahs—it doesn't necessarily even solve that problem—but it ineluctably pushes it elsewhere and pushes it forward. So to look for a resolution to that issue in the third space is not what hybridity is about, because in a way the process of hybridization changes the weightedness, the value, the sign of the historical moment, and that's what I feel happened in the feminist appropriation and reinscription of the issue to raise, from the gendered perspective, a number of issues current today in contemporary race, class, and gender politics in the U.K., issues that affect everybody, not simply the London literati or the Bradford Imams.

13

Culture, State, and the Rediscovery of Indian Politics

Ashis Nandy

A society can conceptualize the relationship between its culture and its state in two ways. The first way is to look for the means by which culture can be made to contribute to the sustenance and growth of the state. The state here is seen as operating according to certain fixed, universal, sociological rules. Elements of the culture that help strengthen the state are seen as good; those elements of the culture that do not help the proper functioning of the state or hinder its growth are seen as defective. A mature society, in this view, is expected to shed or actively eliminate these defective elements so as to improve both the functioning of the state and the quality of the culture.

The second way of looking at the relationship between culture and the state is to do so from the standpoint of the culture. This approach may regard the state as a protector, an internal critic, or a thermostat for the culture, but not as the ultimate pacesetter for the society's way of life. The state here is made to meet the needs of survival or enrichment of the culture; it is never allowed to dictate terms to the culture. Even when the state is used as a critique of the culture and the culture is sought to be transformed, the final justification for the criticism and the transformation is not sought in the intrinsic logic of statecraft or in the universal laws of state formation. That justification is sought in the self-perceived needs of the culture and the people and in the moral framework used by the people.

This dichotomy between the state- and culture-oriented views of society, of course, dissolves if one uses the older idea of the state-as-part-and-parcel-of-culture (as obtains in many traditional societies) or if one refuses to accept the modern idea of nation-state as the only genuine version of state (as is assumed by most modern political and social analysts today). In most nonmodern societies, among people who work with the older concept of the state and not with the modern concept of the nation-state, the culture-oriented approach to state is seen as natural and the state-oriented approach as an imposition.[1] Likewise, in modern societies the nation-state-oriented approach seems natural and rational, and the culture-oriented one looks unnatural, irrational, or primitive. The choice, therefore, boils down to one between the culture-oriented and the nation-state-oriented. However, for the sake of simplicity, I shall use here the expression "state-oriented" or "statist" to mean the nation-state-oriented, hoping that the reader will not confuse this concept of statist with that used in debates between the socialist thinkers and the liberals believing in a minimal state.

You may notice that I am not taking into account in this dichotomy the nature of the state and the nature of culture. These are vital issues, and they need to be discussed fully. For the moment, however, I want to avoid them because I want to be fair to the culture-oriented approach, which believes that a state can destroy the civilization of which it is a part even when the "intentions" of the state are "honorable" and even when it is trying to improve a decaying civilization. When a state becomes ethnocidal, the culture-oriented approach believes, the remedy does not lie only in capturing the state, since it provides no check against the captured state becoming as ethnocidal in scope as it was before being captured.

For the last 150 years, westernized, middle-class Indians have learned to look at the first approach—the one that orients the needs of the culture to the needs of the state—as the very epitome of political maturity, achievement, and development. Since the nation-state system acquired its present global predominance in the last century, most political analysis in the West, too, has forgotten the other alternative. And since a global science of politics became fully operational after the Second World War, the state-oriented attitude to culture has become the only way of looking at culture the world over. Nearly all studies of political development and political culture done in the fifties and sixties have this cultural engineering component built into them. From Talcott Parsons, Edward Shils, and David Easton to Karl Deutsch, Samuel Huntington, and Lucian Pye, it is the same story. So much so that, under their influence, the modern political analysts and journalists are forced to fall back on state-oriented analytic categories, even after the categories have shown poor interpretive power, as often happens when figures like Gandhi, Khomeini, Maulana Bhasani, and Jarnail Singh Bhindranwale (to give random examples) become politically influential.

This is a part of a larger picture. Take for instance, the studies of cultural contexts of economic growth done during the same period. The main function of culture, according to these studies, was to facilitate economic growth. Aspects of culture that stood in the way of such growth had to be ruthlessly excised. In "stagnant" culture, that is, in cultures that did not nurture a thriving modern economy, the engineering challenge was to rediscover or introduce cultural elements that would trigger or sustain economic growth and the spirit of the market that went with it. This was the thrust of the psychological studies of achievement motive done by David McClelland and company and the studies of Protestant-ethics-like elements in non-Western cultures by a drove of social anthropologists. Even the hard tough-minded economists of the period, who did not believe in the relevance of such woolly psychological or cultural anthropological work, never faltered in their belief that a society had to give primacy to the needs of the modern economy, however defined, over the needs of culture. So did the mercenaries among them vending the materialist—read economic—interpretation of history to ensure the centrality of their dismal science in the world of social knowledge. In India, at least, I have not come across a single work of any Marxist economist of the period that challenged the basic priority of economics and sought to restore, even as a distant goal, Marx's original vision of a society freed from the bondage of economism.[2]

An exactly similar case can be made about science. Most science-and-culture studies of the fifties and sixties sought to make the society safe for modern science. For this purpose, all nonmodern cultures were sought to be retooled and made more rational or modern. Thus, scientific criticisms of culture were encouraged, but cultural criticisms of science were dubbed obscurantist.

Occasionally shallow criticisms of the social relations of science were allowed—in the sense that the control over science exercised by imperialism or capitalism or by army generals was allowed to be exposed. But this was done as a part of an attempt to protect the text and the core values of modern science, which were seen as absolute and as the last word in human rationality. As if, somehow, the forces of violence and exploitation, after taking over much of the environment of modern science, hesitated when they encountered the contents of modern science and refused to enter its sanctum sanctorum. Here, too, culture was always at the receiving end, while science kept the company of modern political and economic institutions.

We however are talking of politics at the moment, not of the witchcraft called economics or the megacorporation called modern science. And I want to suggest that, in India, the primacy granted to the needs of the state—seen as a necessary part of a ruthless, global, nation-state system—is not a new idea coined in the late 1940s by the first generation of the post-Independence managers of Indian polity. The primacy of the state was not the discovery of Jawaharlal Nehru or Vallabhbhai Patel, two very different persons who arrived at roughly the same statist ideology through very different personal and intellectual paths. Nor did the primacy-of-the-state theory evolve in the fifties or the sixties when the structural-functional models of political development and positivist-Marxist models of the state endorsed, at two ends of the political spectrum, the primacy of the state. The new model merely relegitimized what had been brewing for more than a hundred years in India and, perhaps, for more than three hundred years in Europe.

The statist model first came to India in the nineteenth century, in the second phase of colonialism, when a more reactive, self-defensive Hinduism began to take shape in response to the consolidation of social theories that saw colonialism as a civilizing influence and as a pathway from feudalism to modern statehood.[3] It was toward the middle of the nineteenth century that a series of dedicated Hindu religious and social reformers first mooted the idea that what Hinduism lacked was the primacy that most forms of postmedieval, Western Christianity granted to the state. Even Islam, they felt, had a built-in space for such primacy. The Hindus did not. That was why, they decided, the Hindus were having it so bad. The sorrow of that generation of reformers was that the Hindu seemed an animal peculiarly hostile and insensitive to the subtleties of the nation-state system; their hope was that the hostility and insensitivity could be corrected through proper cultural and social engineering. This the religious reformers tried to do through a revision of the Hindu personality and way of life.

This effort, because it came as part of a defense of Hinduism, hid the fact that this was the first influential indigenous form of the primacy-of-the-state thesis advanced in India. The thesis, for the first time, brought modern statism within Hinduism, in the sense that the Hindu state of the future was not to be the Hindu polity of the past, but a centralized, modern nation-state with a Brahmanic idiom. Suresh Sharma's recent paper on D. V. Savarkar neatly sums up the spirit of this particular form of Hindu nationalism and the political form it had to later take. It is a measure of the cultural tragedy that colonialism was for India that even a person like Savarkar, after spending nearly 40 years in intense, often-violent, anticolonial struggle and, suffering for it, had to ultimately turn intellectually and culturally collaborationist, purportedly to save the Hindus from Islamic domination with the help of the culturally and politically more "advanced" British.[4]

The earlier generation of reformers, in what can be called the first phase of British colonialism, had pleaded for greater political participation of Indians and also for greater state intervention in the society. But there were externally imposed limits to their enthusiasm; they did not stress the absolute primacy of the state, partly because the state was not theirs and partly because even their British rulers had not yet shown any great ideological commitment to the state system they were running. The state for the first generation of British rulers was mainly a means of making money, not a means of cultural engineering. These rulers feared and respected Indian culture, which they tried not to disturb as long as it did not stand in the way of their greed. Moreover, the raj occupied a relatively small part of the subcontinent and certainly did not give the impression of being the paramount power in the country. The Indians pressuring their British rulers to intervene in Indian society could not internalize a highly activist or an awe-inspiring grand image of the state.[5]

Nonetheless, the first generation of social reformers had provided the base on which the second generation of reformers built their adoration for the modern idea of the nation-state and their suspicion of all grassroot politics. Certainly, these latter reformers did not put any premium on participatory politics, which they accepted theoretically only as a vague, populist possibility. Even when they spoke of mass politics as desirable, they saw it as something that had to come later—after the Hindu had been morally and educationally uplifted and after he had learned to take on modern responsibilities.[6] This shielded them from the awareness that they were unwilling or incapable of mobilizing the ordinary Indians for basic political changes.

The votaries of a Hindu nation-state, thinking that they were pleading for a Hindu polity, were also mostly unaware that the nation-state system was one of the more recent innovations in human civilization and that it had come into being only about two hundred years earlier in Europe, in the mid-seventeenth century. They chose to see it as one of the eternal verities of humankind. Naturally, they diagnosed the Hindu inadequacy in state-oriented politics as a result of a major defect in the Hindu personality and culture, which had to be reformed as the first step to political freedom. (The British in India, for their own reasons, enthusiastically endorsed this priority of the cultural over the political.)

Many of these social reformers, inappropriately called Hindu revivalists, were to later have much sympathy for the anti-British terrorist movements. But that sympathy did not go with any passion for wider political participation of the masses. Indeed, they were always a little afraid of the majority of Hindus who lived in the 500,000 Indian villages. *Hindurajya*, yes, but not with the full participation of all the Hindu *praja*, at least not with the *praja* as they were, and certainly not with the participation of all Hindus in the short run. The conspiratorial style of the terrorists came in handy in this respect, since it automatically restricted mass participation. Even the constant invocation of the Hindu past by the revivalists—the practice that gave them their distinctive name—was a criticism of the living Hindus. It was a compensatory act. It hid the revivalists' admiration for the West and for Middle-Eastern Islam, seen as martial and valorous, and it hid the desperate search for the same qualities in the Hindu past. The political consequence of this admiration for the conquerors of the Hindus was the continuous attempt by many to reeducate the "politically immature," anarchic, living Hindus, so that the latter could rediscover their lost Western and Islamic values and play their proper role in the global system of nation-states. Swami Vivekananda, when he envisioned a new race of Vedantic Hindus who would build a Western society in India, was only being true to the primacy-of-the-state thesis.[7]

I am arguing that the nineteenth-century characters the modern Indians have learned to call revivalists were never truly anti-West or anti-Islam. They were only anti-British and anti-Muslim in the Indian context. Their ideal, in important respects, was Western Christianity or Middle-Eastern Islam. And as for their concept of the state, it was perfectly modern. If anything, they were fundamentally and ferociously anti-Hindu.[8] The only good Hindu to them was the Hindu who was dead, that is, the Hindu who had lived a few thousand years ago. They wanted to enter the world scene with an engineered Hindu who, but for his ideological commitment to classical Hinduism, would be a Western man, a man who would accept the rules of the game called the nation-state system and who could not be short-changed either by the Westerner or by the Muslim.

It was this heritage on which both the mainstream liberal and the official Marxist ideologies in India were to later build. Strange though it may sound to many, there *was* a cultural continuity between the early primacy accorded to the state and the strand of consciousness that was to later seek legitimacy in the popular modern theories of the state in India. Both the liberals and the official Marxists like to trace their origins to the earlier integrationist tradition of social reform, the one beginning with Rammohun Roy (1772–1833) and more or less ending with Rabindranath Tagore (1861–1940) and Gopal Krishna Gokhale (1866–1915). This ignores the checks within the ideological frame of these pioneers. Rammohun Roy, for instance, was a modernizer, but he located the origins of the problems of Hindu personality and culture in the colonial situation and not in Hindu traditions. He believed that the pathologies of Hinduism he was fighting could be found only around the institutional structures introduced by British rule, and, therefore, his own religious reforms and the new Hindu sect he established were directed only at the exposed Hindus, not at parts of the society untouched by colonialism. As he himself put it,

> From a careful survey and observation of the people and inhabitants of various parts of the country, and in every condition of life, I am of opinion that the peasants and villagers who reside at a distance from large towns and head stations and courts of law, are as innocent, temperate and moral in their conduct as the people of any country whatsoever; and the further I proceed towards the North and West [i.e., away from British India], the greater the honesty, simplicity and independence of character I meet with.[9]

In his own crude, unsure way, Roy did try to protect the architectonics of Indian culture. He did not want Indian culture to be integrated into the modern world; he wanted modernity to be integrated into Indian culture. His modern admirers have chosen to forget the checks within him—weak though the checks were. They have built him up as the father of modern India and as a mindless admirer of everything Western.

Thus, as far as the role of nation-state in the Indian civilization is concerned, Indian modernists as well as radicals have drawn upon the ideological framework first popularized by Hindu nationalism. It was in their model that the modern nation-state first became an absolute value and acquired absolute primacy over the needs of the Indian Civilization.

Yet there has always been in India during the last 150 years another intellectual current that has looked at the needs of the society differently. This current sees state-oriented politics as a means of criticizing Indian culture, even as a means of renegotiating traditional social relationships, but it refuses to see such politics as the raison d'être of Indian civilization. However, though a majority of Indians may have always lived with such a concept of politics, for modern India, the concept has survived only as a part of an intellectual underground since the middle of the nineteenth century.

It was only under the influence of Gandhi (1869–1948) that this current temporarily acquired a certain self-consciousness and political dominance. Gandhi has often been called an anarchist. To the extent that he suspected and fought state power and refused to grant it any important role in guiding or controlling political and social change, he *was* close to anarchism. Also, while leading a freedom struggle against a foreign power, he could get away with his antipathy to the state. But this situation could not last beyond a point. His very success dug the grave of his ideology; his antistatist political thought quickly went into recession after Independence. The demands of statecraft in a newly independent nation were such that the national leaders not only began to look with suspicion at the Gandhian emphasis on cultural traditions, they also began to encourage political interpretations of Gandhi that fitted him into the state-oriented frame of politics, neutralizing or ignoring his culture-oriented self as irrelevant saintliness or eccentricity. On this ideological issue, they were in perfect agreement with Gandhi's assassin, Nathuram Godse, an avowed statist. It was not accidental that Godse, though called an ultraconservative, did not feel threatened by the modernists, but by Gandhi.[10]

It is only now that this recessive strain of consciousness is again coming into its own in the works of a number of young and not-so-young scholars—traditionalists, countermodernists, post-

Maoist Marxists, anarchists, and neo-Gandhians. Evidently, an open polity has its own logic. At the peripheries of the modern Indian polity itself, the demand for fuller democratic participation by people who carry the heavy "burden" of their nonmodern culture is becoming an important component of the political idiom.

This consciousness has been endorsed by a political reality having two facets: (1) an increasingly oppressive state-machine that constantly threatens the survival and the ways of life of those Indians it has marginalized and (2) the growing efforts of these marginalized sections to interpret their predicament in terms alien to the modern world and to the state-centered culture of scholarship.[11] There is enough evidence for us to believe that this strain of consciousness may begin to set the pace of public consciousness in India in the coming decades, and the following section is written as a guide and a warning for those pragmatic spirits and hard-boiled modernists of both the right and the left who might have to close ranks to fight this new menace to the modern Indian nation-state. Prewarned, after all, is prearmed.

The first element in this odd strain, which views the needs of a civilization as primary, is the belief that a civilization must use the state as an instrument and not become an instrument of the state. This of course also means that the Indian state should be reformed before the Indian civilization is sought to be reformed. This does not argue out cultural reforms or, even, cultural revolutions. But such interventions are not seen from the viewpoint of the needs of the state. The idea that a civilization can be destroyed or changed beyond recognition reportedly for its own survival in the jungle of the nation-state system is given up here. At the same time, the culture-oriented approach believes that if there is a need either for a cultural revolution or for modest cultural changes in this society, it should begin in deculturized Anglo-India and then, if necessary, end in its externed parts (to translate into English the concept of *bahiskrit samaj* used by Sunil Sahasrabudhe).[12] Culture, in this approach, is the worldview of the oppressed, and it must have precedence over the worldview associated with oppressors, even when the latter claims to represent universal, cumulative rationality and sanctions the very latest theory of oppression.

Second, this approach believes that a cultural tradition represents the accumulated wisdom of a people—empirical and rational in its architectonics, though not in every detail. It does not automatically become obsolete as a consequence of the growth of modern science or technology. In fact, a complex culture has its own ethnic science and technology that are sought to be destroyed by modern science and technology with the help of state power and in the name of the obsolescence of traditional knowledge systems and life styles.[13]

The nonstatists believe that the traditions are under attack today because the people today are under attack. As classical liberalism and czarist Marxism have both by now shown their bankruptcy, many liberals and Marxists have increasingly fallen upon the use of concepts like cultural lag and false consciousness to explain away all resistance to the oppression that comes in the guise of modern science and development. The primacy-of-culture approach fears that more and more models of social engineering will be generated in the modern sector, which would demand from the people greater and greater sacrifices in the name of the state and in the name of state-sponsored development and state-owned science and technology. The culture-oriented approach believes that, when the lowest of the low in India are exhorted to shed their "irrational," "unscientific," antidevelopmental traditions by the official rationalists, the exhortation is a hidden appeal to them to soften their resistance to the oppressive features of the modern political economy in India.[14]

Third, the culture-oriented approach presumes that culture is a dialectic between the classical and the folk, the past and the present, the dead and the living. Modern states, on the other hand, emphasize the classical and the frozen-in-time, so as to museumize culture and make it harmless. Here, too, the modernists endorse the revivalists, who believe in time travel to the past, the Orientalists, to whom culture is a distant object of study, and the deculturized, to whom culture is what one sees on the stage. Such attitudes to culture go with a devaluation of the folk, which is reduced to the artistic and musical self-expression of tribes and language groups. Ethnic arts and ethnic music then become, like ethnic food, new indicators of the social status of the rich and the powerful. Correspondingly, new areas of expertise open up in the modern sector, such as ethnomuseology and ethnomusicology. And cultural anthropology then takes over the responsibility of making this truncated concept of culture communicable in the language of professional anthropology, to give the concept a bogus absolute legitimacy in the name of cultural relativism.

Culture, however, is a way of life, and it covers, apart from "high culture," indigenous knowledge, including indigenous theories of science, education, and social change. The defense of culture, according to those who stress cultural survival, is also the defense of these native theories. The defense must challenge the basic hierarchy of cultures, the evolutionist theory of progress, and the historical sense with which the modern mind works.[15] The modern admirers of native cultures can never accept this radical departure from the post-Enlightenment Western worldview.

Fourth, the culture-oriented approach tries to demystify the traditional reason of the state: national security. It does not deny the importance of national security, even though the statists feel that anyone who is not a statist jeopardizes such security. However, the culture-oriented approach believes that national security can become disjunctive with people's security and may even establish an inverse relationship with the latter.[16] Some of them fear that India is fast becoming a national security state with an ever-expanding definition of security that threatens democratic governance within the country as well as the security of India's neighbors, who are parts of the Indian civilization.[17]

In addition, the culture-sensitive approach to Indian politics seeks to demystify the two newer reasons of state: conventional development and mainstream science (including technology). It believes that new forces of oppression have been unleashed in Indian society in the name of these new reasons of state and the new legitimacies they have created. Those for the primacy of culture believe that these three reasons of state—security, development, and modern science—are creating internal colonies, new hierarchies and recipient cultures among the people, so that a small elite can live off both economic and psychosocial surpluses extracted from the people as a part of the process of modernization.[18] Modernization, the argument goes, has not fallen into wrong hands; built into it are certain forms of domination and violence. The concept of the expert or the revolutionary vanguard is a part of the same story or, as it looks to the nonmoderns, part of the same conspiracy.[19]

It is the feature of the recipient culture sought to be created through the modern state system that the superstitions of the rich and the powerful are given lesser emphasis than the superstitions of the poor and the lowly. This is the inescapable logic of development and scientific rationality today. Only the young, the "immature," and the powerless are left to attack the superstitions of the powerful. (For instance, the belief of the super powers that national security requires the capacity to kill all living beings of the world thirty times over, as if once was not good enough; the belief of our rulers that every society will one day reach the level of prosperity of the modern West, as if the earth had that kind of resources; or the faith of our science bosses that the expansion of

T.V. or nuclear energy would strengthen development without setting up a centralized political control system.) The so-called mature scientists, the ultrarational liberals and professional progressives are kept busy attacking superstitions such as astrology, because they are small-scale enterprises of the ill-bred, native entrepreneurs, not the trillion-dollar enterprises that arms-trade, cosmetics, and pet-food industries are. It is a part of the same game to emphasize the unequal economic exchanges between the East and the West and underemphasize the unequal cultural exchanges between the two, which has already made the modern Western man the ideal of the official culture of India. The culture-oriented activists believe that the latter form of unequal exchange is more dangerous because it gives legitimacy to the "proper" dissenters wanting to lead the masses to a utopia that is but an edited version of the modern West. The first step in the creation of this new set of elites for the future is the destruction of the confidence of the people in their own systems of knowledge and ways of life, so that they become recipients both materially and nonmaterially.[20]

Fifth, the faith in the primacy of culture over the state does not mean the absence of a theory of state. It means another kind of a theory of the state, a theory rooted in the nonmodern understanding of modernity and in a worm's-eye view of the imperial structures and categories that go with modernity. It can also be called an outsider's theory of statist politics. (I have already said at the beginning that this approach does give a role to the state as a protector, an internal critic, and thermostat for the culture.) However, it is an undying superstition of our times that only the modernists can handle the complexities or negotiate the jungle of international politics, ensure internal and external security, and maintain national integration and intercommunal peace. It is a part of the superstition to believe that politics is exclusively the politics organized around the state and the prerogative of the self-declared professional politicians.[21]

The theories of the state used by the outsiders—by those who take the cultural approach seriously—differ in important respects from the dominant theories of political modernization. It is the presence of such alternative theories of the outsiders that accounts for the allegations of irrationality or false consciousness made against these outsiders. These alternative theories look bottom upward toward the modern sector of India, and, therefore, they are not palatable to people who rule India or who want to rule it in future after capturing the state from the present rulers. Such nonmodern theories of the state have no commitment to the ideas of one language, one religion, or one culture for India; nor do they think that such linguistic, religious, or cultural unification advances the cause of the Indian people. Unlike the modernists and the Hindu revivalists, those viewing Indian politics from outside the framework of the nation-state system believe it possible for a state to represent a confederation of cultures, including a multiplicity of religions and languages. To each of these cultures, other cultures are an internal opposition rather than an external enemy. Thus, for instance, true to the traditions of Hinduism, many of these outsiders believe that all Indians are definitionally Hindus, crypto-Hindus, or Hinduized; it sees the modern meaning of the exclusivist concept "Hindu" as a foreign imposition and as anti-Hindu. The culture-oriented do have a commitment to India as a single political entity, mainly because it helps the Indian civilization to resist the soffocating embrace of the global nation-state system and the homogenizing thrust of the culture of the modern West. But they are willing to withdraw the commitment if the statist forces begin to dismantle the civilization to make it a proper modern nation-state and a modern culture, that is, if India is sought to be fully de-Indianized for the sake of a powerful Indian nation-state. This does not imply any innocence about the nature of the global system. It indicates a refusal to accept the games the nations play and an awareness that the problem of internal colonialism in India is a part of a global structure of dominance.

Sixth, it should be obvious from the foregoing that the cultural approach draws a distinction between political participation and participation in state-oriented politics—between *lokniti* and *rajniti*, as some following Jai Prakash Narain put it—and it stresses the former. This is the kind of participation that tries to bring all sections of a society within politics without bringing all aspects of the society within the scope of the state. To those stressing such participation, the politics of the nation-state is only a part of the story, and democratization must have priority over system legitimacy. Alas, this also means that the nonstatists refuse to see the need for democracy as secondary to the need for a strong state. In recent years, this approach to politics has spawned a vigorous civil rights movement in India that is trying to make democratic participation more real to the lowest of the low.[22]

To the statists, this other kind of political participation is a danger signal. It looks extrasystemic and noninstitutionalized—the kind of participation that the modern political scientist, if brought up on the likes of Samuel Huntington, has learned to identify as a sure indicator of political decay—a situation where political participation outstrips system legitimacy.[23] No wonder many of those militantly allegiant to the Indian state would prefer to see the peripheries and the bottom of this society either remain apolitical or, in case the latter are already in politics, systematically depoliticized.[24]

In other words, the culture-oriented approach takes the concept of open society seriously. It knows how the glib talk of culture often hides Third-World despotism. Indeed, the approach takes the principles of democratic governance to their logical conclusion by refusing to accept the definition of civic culture vended by the usurpers or controllers of the state. Culture, this approach affirms, lies primarily with the people. Next door in Pakistan, the dumb general with the toothy smile can find no consolation in the new culturist point of view that is emerging in many traditional societies and, particularly, in this subcontinent. Nor can the senile Ayatollah of Iran in his new incarnation as an Islamic Dracula. Their Islam is a state-controlled set of slogans and gimmicks; it has little to do with Islamic culture, for such a culture can be identified only through open democratic processes. Hopefully, a culture-sensitive polity in India will not stop at mechanical electoral representation of atomized individuals or secularized classes; it will extend representation also to the myriad ways of life in the hope that, in the twenty-first century, Indian democracy will reflect something of the uniqueness of this civilization, too, and pursue the principle of freedom with dignity as a basic human need.

Finally, I must borrow two terms from contemporary philosophy of science to explain the "link" between the worldview that swears by the primacy of the state and the one that swears by the primacy of culture. The former thinks it has an explanation of the latter, which it sees as a product of the frustrations of those who have been displaced from their traditional moorings by the forces of modernity. More, not less, modernity is seen as the antidote for the insane, antiscientific worldview of the disgruntled, culture-drunk, uprooted nonmoderns. This is the tired crisis-of-change thesis. The latter worldview believes that alternative paradigms of knowledge—whether they come from updated Indian traditions or from powerful postmodern theories of the state—cannot be legitimized by categories generated by the presently dominant paradigms of political analysis. There is fundamental and irreconcilable incommunicability between the two sets of paradigms. This is one instance, this worldview claims, where no genuine common language or dialogue is possible. However, the nonmoderns do believe that it is possible for parts of the modern vision to survive in another incarnation, as a subset of a postmodern, and simultaneously more authentically Indian, vision—somewhat in the way the Newtonian worldview survives in the Einsteinian world. With the growing cultural self-confidence of the Indian intellectuals and informed activists, it is possible that the modern West will be seen by a significant number of future Indians the way Gandhi used to see it; as a part of a larger native frame—valuable in many ways, but also dangerous by virtue of its ability to become cancerous.

It is known that when the Newtonian worldview is sought to be explained in Einsteinian terms, elements of it such as mass and velocity retard rather than facilitate communication. This is because the concepts common to the two worldviews are rooted in different theories and thus have different meanings. (This of course is the well-known meaning-variation argument in post-Popperian philosophy of science.) In the context of the issues we are discussing, this means that concepts such as rationality, empirical data, mathematicization, and experimental verification provide no bridge between the state-oriented and the culture-oriented worldviews. Nor do concepts like history, culture, injustice, patriotism, or dissent. No sentiment-laden lecture by the national-security chap on how much he loves his culture is going to appease the activist working among the tribals to protect their lifestyle; nor will the copious tears shed by the ultramodern, rationalist scientist for the Indian villager will move the person to whom the superstitions of the rich (such as the billion-dollar congames involving antidiarrheal drugs or the so-called health-food products like Horlicks and Bournevita) are more dangerous than the pathetic antics of the small-time pavement palmist, being pursued by the urbane rationalists for conning someone out of a couple of rupees (somewhat in the manner in which the village lunatics are pursued by stone-throwing teen-agers while greater lunatics are allowed to become national leaders or war heroes). If you speak to the culture-oriented Indian about the superstitions of the witch doctors or *mantravadis*, he will shrug his shoulder and walk away; he is more concerned about the irrational search for permanent youth that makes the annual cosmetics bill of American women outstrip the combined budgets of all the African countries put together; he is more worried about the superstitious fear of being left behind by other nations, which prompts the Indian sixth five-year plan to invest more than Rs. 9,000 million in only the R&D for space and nuclear programs when the corresponding figure for the R&D for education is 12 million.[25]

The two sides—the statists and the culturists—speak entirely different languages. It is the unmanageable crisis of one worldview—in this case, that of the nation-state-oriented modernity, which has prompted some to switch sides, in some cases willingly, in some cases unwillingly. Call this defection another kind of political realism, or call it an act of faith. I like to call it the latter; after all, faith does move mountains.

Notes

This is a revised version of the Rajiv Bambawale lecture given at the Indian Institute of Technology, New Delhi, on October 13, 1983.

1. In traditional India, for instance, the state was clearly expected to be a part of culture, and the king was expected to see himself not only as a protector of dharma, but also as a protector of multiple ways of life and a promoter of ethnic tolerance. The *Arthashastra* may not provide a clue to this but the Puranas, the folklore, and *lokachara* do.
2. One of the first Marxist thinkers in the Third World to explicitly recognize the primacy of culture was Amilcar Cabral (1924–1974). See his *Return to the Source: Selected Speeches* (New York, Monthly Review Press, 1973). He, of course, drew upon the work of Aime Cesaire and Leopold Senghor. One suspects that the African heritage of the three had something to do with their sensitivity. The disintegrating native cultures they saw around them were more threatened than threatening, something that a Mao Zedong could not say about China. In India, unfortunately, even the Marxism of classical scholars like D.D. Kosambi and D.P. Chattopadhyay have remained in essence another version of Western Orientalism and colonial anthropology.
3. For a discussion of the political consciousness that characterized this phase of colonial politics, and its persistence within the culture of Indian politics as an important strain, see my "The Making and Unmaking of Political Cultures of India," *At the Edge of Psychology: Essays in Politics and Culture* (New Delhi: Oxford University Press, 1980), pp. 47–69; and *The Intimate Enemy: Loss and Recovery of Self Under Colonialism* (New Delhi: Oxford University Press, 1983).
4. Suresh Sharma, "Savarkar's Quest for a Modern Hindu Consolidation: The Framework of Validation," in D. L. Sheth and Ashis Nandy (eds.), *Hindu Visions of a Desirable Society: Heritage, Challenge and Redefinitions* (Tokyo: U. N. University, forthcoming).

   Probably Bankimchandra Chattopadhyay (1838–1894) was the first well-known theoretician of the state-oriented approach in India. I say "probably" because he stated his position indirectly, often through his literary and theological works or through commentaries on the works of others. Sudipta Kaviraj suggests that Bhudev Mukhopadhyaya (1827–1894), a lesser-known contemporary of Bankimchandra, was the first to explicitly accept and plead for a modern nation-state in India.

5. There was also probably the feeling among the Indians that there should be limits to which a colonial state should be involved by its subjects in the matter of social reform. Consider, for instance, the ambivalence of Rammohun Roy (1772–1833), who aggressively worked for the abolition of the practice of sati but who doubted the wisdom of a state-imposed ban on sati.
6. Aurobindo Ghose (1872–1950) in his revolutionary years, when he was under the influence of Mazzini, was a good example of such romantic populism. The revolutionary hero of Sarat Chandra Chattopadhyay's novel *Pather Dabi*, Sabyasachi, is a faithful idealization of this attitude to political participation. The pathological possibilities of the attitude have been explored in some detail in Rabindranath Tagore's *Gora, The Home and the World,* and *Char Adhyay.*
7. It was the same statist vision of India that explains Sister Nivedita's (1867–1911) discomfort with Ananda Coommaraswamy (1877–1947), whom she considered too conservative.
8. This has been discussed in Nandy, *The Intimate Enemy.* See also Ashis Nandy, "The Politics of Secularism and the Recovery of Religious Tolerance," *Alternatives*, Apr 1988, 13(2), pp. 177–194.
9. For example, Rammohun Roy, "Additional Queries Respecting the Condition of India," in Kalidas Nag and Debajyoti Burman (eds), *The English Works* (Calcutta: Sadharan Brahmo Samaj, 1947), Part III, pp. 63–8; see pp. 64–5. Cf. Gandhi's critique of the railways and lawyers in "Hind Swaraj," in *Collected Works of Mahatma Gandhi* (Delhi: Publications Division, Government of India, 1963), Vol. 4, pp. 81–208.
10. Ashis Nandy, "Final Encounter: The Politics of the Assassination of Gandhi," in *At the Edge of Psychology*, pp. 70–98; and "Godse Killed Gandhi?", *Resurgence*, Jan-Feb 1983, (96), pp. 28–9.
11. It is the attempt to grapple with this reality that has revived Gandhian social theory in India, mostly among people who reject orthodox Gandhism of many of the direct disciples of Gandhi. The revival has as little to do with the personal life and the personal successes or failures of Gandhi as Marx's life and his successes and failures have to do with Marx's thought today. The modern Indians naturally like to give the credit for the revival to either "Hindu woolly-headedness" or to the false consciousness generated by "romantic propagandists" like Richard Attenborough.
12. Sunil Sahasrabudhe, "Towards a New Theory," *Seminar*, May 1982, (273), pp. 19–23; and "On Alien Political Categories," *Gandhi Marg*, Feb 1983, 4(11), pp. 896–901. Sahasrabudhe is one of the few serious

Marxists in India who have self-consciously built into their models indigenous cultural categories.

13. In the context of Indian traditions of science and technology, this point has been made indirectly and painstakingly by Dharampal, *Indian Science and Technology in the Eighteenth Century: Some Contemporary European Accounts* (New Delhi: Impex India, 1971); and directly and passionately by Claude Alvares, *Homo Faber: Technology and Culture in India, China and the West* (New Delhi: Allied, 1979). See also Claude Alvares, "Science, Colonialism and Violence," Shiv Visvanathan, "The Annals of a Laboratory State"; and Vandana Shiva, "Reductionist Science as Epistemic Violence," in Ashis Nandy, ed., *Science, Hegemony and Violence: A Requiem for Modernity* (New Delhi: U.N. University and Oxford University Press, 1988).
14. On development, as it looks from outside the modern world, some of the clearest statements are Claude Alvares, "Deadly Development," *Development Forum*, Oct 1983, 9(7); Special Issue on Survival, *Lokayan Bulletin*, 1985, 3 (415); Madhya Pradesh Lokayan and Lokhit Samiti, Singrauli, *Vikas ki Kimat* (Ahmedabad: Setu, 1985); and see also Ashis Nandy, "The Idea of Development: The Experience of Modern Psychology as a Cautionary Tale and as an Allegory," in Carlos Mallmann and Oscar Nudler (eds.), *Human Development in Its Social Context* (London: Hodder and Stoughton and U.N. University, 1986), pp. 248–260; "Development and Authoritarianism: An Epitaph on Social Engineering," *Lokayan Bulletin*, 1987, 5(1), pp. 38–48; and "Culture, Voice and Development," in Yoshikaju Sakamoto (ed.), *The Changing Structure of World Politics* (Tokyo: Iwanami Shoten, in press).
15. In the Indian context, such a point of view was aggressively advanced by Gandhi. See the pioneering essay of A.K. Saran, "Gandhi and the Concept of Politics," *Gandhi Marg*, 1980, 1(1): pp. 675–726. Also Thomas Pantham, "Thinking with Mahatma Gandhi: Beyond Liberal Democracy," *Political Theory*, 1983, 2(2), pp. 165–188; and Ashis Nandy, "From Outside the Imperium: Gandhi's Cultural Critique of the 'West,'" *Traditions, Tyranny and Utopias: Essays in the Politics of Awareness* (New Delhi: Oxford University Press, 1987), pp. 127–162.
16. For instance, Giri Deshingkar, "Civilisation Concerns," *Seminar*, Dec 1980, (256), pp. 12–17; and "People's Security Versus National Security," *Seminar*, Dec 1982, (280), pp. 28–30.
17. For instance, Bharat Wariavwallah, "Indira's India: A National Security State?" *Round Table*, July 1983, pp. 274–285; and "Personality, Domestic Political Institutions and Foreign Policy," in Ram Joshi (Eds.), *Congress in Indian Politics: A Centenary Perspective* (Bombay: Popular Prakashan, 1975), pp. 245–69. Also, Deshingkar, "National Security versus People's Security."
18. For some culture-sensitive Indian intellectuals, the only valid definition of conventional development is the one given by Afsaneh Eghbal in the context of Africa in her "L'etat Contre L'ethnicite—Un Nou-

velle Arme: Le Development Exclusion," *IFDA Dossier*, July-Aug 1983, (36), pp. 17–29:

> Development is a structure in which a centralized power, in the form of a young sovereign state, formally negotiates international funds for rural populations representing ethnicity no external aid, in the field of development, can relate directly to ethnic groups caught in the problematique of survival. All aid is first absorbed and often plundered by state power.

The Indian critic of development will, however, further generalize the principle and affirm that it holds for internal resources, too. Good descriptions of the process of development in India from this point of view are in Alvares, "Deadly Development." For a theoretically alert description of the political context within which such developmental pathologies emerge, see Rajni Kothari, "The Crisis of the Moderate State and the Decline of Democracy," in Peter Lyon and James Manor (eds) *Transfer and Transformation: Political Institutions in the New Commonwealth* (Leicester: Leicester University press, 1983), pp. 29–47.

19. A proper critique of the rhetoric of revolution has not yet developed in India. Revolution could be considered in certain contexts, a reason of a shadow state, the state that would come into being after the present one will have been captured by middle-class, urbane, modern revolutionaries. The sacrifices that revolutionaries demand subserve, in this sense, the class interests of the shadow rulers of a shadow state. However, a critique of statism and a nonmodern awareness of culture has just begun to take shape at the peripheries of the Marxist movements in India.
20. Ashis Nandy, "A Counter-Statement on Humanistic Temper," *Mainstream*, Oct 10, 1981, and *Deccan Herald*, Oct 18, 1981.
21. I must again emphasize that the culture-oriented approach to the state stands for greater democratic participation and, thus, for more politics, not less. It wants to pursue the logic of an open polity to its end, to widen the compass of democratic politics. On the other hand, state-oriented politics, in societies where there are living nonmodern traditions, have often shown the tendency to throttle democratic institutions the moment participation by the underprivileged crosses a certain threshold.

    I should also emphasize that nonstatist politics is not the same as nonparty politics. However, the two can sometimes overlap. The new interest in nonparty politics is not the same that inspired some of the earlier writers on the subject, such as M.N. Roy and J.P. Narayan. The new interest, however, builds upon the old. For a sample of recent writings on the nonparty political processes in India, see D.L. Sheth, "Grass-Roots Stirrings and the Future of Politics," *Alternatives*, 1983, 9(1), pp. 1–24; and some of the papers in Harsh Sethi and Smitu Kothari (eds.), *The Non-Party Political Process: Uncertain Alternatives.* (Delhi: UNRISD and Lokayan, 1983), pp. 18–46, mimeo. On the issue of culture and authoritarianism in India, particularly on how authoritarianism often rears its head in such societies as part of an effort to contain the nonmodern political cultures of the peripheries, see Ashis Nandy, "Adorno in India: Revisiting the Psychology of Fascism," *At the Edge of Psychology*, pp. 99–111; and "Political Consciousness," *Seminar*, 1980, (248), pp. 18–21.

22. See the various issues of the *PUCL Bulletin* for an idea of the scope and concerns of various such groups, the best-known of which are, of course, the People's Union of Civil Liberties, People's Union of Democratic Rights, and the Citizens for Democracy.
23. Evidently, liberal democracy in a multiethnic society has built-in limits on its own commitment to democracy. See Kothari, "The Crisis of the Moderate State."
24. Such depoliticization may come through increasing criminalization of politics or from apathy brought about by the failure of the political opposition to identify the basic social problems. Both can be found in India today.
25. Dhirendra Sharma, *India's Nuclear Estate* (New Delhi: Lancers, 1983) p. 141.

NOTES ON CONTRIBUTORS

David Bennett teaches literary and cultural studies at the University of Melbourne. He is the editor of *The Thousand Mile Stare, Rhetorics of History: Modernity and Postmodernity, Cultural Studies: Pluralism and Theory,* and *Cultural Pluralism?.*

Homi K. Bhabha, of the University of Sussex, is the editor of *Nation and Narration* and the author of *The Location of Culture,* as well as numerous essays on postcolonial criticism and theory.

V. K. Chari, professor of English at Carleton University in Ottawa, received his degrees in Sanskrit and English from Banaras Hindu University. He is the author of *Whitman in the Light of Vedantic Mysticism* and *Sanskrit Criticism.*

Una Chaudhuri, is an associate professor in the Department of English at New York University, where she teaches dramatic literature and theater history. She is the author of *No Man's Stage: A Semiotic Study of Jean Genet's Major Plays* (1986) and *Modern Drama and the Politics of Location* (forthcoming).

Terry Collits teaches in the English Department at the University of Melbourne.

Anita Desai has published stories, essays, children's books, and eight novels. Two of her novels, *Clear Light of Day* and *In Custody,* were short-listed for the Booker Prize. She has been Visiting Fellow at Girton College, Cambridge, and has taught writing at Smith College, Mount Holyoke, and the Massachusetts Institute of Technology.

Jeffrey Ebbesen is currently pursuing his Ph.D. in comparative literature at the University of Connecticut. His primary areas of interest include literary theory and postcolonial studies.

Patrick Colm Hogan is an associate professor of English and comparative literature at the University of Connecticut. He is the author of *The Politics of Interpretation: Ideology, Professionalism, and the Study of Literature*; *Joyce, Milton, and the Theory of Influence*; and *On Interpretation: Meaning and Inference in Law, Psychoanalysis, and Literature.*

Norman N. Holland holds the Marston-Milbauer Eminent Scholar's Chair in English at the University of Florida. He is the author of numerous books and articles on psychoanalytic and literary topics. These include *The Dynamics of Literary Response, Five Readers Reading, Poems in Persons, Holland's Guide to Psychoanalytic Psychology and Literature-and-Psychology*, and *The Critical I.*

Winfred P. Lehmann is Louann and Larry Temple Centennial Professor Emeritus in the Humanities and Director of the Linguistics Research Center at the University of Texas at Austin. He is the author of numerous books and articles, including *Historical Linguistics, Die Gegenwärtige Richtung der Indogermanistischen Forschung* and *Theoretical Bases of Indo-European Linguistics.*

Ashis Nandy is Fellow and Director of the Centre for the Study of Developing Societies in New Delhi. His books include *At the Edge of Psychology, The Intimate Enemy: Loss and Recovery of Self Under Colonialism, Traditions, Tyranny and Utopias, The Illegitimacy of Nationalism, The Tao of Cricket, Alternative Sciences*, and *The Savage Freud and Other Essays in Possible and Retrievable Selves.*

Lalita Pandit is an associate professor of English at the University of Wisconsin at La Crosse. She is the coeditor of *Criticism and Lacan* and a member of the associate editorial board of *College Literature.* Pandit has published on topics in Shakespeare and Indic Studies.

P. K. Saha teaches English and linguistics at Case Western Reserve University, Cleveland, Ohio. Stylistic analysis is one of his main interests.

Darius L. Swann, of the Interdenominational Theological Center in Atlanta, is the coauthor of *Indian Theatre: Traditions of Performance.*

INDEX